Meditator's Field Guide

"I have known Doug for many years now. He has a high-curiosity mind which has helped him dissect and digest much of the spiritual and psychological terrain. What I enjoy particularly is his ability to dive into Buddhist practice and bring his own unique style and understanding to these classical teachings and practices. His many years as a Unitarian minister and as a well-trained psychotherapist makes his view wide as well as deep. I very much respect his views on these teachings."

– John Travis, Senior Dharma Teacher,
Spirit Rock Meditation Center,
Marin County, California

Meditator's Field Guide:

Reflections on 57 Insights that Slip Away

Doug Kraft

Easing Awake Books

Published by Easing Awake Books, 2017
Carmichael, CA 95608
www.easingawake.com

ISBN: 978-0-9986936-4-4 paperback
ISBN: 978-0-9986936-5-1 e-book

Printed in the United States
5   4   3   2   1

In gratitude to my teachers, especially

John Travis
and
Bhante Vimalaraṁsi

Contents

How to Use This Field Guide

Each day is a journey, and the journey itself, home.
— Basho

Many years ago my wife and I bought a home near the American River in northern California. I love to walk through the fields and woodlands along the river or to sit by the rushing water. The region is populated with herons, white-tailed kites, hawks, vultures, turkeys, cranes, rabbits, deer, coyotes, otters, rattlesnakes, salmon, pine trees, purple thistles, sycamores, oaks, lupine, and thousands of other species of flora and fauna. I know a little about some of them and less about others.

A friend gave me a field guide to wildlife in the area. The guide doesn't tell me where to find the paths, meadows, groves of trees, or coves along the river. That's the job of a map. The field guide doesn't instruct me on how to hike or what to bring or leave behind. It assumes I know enough to get around. Instead, it focuses on the wildlife itself: how to identify creatures and plants, what they do, what's important to them, and how understanding them is "a key to unlock the gates to greater understanding of the world around us."[1]

---

[1] *The Outdoor World of the Sacramento Region,* complied and edited by Jo Smith, et al. (The American River Natural History Association, 1993.). p. 1.

I wrote this *Meditator's Field Guide* in a similar spirit. However, rather than focus on the world around us, it focuses on the world within us — the inner landscape revealed by spiritual practice, particularly meditation. Like other field guides, it doesn't provide a detailed map or beginning instructions. I intend it to be a companion for "hikers" already on a spiritual trail. I imagine you have a few miles behind you already. My earlier books, *Buddha's Map* and *Beginning the Journey*, offer an extensive map and detailed instructions should you need them. (See the resource list on p. 353.)

However the path we imagine in the beginning is never quite the one we discover along the way. Once we have some familiarity with the landscape, it becomes possible, perhaps essential, to reflect on the insights and experiences that arise during our journey.

Each of us is unique with different temperaments, aspirations, concerns, inclinations, and history. Each of our journeys is unique, so I assembled this field guide in a way that is easy to jump around to diverse topics in whatever sequence works best for you. Though all the chapters are interconnected, each is written to stand on its own. For your convenience some chapters repeat key points. Similar to most field guides, this one doesn't have to be read linearly from front to back.

Every part of meditation is directly or distantly related to every other part. Each reflection is connected to all the others; that is how Buddhism works. You can start anywhere and read in any direction. Better yet, you can look for the topics most relevant to your life and practice and start there. At the end of each chapter you'll find references to other closely related chapters.

Wise Effort and the Six Rs

You'll find references throughout this book to a process called "The Six Rs." Let me introduce you to them now.

A wide variety of meditation styles are practiced today. Most are helpful to some people at various times. The Buddha himself taught several different methods. In recent years I've favored a combination of kindness and wisdom practices that the Buddha described in the earliest records of his talks. You'll find mention of this combined practice throughout the field guide, though most of the reflections are helpful for many styles of meditation.

Every meditation practice I have tried or heard about has one element in common: hindrances to the practice. It's safe to say that all meditators stumble over distractions. How we handle them is essential. The Buddha recommended Wise Effort (*sammā vāyāma*). Effort is easy. Wisdom is not always easy.

The most effective approach to Wise Effort that I've found is a six-phase process I learned from one of my teachers, Bhante Vimalaraṁsi. It's so familiar that we fondly call it "The Six Rs." It works like this. When you realize that your awareness has been taken over by a distraction, you:

- **Recognize** that your attention has been drawn away;
- **Release** the distraction by just letting it be as it is;
- **Relax** any tension;
- **Re-Smile** or bring in uplifted qualities such as kindness, compassion, joy, or peace;
- **Return** to the primary object of meditation; and
- **Repeat** the process as often as needed.

The Six Rs can be useful with a wide variety of meditation practices. I include a description in Appendix A (see p. 287), so that you can have it at your fingertips.

It is my hope that this field guide to meditation will help you find depth, ease, wisdom, and kindness in meditation and in life.

May your vision be clear, your footing steady, and the journey itself your home.

Introduction

Truth waits for eyes unbound by longing.
– Ram Dass

Slippery Fish

I laugh when I hear the fish in the sea are thirsty.
— Kabir

During the 1990s I had a wise and wonderful psychotherapist who helped me work through the remainder of the depression that had haunted me since childhood. She had ways of looking at my inner dynamics that were new to me. Yet they often rang true.

© Jens Tröger

I came to trust that she had a deeper and more sympathetic understanding of me than I had of myself. Some of her insights shook me to the core. "Wow," I thought, "I'll never forget that."

Yet I often did forget. Some insights never left. Others faded in a few minutes. For the life of me, I couldn't remember what she'd said – only that it was important. "Can you say that again in as few words as possible so I can memorize it by rote?"

She'd laugh. "We found a slippery fish. Since they challenge your core character structure and beliefs, they are as difficult to hold onto as a bar of soap or a slippery fish. They are probably true, otherwise the mind wouldn't push them aside so adroitly. We're onto something valuable."

I found similarities in meditation. Some insights resonated deeply and never floated away. Others rattled my core and faded like a dream.

When I began teaching, I was surprised to find the same phenomenon with yogis. I had to offer some teachings over and over like, "Meditation is not about getting rid of anything," or "It's not personal. Nothing is personal." No matter how emphatically I repeated these, the next day or next week, I had to say them again. "Oh yes," the yogi would say, "I forgot."

I began collecting these slippery fish and reducing them to a few words so they'd be easier to remember. Traditionally they are called "gathas" – short phrases designed to illuminate the meditative process or spiritual understanding. Then I'd find images or stories to give them life.

My collection of meditative slippery fish is the core of this field guide. Each chapter is a reflection on one of them. Each chapter begins with a gatha. The gatha is either the chapter title itself or is displayed immediately after the title. The appendices include a list of them (see p. 355).

Some of the insights fade more quickly than others. But all reflect an essential meditation understanding that can slip away without so much as saying goodbye. I hope this field guide will help bring them back to life.

Overview

Each reflection is written to stand alone without the support of the others. They can be read in any order depending on your need and curiosity. However, a book requires a linear sequence. So I grouped the reflections into five sections:

Section I: Finding a Compass

Section II: Getting Our Selves Out of the Way

Section III: Glowing Like a Candle

Section IV: Cleaning Up Our Act

Section V: Expanding Infinitely

Organizing the field guide this way reflects how I've seen yogis travel the Buddha's path. And it roughly parallels the Buddha's descriptions of his Four Ennobling Truths and Eightfold Path. The chapter on "Three Essential Practices" (pp. 3-14) and Appendix F (p. 317) explore the Four Ennobling Truths and the Eightfold Path in more detail. For now, let's unpack the five sections of this book.

I. Finding a Compass

If we want to travel from New York to San Francisco and head south, it will be a very long journey, no matter how mindfully we take each step. On the spiritual journey, we must develop a compass — get our general direction — right from the beginning lest we wander aimlessly.

It's especially important when we consider what motivates us to begin a spiritual journey in the first place. Today, as in the Buddha's time, we're less likely to feel drawn by lovely possibilities than to feel pushed by gritty realities we want to transcend, escape, heal, or alleviate. Sometimes the pain is obvious: illness, injury, loss of a job, death of a friend, or breakup of a relationship. Sometimes the pain is quiet: loss of meaning, vague dissatisfaction. As Aldous Huxley wrote, "There comes a time when one asks even of Shakespeare, even of Beethoven, is this all?"

In good times we may muse about peace, enlightenment, and spiritual realization. But usually it takes a wake-up call to get us to take the first step. That wake-up call is often some kind of pain or dissatisfaction.

Millions of years of evolution have bred us to flee pain. Pain jolts us to move us along. If the problem is a large predator, flight may be the best solution. But if the problem is internal anguish, the urge to tighten up and run away is not so helpful. As Buckaroo Banzai put it, "Wherever you go, there you are." [2]

So the Buddha's teachings begin with suffering and how to understand and deal with it effectively. He never said life *is* suffering. Only that suffering *is a part of life* (see p. 4). It's woven into the fabric of the unstable world in which we live. Everything breaks, nothing lasts forever, and all that we love will fade eventually. Since we can't always dodge suffering, it's best to understand how the mind-heart responds to it and figure out how to engage it wisely.

---

[2] Buckaroo Banzai is the lead character in the 1984 film *The Adventures of Buckaroo Banzai Across the 8th Dimension*, written by Earl Mac Rauch.

It's difficult to understand something if we're avoiding, denying, ignoring, or trying to control it. Avoidance creates tension. To truly understand a difficulty we have to turn and face it. And since tension distorts our perception, we must first relax.

It's not so easy to relax the mind and open the heart in the face of suffering. But if we don't, we'll have no wisdom to guide us.

The Buddha takes it a step further. If suffering is an illness, he said the disease is incurable. It's inherent to life in this relative world in which we live. His solution was to get rid of the patient. If there is no one to suffer, there is no suffering.

His logic may be clear. But what it means to "get ourselves out of the way" may be mystifying in this context. It doesn't sound like what we had in mind when we started on this path. We'd prefer improving ourselves, finding a true self, or realizing our highest nature. But as we engage this path, it gradually becomes clear that full awakening cannot happen until we see our self to be as ephemeral as a cloud in the sky or a sandcastle under a wave.

The Buddha called this "Wise View" (*sammā diṭṭhi*). In a nutshell it means seeing the impersonal nature of all phenomena. There is no permanent, enduring self-essence separate from everything else.

So the first section of this field guide, "Finding a Compass," explores the challenges of turning toward difficulty, relaxing into it, and seeing the impersonal nature of all phenomena including the self. This is the compass bearing the Buddha offers.[3]

---

[3] This first section relates roughly to the first of the Four Ennobling Truths (understanding suffering) and the first two folds of the Eightfold Path (Wise View and Wise attitude).

II. Getting Our Selves Out of the Way

The second section takes this direction and puts it into practice. It's about the actual techniques and attitudes that naturally soften tension and allow the ephemeral self to lose its illusion of solidity, like a mist evaporating in the morning sun.

The Buddha said the root of our experience of difficulty is a preverbal, instinctual tightening called *taṇhā*. He encouraged us to abandon this tension. He didn't counsel us to turn away from suffering but to relax the tension it brings.

This leads to what he called "Wise Attitude" (*sammā saṅkappa*): the attitudes and intentions that flow from seeing the impersonal nature of phenomena. These, in turn, lead to wise effort without strain, awareness, and stability of mind.

The section explores all of these themes: abandoning tension, relaxing the sense of self, effort without strain, cultivating awareness, and allowing the mind to stabilize itself. This is how we learn to get our selves out of the way.[4]

III. Glowing Like a Candle

As we relax tension and give up on improving, fixing, preening, bolstering, or elevating our sense of self, we're left with a mind-heart that glows. We find an awareness that is soft, clear, kind, wise, and wide open. Suffering fades into a sense of simply being with what is.

We still engage the conventional world, love our children, go to work, buy groceries, and discuss events of the day. But we don't get thrown off balance as easily as before. And when we do, we recover more quickly.

---

[4] This second section relates roughly to the second of the Four Ennobling Truths (relaxing the tension that creates suffering) and the second, sixth, seventh and eighth folds of the Eightfold Path (Wise View, Wise Effort, Wise Awareness or Mindfulness, and Wise Collectedness (*samādhi*).

This third section of the field guide offers tips to help us stay with this luminous awareness more easily and deeply.[5]

IV. Cleaning Up Our Act

However, no matter what we do, the luminous, pure awareness doesn't last. We touch something lovely outside of time itself. Then it fades. Peacefulness expands into spaciousness; then it collapses into a muttering, discursive mind.

With all its qualities, the glowing mind-heart can shine light on old wounds hiding in the shadows. Mark Twain remarked how self-knowledge is bad news. Old habits rise to the surface. Old neuroses get restimulated. Old ways of thinking disrupt equanimity.

Most of us spend a lot more time outside meditation than in it. The mind that grumbles in the rush-hour traffic keeps grumbling in the meditation hour. The strains of life play out in our practice.

Gradually it becomes obvious that meditation alone is not enough. We need to clean up our act. We need to get to work on what Ram Dass calls our "uncooked seeds."

As important as it is to figure out how to engage life in the world, most of us do not need a code of ethics or list of precepts to know that it's not helpful to kill, lie, steal, seduce the neighbor's partner, or go on a drunken binge.

However, in the relative world, there are no absolutes. There are no rules that we can follow rigidly and always be safe. It's these gray areas that throw us off.

So rather than lead you through specific precepts in separate short chapters, this section has longer but fewer chapters exploring the relationships between skillful behavior and

---

[5] This third section relates roughly to the third Ennobling Truth (realizing the well-being of cessation as discussed on pp. 7-12) and the last three folds of the Eightfold Path (Wise Effort, Wise Awareness, and Wise Collectedness).

wholesome mind-states. And it looks at the importance of kindness as an overarching guide.[6]

V. Expanding Infinitely

During the Buddha's time, the most advanced societies had slavery or rigid castes; women were considered chattel; the world was thought to be flat; and science, religion, art, and ethics were fused in an undifferentiated mass. The scientific method would not emerge for two millennia. Modern psychology wouldn't emerge for several centuries beyond that.

The people in the Buddha's time weren't stupid. Their brains were the size of ours. Many people had great wisdom. But the way the average person thinks about and understands the world has evolved dramatically since 500 BCE.

Were the Buddha alive today, he'd probably have a few new tools for us. He'd have other ways to help us get out of our way. In this last section we'll explore one of those: the infinitely expanding self.

Collection of Slippery Fish

This book is a collection of reflections on the tips, hints, gathas, guides, and tools to deal with slippery fish found at many different stages of the journey toward kindness and wisdom.

I hope you will be inspired to write about your own slippery fish. Taking the time to articulate insights that slip away can deepen the investigation of gifts that otherwise fall back into the sea.

Before turning to specific slippery fish, I'd like to guide you through an exploration of who the Buddha was and how Buddhism first entered the world. Seeing the origin of these

---

[6] This fourth section relates to the three middle folds of the Eightfold Path. The third fold is about how we communicate with one another (skillful speech). The fourth fold is about how we treat those around us (skillful actions). The fifth fold is about how we engage the world as we take care of ourselves (wise lifestyle).

teachings and the people the Buddha was addressing can help us understand the depths of what he was trying to convey.

Related Chapters

1. Three Essential Practices, p. 3
2. Resilience, p. 15

How Buddhism Entered the World

Like a dream, an illusion, a bubble, a shadow,
a drop of dew, a flash of lightning.
This is how to contemplate all phenomena.
— The Buddha, *Diamond Sutra*

© Aaron Burden, Unsplash.com

It's hard to project ourselves back two and a half thousand years into another time, another age, another continent, another country, another economy, another political structure, another social system, and a whole other worldview, and try to intuit the innermost thoughts of a spiritual innovator like the Buddha. However, if we can understand a little better what he experienced and how his contemporaries understood his instructions, we can better know how his teachings relate to us. So before we get to some of the insights, let me share with you some of his story.

Much of the information in Buddhist tradition and lore is helpful. But some is contradictory or easy to misread. For example, we don't actually know his given name. Buddhist tradition says it was "Siddhārtha." But this may not be true. "Siddha" means "accomplished" and "Aretha" means "goal." "Siddhārtha" means "one who accomplished his goal." It sounds like a second, spiritual name given later in life to a seeker who has attained something wonderful. It's hard to imagine parents gazing at their newborn and saying, "Look at what you've achieved! We're going to call you 'one-who-has-accomplished-his-goals-in-life'."

We are confident that his family name was "Gautama." So I'll call him "Sri Gautama." His clan name was "Shakya." The Shakya were warriors in the north of the Ganges River valley two to three thousand years ago. He was born into a tribe of fighters.

Buddhist tradition says his father, Śuddhodana, was a king. But he wasn't a king as we understand it. Twenty-six hundred years ago, the Ganges valley was a collection of small, autonomous principalities. Śuddhodana was a head guy — more of an independent duke than a king. Think of him as a clan chieftain. He was well respected; it would take an esteemed man to hold together a tribe of warriors.

Tradition says Sri Gautama grew up in a big palace. But there were no drawbridges, ramparts, or towers. Several years ago, my wife and I were on a pilgrimage to sites in the Buddha's life. One afternoon we had lunch at his house – at least what was left of it. His homestead in Kapilavatthu had all but disappeared until archeologists located the site in a seemingly empty field. They excavated down several feet to expose the base of the walls. Sitting there eating a sandwich, we could see the footprint of the homestead. A wall enclosed the family compound on four or five acres. The house walls were not thick enough to support more than a few stories, much less towers. Think of it as a spacious villa.

They lived much closer to nature than we do. There are 50 to 100 times more people living in the Ganges valley today than back then. There was more nature per capita. His agrarian culture was attuned to the cycles of nature.

And nature was generous. The fertile valley produced more food than was needed. It was a prosperous period. There was time for leisure, arts, music, poetry, contemplation, and study of the ancient Vedic scriptures.

It was also a time of social innovation. People could move into the small cities and, with entrepreneurial determination, rise above the traditional expectations of their caste.

Hippie-like wanderers could drop out of the workforce altogether and beg for food — there was plenty to go around. However, most dropouts were older men who turned the family farm or business over to the children and drifted off in search of spiritual fulfillment. People lived in large, multi-generational clusters with all the hubbub of big family dynamics. Those who wanted peace and quiet had to wander off into the woods.

These wanderers were called "bhikkhus." Later, the English translated "bhikkhu" as "monk" because modern bhikkhus wear robes and walk with contemplative deportment. But the term literally means "beggar." Back then they had a more reverential attitude toward beggars than we have today.

With all those seekers, it was a time of spiritual as well as social innovation.

Tradition says Sri Gautama grew up in a 5th century BCE version of the 20th century CE movie, *The Truman Show.* In the movie, Jim Carey played a baby raised in a reality TV show of actors in a massive movie set. For the first 29 years of his life, Truman thinks it's all real.

For the first 29 years of his life, tradition says Sri Gautama grew up in a palace sheltered from the harshness of life. Then he saw disease, old age, death, and a monk and was inspired to become a monk and seek a holy life.

This story is probably fanciful.

In reality his mother died shortly after his birth. He lived on a large farm with inevitable exposure to birth and death. His large extended, close-knit family respected elders rather than hid them from the kids. He would have seen plenty of people aging. The members of his warrior clan must have talked about wars and bloodshed. After Sri Gautama became a spiritual superstar, his brother-in-law and cousin, Devadatta, tried to kill him several times. When he wasn't plotting homicide, Devadatta tried to split the saṅgha of monks. Surely there must have been some signs of family dysfunction in the early years. Sri Gautama grew up in a political family and must have seen some of the political intrigue that we know flowed around him.

To believe Sri Gautama was unaware of the harsher aspects of life suggests he was naïve, unobservant, dim-witted, and prone to idealistic fantasies. The evidence suggests the opposite. He was wise. He was a keen observer of life – his talks are filled with similes of the details of ordinary life. He was smart and able to adapt his teachings effortlessly to people's quirks and gifts. And he had no interest in idealism – he refused to talk about metaphysics or ideals and instead focused on the practical, down-to-earth problem of finding happiness in the world as it is.

The records of his early life are sketchy. He was born in a higher caste. But he didn't grow up in a monastery or a BCE version of a reality TV show.

I didn't grow up in a sheltered family either. So I find it encouraging that Sri Gautama became fully enlightened despite being exposed to the rough and tumble of life.

This was the world Sri Gautama knew. To understand his message, it helps to understand the world he lived in, how the people he taught would hear him, and the family dynamics that shaped him.

Rāhula

The records of his life become more detailed starting in his late 20s. They offer a different version of his venturing forth into the life of a monk. In his 29th year his wife, Yasodharā, gave birth to Rāhula. One evening Sri Gautama looked in at his sleeping infant. He wanted what most parents want for their kids — the deepest happiness and fulfillment. But he didn't feel he had it to give.

Remember, he lived in a wealthy family in an affluent time. His father was wise. His friends were cultured. His home was in a beautiful valley. He had at his fingertips the best his culture had to offer.

Still, things got messed up: crops failed, roofs leaked, bodies sickened, relationships drifted, cousins could be mean, mothers and friends died. As the songwriter Paul Simon put it, "Everything put together sooner or later falls apart."

His lifestyle wasn't leading him to the deep contentment he wanted for himself and his son. He'd have to look elsewhere.

What else was there?

Those wandering bhikkhus offered an alternate model of how to seek the best in life. It was unusual for a young man to take this path. But the wanderers were an inspiration. It seemed worth a try.

His love for Rāhula was so strong that he worried if he didn't leave right away, he might never venture forth. Yet he knew there was no enduring foundation for happiness in the people and things around him.

So he called his bodyguard, Channa, and snuck out of the family compound in the dead of night. When they were far enough away, he exchanged his clothes for monk's robes, shaved his head, and sent Channa back to the compound with his horse. He traded the life of a well-to-do warrior for the life of a barefoot monk on a spiritual quest. His attention shifted from the outer to the inner world. Now we can call him "Venerable Gautama."

Today some people view him as a deadbeat dad walking away from his parenting responsibilities to pursue his own selfish interests. To make this case we have to ignore his motives and cultural context and project ours onto him. I suspect he was genuinely torn. He didn't run off with the family fortune. He left it with his wife and child who would be loved and cared for in a large, caring, well-to-do family. And not unlike an alcoholic father going off to rehab, he had his son's deepest, long-term happiness at heart. After his enlightenment, he returned to the family and reconnected with his son. Rāhula chose to become the youngest monk to join the saṅgha. Eventually he awakened completely. The Buddha brought his son to a deeper contentment than he could have as a lay dad.

But I am getting ahead of the story.

Seeker

For eons saints and seekers had explored the inner world and developed practices that created deeper and longer-lasting comfort than the outer world provided. These seekers believed that spiritual and worldly forces competed with one another. If we suppressed the worldly forces — body and emotional instincts — they believed the spiritual became stronger. This approach appealed to the warrior mentality of suppressing the restless mind, fiery emotions, and bodily appetites for the sake of spiritual peace.

One of Venerable Gautama's teachers was the famous Alara Kalama. From him he learned how to suppress the bodily, emotional, and mental activity until he entered a deep state of mental absorption called "The realm of no-thing-ness." He became so adept that Alara Kalama invited him to help lead his saṅgha.

I once tried to cultivate a deep state of mental absorption by counting 100 breaths without letting my attention waver. If it even flickered, I'd begin again. I'd start, "Breathing in. One. Breathing in. Two." And so forth. At some point my mind would say, "Breathing in. Fifty-two. I'm doing pretty well. Oops. I drifted. Breathing in. One ..."

It took me nine months before I could somewhat reliably count 100 breathes without wandering once. When I looked at the quality of my mind, it was like a steel trap. It was rigid, tightly constrained, and opaque. I thought, "This is worthless."

I can imagine the Venerable Gautama mastering even deeper absorption states and thinking, "This isn't helpful." So when Alara Kalama invited him to co-lead the saṅgha, he declined.

Despite the equanimity of the realm of no-thing-ness, it was only a temporary state. Inner bliss was not eternal bliss. Like worldly pleasure, it was put together and "everything put together sooner or later falls apart." When he came out of that state, he recognized he still had greed, aversion, and delusion within.

So he left Alara Kalama.

His next teacher was Uddaka Rāmaputta. "Putta" means "son of." Rāmaputta was the son of Rama, a deceased teacher who had known a deeper state called "The realm of neither-perception-nor-non-perception." From his father, Uddaka had learned the instructions for getting into this sublime state. But he had not mastered it. He gave Venerable Gautama the instructions. Gautama mastered neither-perception-nor-non-perception. He went further than any of his living contemporaries. Uddaka Rāmaputta offered to step aside and turn his saṅgha over to Venerable Gautama.

Again, Gautama declined. Despite the bliss of the state, it too was put together and fell apart leaving him with the seeds of greed, aversion, and delusion.

He gave up on teachers and went to practice with a group of ascetic monks in the hills of Rājagaha. He continued his meditation along with ascetic practices of denying himself food, clothes, contact with women, and in other ways suppressing bodily and emotional desires.

Eating only a few calories a day, his body shriveled, his skin blackened, his eyes sunk, and his hair fell out. He was on the brink of death. Yet lasting peace still eluded him. If he went any further he would die and his spiritual quests would remain unfulfilled.

After six and a half years of practice, he rejected the path of ascetic denial and the spiritual warrior. Frail and famished, he wandered out of the hills and onto the Ganges plain. Too weak to take another step, he sat down and leaned against a tree in the center of a small village. Death was near.

Sujata

At that time, the folk religions in this region centered on tree spirits called devas. Each village had a tree that was home for a deva. Young women married the deva. The tree spirit would remain true to the woman through thick and thin. Later, she might marry a human. Who knew if he'd be faithful? But her first husband, the deva, would always look after her.

Sujata was a young woman who had married the local deva and more recently married a young man. More than anything else, she wanted a child.

As Venerable Gautama left the hills of Rājagaha, Sujata realized she was pregnant. She was overjoyed. She made a gift of kier — a pudding of rice, milk, and rose petals that tastes like human breast milk — and took it as an offering to the tree spirit.

When she arrived at the village center, a being with a huge aura sat beneath the tree. Its body was shriveled, dark, and only vaguely human. She was sure it was the tree deva and offered it the kier.

It was, in fact, Venerable Gautama.

Her gift created a dilemma for Gautama. His training turned him away from the world, away from women, away from luxurious foods. To accept kier from this young, beautiful woman would be scandalous.

But he'd become disillusioned with ascetic attitudes and repressive practices. They were literally killing him. What should he do?

He accepted the kier. With this act Buddhism was born. If there was a symbolic moment when Buddhism appeared in the world, it was in that simple gesture of accepting Sujata's gift. He symbolically embraced the feminine as well as the masculine, the earth as well as the sky, the dark as well as the light. It was a movement away from the religion of extremes toward a spirituality of the middle way, a spirituality of embrace rather than denial, of being with what is rather than striving for something beyond, of turning toward rather than turning away.

Eventually Sujata realized he was a famished ascetic rather than the deva. But she returned each day anyway to offer him food. She nourished him back to health.

After a week his strength returned enough that he could get up and walk a half-mile to the Nirañjarā River. The river was 50 to 60 feet wide and a few feet deep. He waded across and came to a grove of fig trees. It was a quiet, comfortable, and beautiful place to meditate in the shade near the river.

Bodhi Tree

He sat down at the root of a tree in the late afternoon. All that he had learned and sought seemed to be coming together. He closed his eyes. He was no longer tempted to

© Adam Eurich

push the world away or to push his thoughts and feelings aside. His attempts to shape the body and mind had failed and nearly killed him. Rather than trying to control the mind-heart, he decided to observe it so he might understand how it worked. He didn't push or pull or work to make anything different than it was. He observed, released, relaxed, quieted, and opened so that he might see more clearly.

Imagine holding a beach ball under water and then relaxing. What happens? The ball rushes to the surface and flies into the air.

This is what happened to Venerable Gautama. For six and a half years he had held defilements at bay, pushed aside yearnings, desires, fears, irritations, confusions, and delusions. Sitting under the fig tree, he stopped suppressing them — he stopped holding them under the water. They all flew up into his awareness.

Venerable Gautama had a massive hindrance attack. In his day they didn't have the language of modern psychology. The processes of the mind-heart were described as people or beings. After all, that is what they feel like. He said it was like being attacked by ten thousand demons and allured by ten thousand fair maidens. His mind was a swirling storm of all the desires, dislikes, and delusions he'd been pushing away for so long.

He didn't indulge them or fight them or try to push them aside. It was a middle way of neither indulging the story lines nor trying to control them. He just saw each one as clearly as he could and allowed it to do what it wanted. He relaxed so that he could observe it more clearly. He let his mind-heart expand so it could see even more sensitively.

They kept coming and swirling and buffeting and draining his energy. His faith weakened. "Surely, I need to control them a little. Who am I to think peace is possible?" His confidence waned.

Then he remembered an afternoon when he was a young boy. His father had been leading an agricultural ritual in the fields. He'd been left alone with an attendant beneath a rose apple tree. He'd relaxed into the peacefulness of the day. His mind-heart gently expanded out into a quiet, luminous spaciousness. It was sweet, loving, kind, clear, and effortless. All he did was relax into what was already there.

Sitting under the fig tree beside the Nirañjarā River with his mind swirling with distractions, he remembered the sweetness of that afternoon beneath the rose apple tree. Peace was possible. It required no strain. In fact, without ease peace was impossible.

That memory gave him the faith to not push the inner whirlwind away but to relax into it. As he did so, it slowed down. He observed and relaxed more and it slowed down more. Maybe all that turmoil was just the result of the strain of attempting to control the mind-heart.

He surrendered into the swirl and it became a quiet breeze. The hindrances that had felt like spears and arrows didn't stop. However, now they seemed more like flower petals gently drifting by: no longer a problem.

When I was meditating in Thailand, there were lots of dogs in the wats (monasteries) where I practiced. The Thai don't have dogs or cats for pets because they are too expensive to feed. But there are lots of dogs and cats in the country. They are all feral. They aren't treated very well.

However, the people in the wats cultivate friendliness and compassion toward all creatures. They feed the animals and treated them kindly. So dogs take up residence in the wats. Their hierarchical and territorial instincts are intact. Sometimes a few dogs would try to kill each other on the doorstep of my kuti (meditation hut). During the night they barked and howled at any movement or rustle.

At first the ruckus of all the yelping was a huge hindrance for me — as distracting as having spears and arrows flying through my mind.

But after ten days, the ruckus was gone. I was pleased. And I wondered what had happened. So I listened more carefully. In fact, all the noise was still there. But I was so relaxed and peaceful they felt like the sounds of life gently flowing around me. I didn't fight them. And they no longer disturbed me. They were like soft petals in a gentle breeze — not a problem.

As Venerable Gautama sat through the night beneath that fig tree, the distractions in his mind-heart seemed less like threats and more like the soft flow of life itself. As he quieted he saw subtler and subtler tensions buried deeper inside. He didn't try to analyze them or tell a story about them. He just saw them, let them be, relaxed, settled into a quiet joy, and let a luminous peace spread out.

Eventually, nothing was left. He was in that space of no-thing-ness without any control. Yet the tiny effort to perceive no-thing-ness created tiny ripples. So he let go of perception and softened more. He went into a peaceful version of neither-perception-nor-non-perception. He relaxed further until everything ceased — no perceptions, no awareness, no memory, no feeling ... truly nothing. Without memory, perception, or consciousness, there was no suffering. Soon even the sense of no-thing-ness disappeared.

When the sun arose over the fig trees in the morning, the turmoil was gone. The tension was gone. And he knew it would never return. It was all so simple and had been there all along waiting to be released.

His relief was profound yet as natural as that day under the rose apple tree. He had become Siddhārtha — one who had accomplished his goal. He had become a Buddha.

Awakening is not easy. Without ease it is impossible.

Buddha

Now what?

What he'd discovered was so sublime that he hung out in the fig grove for weeks absorbing its ramifications. Awakening left him very comfortable with solitude. His realization seemed too subtle for others to understand.

In truth, the path he had taken was nearly impossible. A Buddha is somebody who works out liberations without guidance from anyone. It's very, very difficult to do.

Gradually he realized there were some people close to awakening. Perhaps it would take them a long time to work it out on their own. Perhaps they wouldn't make it. But with a nudge or a pointer in the right direction from him, they might do well. So he set out to teach.

Upaka

The first person he came upon was a young yogi named Upaka. As Upaka approached him on the road, he recognized something extraordinary about the Buddha and asked, "Who are you?"

The Buddha replied, "I am one who woke up." That's what "Buddha" means: "one who woke up."

Upaka asked, "Who is your teacher?"

The Buddha answered him truthfully and with such inspiration that the words came out in verse. *Majjhima Nikāya* 26.25 records these verses:

> *I am one who has transcended all, a knower of all*
> *Unsullied among all things, renouncing all,*
> *By craving's ceasing freed ...*
>
> *I have no teacher, and no one like me*
> *Exists anywhere in all the world*
> *With all its gods, because I have*
> *No person for my counterpart ...*

He continued like this for several minutes.

Put yourself in Upaka's place. You're walking along a public thoroughfare — perhaps a subway. You see a glowing stranger and offer a polite greeting. He replies, rapping in cadence:

> *I am the Accomplished One in the world,*
> *I am the Teacher Supreme,*
> *I alone am a Fully Enlightened One*
> *Whose fires are quenched and extinguished ...*

What would you think? Would you suspect he was on drugs?

The sutta (discourse) describes Upaka's reaction: "When this was said, the ascetic Upaka said: 'May it be so, friend,' Shaking his head, he took a bypath and departed." He took the Buddha for a nut case and politely scooted away. ("Upāli Sutta," *Majjhima Nikāya* 26.)

As the Buddha watched him scuttle away, he must have thought, "Well, that didn't go so well."

Do you know that feeling?

For more than 25 years, I was an active Unitarian Universalist minister. Each summer, I had a month of vacation and a month of study-leave to prepare for the coming church year. When I returned to the pulpit in September, I felt refreshed and inspired with new ideas and insights to share. I poured my heart into those first fall sermons.

Afterwards people greeted me at the door with blank smiles and polite remarks: "Very nice." "Wonderful effort."

"Well, that didn't go so well," I'd think. "They didn't get it." The problem was I was more connected with my insights than I was with them.

As I reconnected with my congregants in the following weeks, I held two questions in the back of my mind: "What are their concerns?" and "Do I have anything useful to say about them?"

Within a few weeks, they were greeting me after the service with eye contact, presence, and reflections about the morning's topic. We were back in the groove together.

Most of us have had that kind of experience: being so inspired that we don't really connect with the people we're talking to. We talk right past them.

Being enlightened didn't mean the Buddha knew everything about everything. So as Upaka disappeared down the path shaking his head and muttering under his breath, I imagine the Buddha thinking, "That didn't go so well. I need another approach."

Getting the Ball Rolling

A few days later, in the outskirts of the little town of Sarnath, the Buddha came upon the group of five ascetic monks who had been old friends on the path. This time he paid careful attention to who they were and what their concerns were. He spoke in terms they'd relate to. This time, his words connected.

The world has not been quite the same since.

By the end of that talk, one of the monks, Kondañña was fully awakened. The others had to practice what he'd told them for a few days. Then they too awakened.

I'm grateful to Kondañña and his friends for their attainment. If the Buddha had been unsuccessful with them, he might have returned to the fig grove and disappeared from history.

If accepting Sujata's gift marked the birth of Buddhism, the talk to the five ascetics in a wildlife refuge in Sarnath marked Buddhism's entry into the world. The talk is known as "The Dhammacakkappavattana Sutta: The Discourse on Setting the Wheel of Dhamma in Motion." We can think of it as "Getting the Ball Rolling."

In it the Buddha laid out the core of a meditation practice. The Buddha became famous for tailoring his teachings to suit his students' temperaments and proclivities. The discourse contained the foundation practices that appear in various ways in all his teachings. It describes what we all have to do one way or another to wake up.

Wouldn't it have been nice if someone had taken a few notes?

While the five monks didn't take notes, they repeated what they remembered to others who repeated it to still more people. It was passed along imperfectly for several hundred years until somebody finally wrote it down.

We can find that version in the *Saṃyutta Nikāya,* Sutta 56.11.[7] In the next chapter, we'll look at the essential practices that the Buddha laid out in that seminal talk.

---

[7] On my website (www.dougkraft.com) is an article called "Turning Toward" which examines that talk line by line.

360 Degree Awareness

One of the many inspirations of the story of how Buddhism entered the world is his emphasis on a wide open 360° field of awareness rather than a tightly focused, one-pointed concentration.

A common technique in his day and ours is to place our attention on a single object like the breath, a kōan, a mantra, or feeling of kindness. We are encouraged to exclude everything else until our awareness is "absorbed" into this one item. In this way hindrances and unwholesome states are suppressed, leaving the mind blissful.

In his own training, the Buddha developed one-pointed concentration to a higher degree than any of his contemporaries. He found it didn't work.

I find it hard to imagine the Buddha teaching a technique that had failed him.

On the other hand, a quiet, collected, stable awareness called "*samādhi*" is very helpful. One way to cultivate samādhi is to use a single object such as the breath or kindness as a home base to return to when the mind wanders. This can be skillful if it does not become the exclusive object of attention. We return to our home base to help the mind-heart find its natural stability. But we don't suppress other objects. An easy way to do this is with the Six R process (see p. 287).

This is a middle way between one-pointedness and aimless mental wandering. These distinctions are important. The Buddha found that learning to observe how the mind-heart works is liberating while trying to control how it works is entrapping (see p. 105–112). If we see only one object, we won't see how the mind naturally operates. But if we have no stability, awareness won't see anything very deeply — it just bounces around reactively.

Over-concentration creates tension while bouncing around does nothing to release tension. The middle way is to release tightness so that awareness naturally settles while remaining wide open to see what's going on.

After all, meditation is ultimately about awareness rather than a single object of awareness like the breath or a mantra. As we relax the tightness in the mind-heart, natural awareness remains behind — pure, clear, kind, intimate, impersonal, luminous, and stable.

When you try to stop activity to find stillness,
your very effort fills you with activity.

–Sengstan

Related Chapters

1
Finding a Compass

When liking and disliking are both absent,
everything becomes clear and undisguised. Make
the smallest distinction, however, and heaven
and earth are set infinitely apart.

—Sengstan

© Adam Eurich

1. Three Essential Practices

Turn toward. Relax into. Savor peace.

These three attitudes and essential practices – turning toward, relaxing into, and savoring peace – give Buddhism its distinctive flavor. The Buddha adapted his instructions to fit the gifts and vulnerabilities

© Adam Eurich

of his followers, but most of the practices he taught have these three elements in common.

Context

The Buddha first articulated the three practices in his talk to his old meditation buddies — the five ascetics — in the deer park in Sarnath not long after his awakening (see pp. *xvii–xxxii*). He began by introducing them to his concept of the middle way. Then he went on to describe these practices. They have been passed down to us as the "Four Noble Truths." Most Buddhist scholars and teachers agree that they are the foundation of Buddhism. But titling them "Four Noble Truths" can be misleading.

First, the "Four Noble Truths" aren't "Truths" with a capital "T." They aren't declarations about ultimate reality. They are simple observations about ordinary life – things like, "we all hurt from time to time," and "ease feels better than uptightness."

Second, they aren't noble. In *Pāli*, the original language of the *suttas* (discourses), the word "noble" doesn't refer to the truths/observations but to the mind of a person who engages them wisely. Each observation has a practice associated with it. These practices ennoble or uplift the person. The teacher and scholar Stephen Batchelor refers to them as "The Four Ennobling Truths" to shift the emphasis from the observations to the way we engage them.

And finally, there aren't four. The supposed fourth is the Eightfold Path. That's not a truth or an observation but a useful checklist. It's a construct. If we practice the first three wisely and get stuck, the checklist gives eight areas we can reflect upon to help fine-tune our meditation.

In the West, religion is usually defined by sets of beliefs, statements of faith, or metaphysical manifestos about ultimate reality. The Buddha was not interested in such views. He was interested in how we engage our experience.

Early Western translators did not understand this about Buddhism. They elevated the mundane observations to capital "T" Truths and skipped lightly over the practices associated with each.

However, the three practices are the foundation of the Buddha's meditation instructions and the common elements that appear over and over in his various teachings.

To understand the three practices, it helps to understand three Pāli words — *dukkha, taṇhā,* and *nirodha.* And it helps to understand three practices — understanding, abandoning, and realizing. The Buddha said, "Dukkha is to be understood. Taṇhā is to be abandoned. Nirodha is to be realized."

Let's look at each.

Understanding Dukkha

The first practice is understanding *dukkha.*

Dukkha is a Pāli term most often translated as "suffering" or "dissatisfaction." Leigh Brasington, a scholar and teacher, translates it as "bummer."[8] The Buddha didn't say that life is

---

[8] His website, http://www.leighb.com, contains a fun and

suffering or that life is a bummer — only that it has bummers. Anyone never been bummed out? Anyone never suffered? It's not a profound observation. There is nothing noble about bellyaches, abscessed teeth, broken bones, broken hearts, disappointment, grief, loss, anxiety, or bummers of any kind.

To fully understand someone, we have to do more than diagnose them or draw an intellectual conclusion. We have to know the person empathetically and intimately from the inside. We have to know how they tick, what motivates them, how they see the world, what frightens them, what they aspire to.

To fully understand ourselves, we need the same kind of empathy for ourselves.

Similarly, the Buddha said that to awaken we must fully understand the nature of suffering, dissatisfaction, and bummers. Arms-length analysis is not enough. We have to know how suffering feels, what makes it tick, how it arises, how it moves, how it passes away. It's not helpful to get wrapped up in the stories and concepts behind the bummers. But it helps to see their processes.

We'll never find this deep knowledge if we're running away or trying to shield ourselves from dukkha. We must experience it intimately without resistance.

The five ascetics had been trying to rise above the waves of suffering or push suffering below the waves like a beach ball that would pop back up when they relaxed. The Buddha said, "Turn toward the bummers. Relax into them. Let go of your ideas and see anew. Dive in until you know their true nature. You must fully understand."

When we engage dukkha openly this way, we come to see how suffering arises and passes. And we see that the experience of suffering is rooted in *taṇhā*. This brings us to the second of the three practices.

---

illuminating discussion of this translation.

Abandoning Tanhā

The Buddha said, "The origin of the experience of suffering is taṇhā. Taṇhā must be abandoned."

Taṇhā is a preverbal, precognitive, instinctual tightening. When we are about to step off the sidewalk and notice a car coming our way, the body tightens. We don't think about it, contemplate it, or decide to stiffen. It just happens. When we see something delicious, the body and mind tightens slightly to prepare to move toward it. We may not notice the tightening because our focus is on the treat out there and because the inner tightening can be subtle.

The tightening is not willful — it's not something we decide to do. It may be followed by thoughts and decisions. But taṇhā itself is a preverbal, preconceptual, complex reflex. This tightening is the root of a sense of self — identifying various phenomena as a part of "me" or belonging to "myself."

Taṇhā is often translated as "craving." It can be large and powerful, like a junkie with darting eyes and trembling hands craving her next fix. But it can also be as subtle as an inclination, as wispy as a soft yearning, as quiet as a worry, as light as a fantasy. Sitting in meditation we sometimes feel the mind-heart lean subtly toward or away from an idea, image, feeling, or experience. When we're bored, we may feel the mind thicken into a fog. These are different flavors of taṇhā.

When we fully understand dukkha, we see that it arises out of taṇhā: suffering arises out of tension.

Taking this on faith, recognizing this in our own experience, or even fully understanding taṇhā is not enough. It has to be abandoned: we relax physically, emotionally, and mentally.

Notice that we don't abandon the suffering; we don't try to walk away from it, rise above it, turn lemons into lemonade, push it under water, or grin and bear it. We understand the suffering and let it be what it is.

It is the tension that we abandon by softening. This does not always bring immediate relief. But without tension, the suffering runs out of fuel. When there is no more desire, aversion, or confusion, new suffering does not arise.

To say this succinctly, seeing the source of suffering is not uplifting. Relaxing into the tension is. The Buddha is not asking us to accept or verify an observation. He's inviting us to engage the observation by relaxing the physical, emotional, and mental tightness that gives fuel to so much difficulty.

Taṇhā is not something we accept. It is something we abandon. And when we do, we experience the third observation and its practice.

Nirodha

The Pāli term "nirodha" is usually translated as "cessation." When we abandon the tension in taṇhā, it ceases. Taṇhā comes in three brands — desire, aversion, and delusion. Nirodha is often defined as the absence of these three.

This is accurate but not necessarily informative. It's like describing a lovely day as the absence of sandstorms or a wonderful camping trip as the absence of rape and pillage. The absence of greed, aversion, and delusion tells us what nirodha is not, but not what it is.

The experience of nirodha begins as pure awareness — awareness without tension or distortion. It's clear and perceptive. It has no agenda — it just sees things as they are. It doesn't judge or compare. It feels kind and loving. It's relaxed, soft, and spacious. It's uplifted and gently luminous. And it does nothing to draw attention to itself. Notice that each of the Six Rs resonates with a quality of pure awareness.[9]

---

[9] **Recognize** resonates with clear perception. **Release** or letting things be as they are resonates with awareness without an agenda or need to compare or judge. **Relax** implies a relaxed awareness. **Re-smile** generates uplifted qualities. **Return** is about returning to the practice of sending out luminous qualities. And **Repeat** suggests an awareness that is patient and has no need to make a fuss or draw attention to

Sitting under the rose apple tree, the young Gautama felt kind, loving, accepting, spacious, relaxed, uplifted, and luminous (see pp. *xxv–xxviii*). When we experience this pure awareness, we realize that it's been here all along.

It's as if we're in a classroom of rowdy kids who are banging chairs, throwing erasers, yelling, and punching. Over in the corner someone is writing poetry. We don't notice her because of the hubbub.

Then one morning we arrive early to class. The room is empty except for the young poet. We talk quietly with her or sit silently as she composes. Gradually the other kids enter with their boom boxes and carrying on. Soon the room is back to cacophony.

However, now, even with all the noise, we can sense the poet because we know what she feels like.

Like the poet in the classroom, pure awareness is always with us. Without pure awareness beneath it, there would be no awareness of any kind. Distorted awareness is pure awareness covered with junk.

We can't create nirodha or pure awareness because it's already here. Anything we do to create it just adds tension and distortion. All we can do is relax into it. Relaxing allows the tightness to soften and the distortions to dissolve into pure awareness.

Here's a way to demonstrate pure awareness:

Hold up your forearm. Then let it relax and flop into your lap. ...

Now, do it again. But this time, as the arm relaxes, relax all your thoughts at the same time. ...

Do it again — just release all the contents of the mind as you release the arm. ...

Try it a third time.

---

itself. See "Appendix A. The Six Rs and Five Ss Overview," p. 287 for more details on the Six Rs. Also, the "Pure Awareness" section on p. 160 is helpful for comparing pure awareness and the Six Rs.

Did you notice a moment when the mind was relatively free of content? The Tibetan Mahāmudrā tradition calls this "the natural mind." After a short time, maybe less than half a breath, the thoughts start up again. But for a moment, the mind has no content, just pure awareness of awareness. This is a form of nirodha — awareness without tension or distortion.

Now, relax as you look around the room. As you notice various objects, see if you can feel that quiet, open space of pure awareness — the natural mind — behind your thoughts and perceptions. As you notice various thoughts and images in the mind, see if you can feel the awareness that holds them. It's like shifting your attention from clouds to the sky that holds them (see p. 77).

Pure awareness is not just an absence. It has a feel and texture of its own. As we know it more intimately, we can let the mind rest there in meditation. It can help guide our practice.

Realizing Nirodha

When we talk about realizing nirodha in this context, "realize" means "making it real" as in "making it known through direct experience."

There are various depths of realizing nirodha. Some only show up in advanced practice. If you aren't familiar with them now, you can look forward to them as your meditation deepens. But I want to mention them all now for the sake of completeness.

Savoring

The lightest experience of nirodha comes from savoring quiet moments.

When we abandon tension, tension subsides. The remaining peacefulness may be so quiet that we don't notice it. The mind is drawn to tension. Nirodha has none. So awareness may slide right over it. Sitting in meditation or walking in the woodlands, sometimes my mind becomes soft and luminous without my knowing it. I'm more familiar with striving and figuring things out. Peacefulness doesn't jump up and down and wave its arms crying, "Notice me! Notice me!" Sometimes I'm oblivious to the glowing, lovely quiet.

The lightest nirodha comes from noticing the quiet and savoring it — not attaching or holding on to it, but relaxing and enjoying it. This helps us know it is real — we realize nirodha.

When our kids were growing up, my wife and I tried to keep them away from soda and other sugar as much as we could. But we didn't want them to develop a big complex about it. So once a week, they could have a small glass of soda. Usually it was on Saturday morning.

Damon, our youngest son, would look at the little glass of cola, smell it, take a tiny sip and let it swirl around on his tongue. He'd close his eyes and savor it as fully as he could while it lasted.

In the beginning, savoring nirodha means just absorbing the loveliness of the relative quiet.

Fading of Desire

As nirodha goes deeper, we begin to realize where it came from. Imagine we'd been hungering for something sweet all day. Finally we get a first bite of a mango or chocolate: "ah." The taste brings bliss — at least for a moment until we start hankering for a second bite.

The problem is that we may believe that happiness comes from getting what we want. The advertising industry preaches the philosophy of trying to get what we want and get rid of what we don't want.

But if we shift our attention from the chocolate or mango to the quality of awareness, we see that with that first bite, the hankering disappears. We no longer want it because we have it. Too often we confuse getting what we want with not wanting. So rather than savor that lovely state of mind, we focus on getting the next bite. Aversion and greed are back all too soon and bliss is gone.

So a deeper quality of nirodha comes from realizing that the happiness didn't come from a mango tree or a cocoa tree. It didn't come from "out there." It came from "in here" when the mind-heart abandoned the tension of liking and disliking.

Ever-Present Well-being

An even deeper realization comes from feeling the quiet happiness that is with us all the time. Like the poet in the noisy class, it's here to be experienced each moment we aren't distracted by the hubbub.

With this realization, we stop fighting the noisy kids and shift our attention to the ever-present quiet. We recognize the distractions, release them — let them be without holding on or pushing away — and relax into the background stillness enveloping us.

Sometimes this appears as a figure-background shift. Rather than sitting in our rumbling mind and looking at a distant peacefulness, we are sitting in the peacefulness seeing a distant rumbling. Rather than sitting in the rambunctious class looking out into the peaceful grounds outside, we are sitting outside, enjoying the trees and the sunlight while gazing in at the noisy classroom.

Gael Turnbull wrote a poem that hints at this deeper experience of nirodha:

> *I remember once*
> *in a far off country*
> *it doesn't matter where*
> *or even when*
> *it had been a hot day*
> *and a lot of work to be done*
> *and I was tired*
> *I stopped by the road*
> *and walked across a field*
> *and came to the shores of a lake*
> *the sun was bright on the water*
> *and I swam out from the shore*
> > *into the deep cold water*
> > *far out of my depth*

and forgot
for a moment
I forgot
where I had come from
where I was going
what I had done yesterday
what I had to do tomorrow
even my work
my home
my friends
even my name
       even my name
       alone in the deep water
       with the sky above
and whether that lake was a lake
or the shore of some great sea
or some lost tributary of time itself
for a moment
I looked through
I passed through
I had one glimpse
       as it happened
       one day in that far off country
       for a moment
       it was so

Winking Out

Some have experienced a deeper form of nirodha where the mind becomes so relaxed that perception, feeling, and consciousness relax and fade. I call it "winking out."[10] This is a more advanced practice that arises on its own as our meditation deepens beyond the eighth *jhāna,* or eighth stage of practice.

The Buddha's third essential practice includes savoring peacefulness, noticing the fading of desire, recognizing the well-being that is always with us, and winking out. These are what he meant by realizing nirodha.

Interwoven

These practices are closely woven together. Understanding dukkha, abandoning taṇhā, and realizing nirodha form a foundation for meditation. And they form an attitude toward all of life.

At its core Buddhism is not a practice, set of beliefs, code of conduct, or set of rituals. It has all of these. But in essence Buddhism is an attitude of turning toward whatever life brings our way, relaxing into it, and realizing the pure awareness that is always here.

There is one caveat: if we're freaked out and upset, then looking at what's going on through that disturbed, tense awareness doesn't help. Whatever we see will be distorted by that tension. We have to turn toward life with a relaxed mind and open heart.

So, if the mind-heart is uptight and we can't relax it, it's wise to do whatever we can to help it settle and stabilize. This is where so many practices come from — different ways to stabilize the mind. Techniques range from koans, to breath awareness, to sending kindness, to contemplating the ephemeral nature of our lives and all we experience.

---

[10] In *Buddha's Map* [2013], Chapter 20 I discuss the phenomenon of winking out in the context of meditation.

But it's very important to realize that if all we do is stabilize the mind, that's not enough. It is essential, but not sufficient by itself. The Burmese meditation master Sayadaw U Tejaniya says, "If the awareness never comes off the object of awareness and turns to awareness itself, your meditation won't go very far."

So by all means, do what needs to be done to find a little relaxed, open, stable peace. Then use that wholesome awareness to look into what's going on in meditation and life outside of meditation.

If we aren't aware of the qualities of the mind-heart, we won't realize the depths that are possible — the depths and heights that are here all the time just waiting to be savored.

These three essential practices are embedded throughout this *Meditator's Field Guide*. Turning toward is fundamental to the section "Finding a Compass." Relaxing into is fundamental to "Getting Our Selves Out of the Way." Savoring peace is fundamental to "Glowing Like a Candle" and "Expanding Infinitely." And all these practices help in "Cleaning Up Our Act."

Related Chapters

2. Resilience

It is due to our choosing to accept or reject that we do not see the true nature of things.

— Sengstan

The essence of Buddhism is not a religion, philosophy, meditation practice, or code of ethics. Buddhism has all these, but at its core it is an attitude of turning toward whatever life brings along, softening into it, and savoring peacefulness (as discussed in the last chapter, pp. 3-13).

I was looking for a story, image, or piece of poetry that captured this attitude without using words like "mindfulness," "acceptance," or "insight." If the Buddha had anything useful to say (and I think he did!), it wasn't useful because he *invented* it, created, it, or made it up. It was because he *discovered* it in the core of human experience. If his teachings are truly universal, there must be other people who found and expressed something similar without using Buddhist lingo.

I recalled the refrain of a song by Jim Scott. Jim is a world-class acoustical guitarist who played with the Paul Winter Consort. He's also a composer who recorded several albums of his own music.

When he was touring California several years ago, I set up a Sunday afternoon concert for him as he passed through Sacramento.

Just before the concert, Jim and I were checking the stage, microphones, and equipment. He was talking about his life – personal struggles, family concerns, and anguish. He was very open. As he stood in center stage, emotions rose to the surface and a few tears slid quietly down his cheek.

After a few minutes I interrupted, "Jim, there's a few hundred people here watching us. The concert was supposed to start a few minutes ago."

"Oh," he said. He sat down, turned on the mic, picked up his guitar, and for the next two hours delivered an exquisite concert in which he was totally present and attuned to the audience. Music flowed through him from somewhere beyond.

I wondered if this was what it was like to be with Mozart. Reportedly Mozart's personal life was a mess. But when he composed or played, he got completely out of the way and let the beauty flow through him. Jim did this easily.

There's a Way

The lead song on one of Jim's albums is "There's a Way."[11] The refrain goes like this:

There's a way and there's an ease to the life we lead,
There's a dream of peace not so far away.
There's a force and there's a flow to the life we lead,
If we will just release and let it be that way.

Most of our lives have struggles, concerns, anguish, and poignancies. We may hope meditation will fix them or offer protection from difficulty. But usually it makes us more sensitive without actually fixing anything.

The Buddha's practice starts from a radical proposition: there is nothing that needs to be fixed. There is a love, wisdom, power, flow, and ease that are with us already. They will take care of us, "if we will just release and let it be that way."

The trick is to release and get out of the way. Not so easy.

The next morning, Jim and my wife Erika were standing in our kitchen. Erika is also a musician. She was telling Jim how much she enjoyed his music. Even though it is technically challenging, he plays and sings with an easy flow.

Jim smiled shyly and said, "I took private." This alluded to high school bands where most kids were taught in a group setting and stumbled around learning to play as best they could.

---

11 "There's a Way" appears on *Earth, Sky, Love and Dreams,* © 2002, www.jimscottguitar.com.

A few kids stood out and got first chairs and solos. When asked, "How'd you get so good," they said, "I take private," meaning they took private lessons with a teacher who gave them more individualized training and discipline.

At the core of meditation is a similar paradox: it may take discipline to learn how to get out of the way.

Waves

To help us learn, we turn to another artist, a spiritual artist named Siddhārtha Gautama of the Shakya clan. Over 2,500 years ago he left detailed, step-by-step instructions on how to get out of the way.

The essence of his guidance is another paradox: to get out of the way, we don't turn away – we turn toward. Whatever disturbances come into our lives, we turn toward them and relax into them. In meditation, this is our job: open to whatever arises, soften into it, and savor the peace that follows. (See pp. 3–14, for more details of how the Buddha described these practices.)

Here's an image of these processes:

I was born in Boston, Massachusetts, and moved to Houston when I was seven weeks old. I lived in Houston for sixteen years. Once or twice a week in the hot summers, my three brothers, one sister, and I tumbled into our blue-and-white family Chevy station wagon and our mother drove us to Galveston so we could play in the Gulf of Mexico.

Houston is sixty miles from Galveston and sixty feet above sea level. The land slopes downward at a rate of one foot per mile: about as flat as one can imagine.

The Gulf floor is only a little steeper. We could wade out several hundred feet and only be waist deep.

When big waves came, trying to escape them was futile. Running through water was exhausting, and the shore was too far. If we tried to get away, waves caught us from behind and knocked us flat.

So we planted our feet and braced as the waves crashed upon us. This worked for the small waves. But water is heavy. Big waves outweighed us ten to one. We weren't strong enough to stand up to them.

Finally we learned that the best way to greet a wave was to relax into it. When the wave was really big, we'd relax and dive into it.

As scary and frothy as the waves seemed when they roared toward us, if we relaxed into them, the surf passed over and left us in the essence of the wave: sea water, plain old sea water. Not so bad.

Then our natural buoyancy brought us to the surface so that we floated in that little trough of peace between the waves.

Resilience

If you thought this meditation practice would protect you from the slings and arrows of misfortune, my condolences. I'm sorry for your loss. As far as I've been able to discover, there is nothing to protect us from the ocean of life with all its ups and downs. It's where we live.

But meditation can give us a healthy and wholesome way to respond to waves so we don't tumble as much.

When I trained with the Korean Zen master Sheng Sean, he had a wooden statue of a Buddha with a rounded bottom. He had stapled one end of a piece of elastic to that bottom and the other end to a board upon which the Buddha sat.

Sheng Sean swung the back of his hand and knocked the statue over. The rubber band pulled it back upright.

He said, "Nothing can protect us from what life brings along. We all get whapped. But meditation can be the rubber band that brings us upright more quickly. Meditation gives us resilience."

So we escape nothing in this practice. But hopefully, it'll give us a little more resilience – and maybe even a few surfing tips.

And it all begins in this attitude of turning toward, softening into the waves that come our way and savoring peacefulness.

In time, we learn to rest in the waves themselves.

© Julia Caesar, unsplash.com

When you don't care where you are, anywhere is home.
– Inscription on a backpack

Related Chapters

3. Rest in the Waves

[The duck] can rest while the Atlantic heaves,
because he rests in the Atlantic ...
He has made himself part of the boundless,
by easing himself into it just where it touches him.

– Donald C. Babcock,
The New Yorker Magazine, October 4, 1947

Many people come to meditation looking for some peace or well-being. They have felt buffeted by the surf and want to calm the waters of their lives.

Unfortunately, calming the waters for more than a few moments is unlikely. As far back as we can see in history, there have been waves: failure, death, famine, war, disease, heartbreak, violence, and tragedy. It's likely these will continue into the future. They are part of this world.

Fortunately, inner calm, peace, and well-being don't require stopping the waves. Like the duck sitting in the waves in Donald C. Babcock's poem, the art is learning how to rest in whatever comes our way: "He can rest while the Atlantic heaves because he rests in the Atlantic." Whether faced with sorrow, joy, fear, delight, peace, or restlessness, all we have to do is see the truth of the moment. Then, rather than trying to control our experience, we let it be, relax, and soften into it.

Unhappiness does not come from the waves. It comes from resisting them or wanting them to be different than they are. When we are content with whatever life brings, our contentment is as boundless as the ocean.

My teacher John Travis used a different metaphor to remind me of this. I had just told him my life felt fine at the moment. But an avalanche of projects and deadlines was heading toward me. I was running downhill and staying ahead of it. So I was fine right now. But if I stopped running I'd be buried.

He looked at me quietly for a moment. "Your delusion," he said with a twinkle, "is thinking you have to sit still in order to be at peace."

Sitting meditation is learning how to rest in the waves that pass through us. Meditation in active life is learning how to relax even when we're on the move.

Don't resist or push. Soften.
– Bhante Vimalaraṁsi

Related Chapters

4. Nothing Is Difficult, Some Things Take Time

It is idle, having planted an acorn in the morning, to expect that afternoon to sit in the shade of the oak.

– Antoine de Saint-Exupery,
from *Wind, Sand, and Stars*

I awoke around 12:30 in the morning, rolled over, and began to slide back into slumber. A thought drifted lightly through the side of my mind: "He's an emotional coward."

"He" referred to a man with whom I'd had a difficult relationship. I'd handled it with equanimity, empathy, and compassion. I had been a paragon of kind maturity.

The phrase "emotional coward" captured the essence of what I'd found difficult. The angry vapors seeping out of the phrase brought me back from the edge of sleep. "Send him an email. Tell him he's an emotional coward," I thought.

I no longer felt like a paragon of compassion. "I'd like to stick a finger in his eye." Beneath my spiritual sensibilities was a tantrum I had been quietly pushing aside.

I might have been able to subdue the ire. But when I try to fight the truth, I always lose sooner or later. And the truth was I was angry. The genie was out of the bottle, and I had no desire to push it back in.

Now I was thoroughly awake. I got out of bed, wrapped up in a blanket, and sat down to meditate. I recited the refuges, precepts, and two aspirations: "I seek to observe the mind without preference." "I seek clarity and acceptance."

My object of meditation was equanimity spreading in all directions. After a short while, it began to thin out into clear mind.

Then a thought erupted: "I want to tell him this, this, this, and that." I didn't really want to poke him in the eye. But a good tongue-lashing would feel satisfying.

I recognized the flush of anger. Meditation is a purification process. As the mind-heart quiets down, psychic toxins can rush to the surface. It's healing.

So I just let the feelings be. I released them in the sense of not trying to hold onto them or push them away. But I gave them plenty of space to romp around inside. At the same time, I relaxed the tension in them: it felt like relaxing into the anger. I smiled slightly and sent out a little equanimity.

"This would be a better way to say it," I thought. "That'll get him."

An hour later, waves of righteousness continued to rise through me, followed by moments of quiet, followed by more waves. I just tried to stay out of the way and let them do their thing. They'd throw me off balance for a moment. I'd feel it, release it, relax into it, and return to equanimity only to have another wave throw me against the rocks.

I had hoped this would gradually subside, but it kept going. I felt discouraged. I recognized the discouragement as just another impersonal energy, released it, let it be, softened into it, and smiled.

Fifteen minutes later I noticed the thoughts no longer had any specific content. They still reverberated like buffalo stampeding across the plains. But I couldn't make out individual animals anymore. There weren't specific thoughts, just thundering hooves.

Then the rumbling ceased. There was still aversion without content. I continued to recognize what was going on in the mind-heart, release it, relax into it, smile softly, and send out peacefulness.

Then it was all gone. There was only a pervading quiet and ease. I vaguely remembered that I had been upset about something. But it took effort to recall what the fuss was about. "Oh yes, that guy." Compassion welled up for his suffering that had made him behave so poorly. There was nothing I could do about him. So I let it drift away like the last clouds fading into a clear sky.

There was a slight luminosity in the back of my mind. I thought it peculiar that I found it easier to recognize the upset than this quiet glow. So I relaxed into the glow.

In a while I winked out — my awareness disappeared for a few minutes. When I came back, the mind-heart was soft, quietly joyful, and expansive. And my body was fatigued.

It was 2:30 in the morning. I'd been meditating for two hours. I crawled back into bed and slid into a deep and peaceful sleep.

Presence and Patience

One of the paradoxes of the Buddha's spiritual path is that it grinds to a halt if we try to rush. However, it unfolds quickly when we aren't in a hurry to get anywhere.

The path thrives on presence. And presence thrives on patience: just letting things be as they are. Patience feels like relaxing into what is, even if it's anger or discouragement.

There are many ways to not be present. Paul Simon wrote a song called "50 Ways to Leave Your Lover." There are at least 50 ways to leave the present. These may be the top five:

• Resistance: deliberately ignoring what we experience because we don't like it.

• Impatience: anticipating where a feeling might lead and trying to get out in front of it rather than letting it unfold at its own pace.

• Tensing: tightening either to resist what is or to get ahead of what is.

• Storytelling: making up stories and ideas about what's happening and focusing on those tales and concepts rather than just being with the unedited moment.

• Selfing: creating an image of who we think we are, who we'd like to be, or who we're afraid we are and comparing our experience to that image.

When we are present with what is, it feels like relaxing into our experience. Perhaps the present feels like a tantrum,

water crashing on the rocks, or a quiet glow. It doesn't matter. Whatever is, we just soften into it as it is.

When we don't do this, the path feels very difficult. When we truly relax into it, it feels very simple and easy. As the cellist and educator David Darling said to me once in a workshop, "Nothing is difficult. Some things take time."

Related Chapters

5. A Vote for Kindness: No Unchanging Self

Does this path have a heart?

– Carlos Castaneda

Following a path is a common metaphor for maturing spiritually. The further we go, the wiser we become. The wiser we become, the more contentment we enjoy. The destination is enlightened well-being. The image of the path is one of a traveler on a journey to a goal. It assumes there is somewhere to go and someone to go there.

Carlos Castaneda's teacher, Don Juan, critiqued this metaphor. He said contentment is found in how we travel, not in where the travel ends, because the path has no particular destination.

The Buddha agreed: how we experience each moment is more important than an imagined endpoint. But his analysis is more basic and perplexing: the problem is not the path but the assumption that we have an independent self-essence that walks it. The Buddha said that ultimately we have no separate self.

This teaching is captured in a single word, *anattā*. In Pāli, the language of the earliest records of the Buddha's talks, "attā" means "self," and "an-" is a negation. So anattā literally means "no self" or "non-self." In English, this sounds like nonsense: if I have no self, then who or what is the self who experiences this self I don't have?

Richard Gombrich is a Buddhist scholar who suggests that the confusion arises out of an incomplete translation.[12] *Attā* (or *atman* in Sanskrit) means more than the English word "self"

---

[12] Richard Gombrich, *What the Buddha Thought* (Sheffield, United Kingdom and Bristol, Connecticut: Equinox, 2013), 8–11.

implies. It refers to an eternal, unchanging, higher self that is our true, absolute essence. The goal of the spiritual path for the Buddha's contemporaries was finding this unchanging attā.

What the Buddha meant was that we have no *unchanging* self (no attā). To the Buddha's contemporaries, "no unchanging attā" would have been redundant. But in modern English, this nuance is lost unless we insert "unchanging" into the phrase so it reads "no unchanging self."

The Buddha didn't say that we don't have a self. In the relative world we obviously do. My self is typing these words. Your self is reading them. But in absolute reality, we have no enduring self.

After we've put so much time and energy into a spiritual path, the news that we have no lasting self-essence may be discouraging. The Buddha responded by recommending kindness, compassion, joy, and equanimity. Carlos Castaneda did too when he shifted the focus from where the path leads to how it feels to walk it: does this path have heart? Kindness is all that matters. Kindness is not a destination; it's a way of walking.

Self As Time

Still, the distinction between having a relative self and not having an absolute self can be confusing. One way to sort this out is to consider self in the context of time. As a reified concept, self can be said to exist or not. But when placed in the context of time, self is relatively real but not absolutely real.

Here is a thought experiment to illustrate:

Imagine that you lived for a hundred years. Every day a few pictures were taken of you. The pictures were made into a movie that shows a hundred years of body changes in twenty minutes.

To make this more interesting, imagine the film starts several decades before your birth and continues a century beyond your death. What would we see?

At first there would be nothing – or perhaps your mother and father. Then your mother becomes pregnant. Her body swells rapidly, and out you come. During the next few film moments, that tiny body does little but nurse, pee, poop, sleep, and gurgle. Nevertheless, as food flows through, it stretches, swells, and grows. Over the next several minutes of the movie, the body gets up, straightens out, fills out musculature, and grows hair. As the film goes on, the body matures sexually. Its frame, eyes, and skin become vibrant with youth and young adulthood. It comes into full stature.

Then the growth slows down. The hair thins a little. A few blemishes appear. The skin sags here and there.

A dozen minutes into the film, the shoulders slump. The eyes are clear but some of the body tone is gone. There is a little extra fat.

Then the body shrinks. The parts don't line up as smoothly – the symmetry is gone. The hair loses its color. The skin is uneven and blotchy. The frame becomes frail. The eyes turn watery.

Suddenly, the body is lying down with closed eyes and no sign of life. It's dead.

The film continues. We watch the skin dry out and shrivel. It wastes away. In a few film moments, there is little but bones. Over the next several minutes, the bones dry out, crumble, and blow away.

During the last long minutes of the movie, there is nothing on the screen. Even the bone dust is gone.

The film ends with a question stretched across the screen, "Do you exist?" The question fades into another, "What matters?"

How you answer the first question depends on the time period we are talking about. In some timeframes you obviously exist as an infant, a maturing young adult, a middle-aged person in the prime of life, a frail sage. The self looks different at different times. It feels differently, thinks differently, and views life differently. Still, it's clearly there.

Yet ultimately, the self doesn't exist. It has no essence. It has no core that goes on for eternity. The sense of self arises out of various conditions. Its nature is to fall apart.

If we are anything, we are like a sand castle on the beach. When the tide washes over, nothing essential is lost. Every grain of sand remains somewhere. But the configuration is gone. We have no permanent configuration apart from everything else. There is no eternal self-essence.

Weird

Intellectually we all know this. But it's hard to hold the thought that we arise out of nothing and that in not too many decades we'll be dust blowing in the wind or absorbed by the earth.

The reality of this first touched me when I was seven and then again as a teenager.

When I was seven years old, my mother told me where babies came from: the sexual act, eggs, sperm, the whole business. I had a normal seven-year-old response to this information: "Oh Gross!"

But later that night as I lay in bed gazing at the ceiling, I thought, "What if my mom and dad had not gone to the University of Michigan at the same time? They might never have met. I would not have been conceived. I would not exist." Nonexistence was pretty weird for a seven year old to think about.

"What if they had met but not fallen in love? What if they had not decided to get married? What if they had not been in the mood to start a baby on a particular summer day in August of 1947? What if a different one of the 50 million sperm had reached the egg first?"

I could think of millions of ways by which I would not have come into existence!

Maybe my parents would have had a different second child. They might have even given it my name! No one would miss me. No one would know anything about me. No one would even notice that I didn't exist because ... I didn't exist.

We may think we're part of a larger plan. But I saw no evidence of that. Life itself may be inevitable, but our particular organism is a mathematical improbability. Our individual existence is a fluke. That's what I thought. Pretty weird.

Flash forward eight years:

During my junior year in high school, something happened that I had never experienced: a guy in my circle of friends ceased to exist.

Larry was smart and thoughtful. One morning Paul told me Larry was dead – he'd been killed in a car crash.

Four days later an even stranger thing happened: we had our French midterm exam right on schedule. Larry used to sit up front on the right side of the classroom. During the test I looked around and wanted to yell, "Has anyone noticed that Larry has vanished? Does his life make any difference?" I wanted to write across my test, "Laurence est mort! Laurence est mort!"

But I didn't. It had begun to sink in that when I die, 99.999 percent of the billions of people on Earth will not notice. Yes, a few will mourn my passing for a few months. But in the following days, they will probably eat breakfast, read books, go to movies, complain about politics, and go on with their lives. The sun will rise each morning, the birds will sing each spring, clouds will continue to float in the sky. Five or ten years after I die, the traces of my existence will dissolve into the larger flow of life as if I had never existed.

Kindness

I'm not trying to bum us out. But it's wise to have a sober perspective to reflect on what really matters in life.

Given the millions of billions of creatures on the planet, given the over 13.5 billion years this universe has been growing, given the incredible expanse of time and space, our individual lives are less than a single flash of a lightning bug on a summer's night in a field of billions of fireflies. Our existence is a statistical fluke that vanishes so quickly.

What difference do our lives make? Perhaps nothing matters.

But if there is anything that influences the arc of life toward the good, I think it is kindness: simple, ordinary, unpretentious kindness. Perhaps nothing is more important than being gentle, clear, and kind to ourselves and one another. This sends ripples of healing kindness into the world with everything we do.

So I agree with the Buddha and Carlos Castaneda. There are paths we can travel. And they all lead to our dissolution. But if the way there is suffused with heart, kindness, and friendliness, then it's okay.

I vote for kindness.

Does this path have a heart? If it does, the path is good; if it doesn't it is of no use. Both paths lead nowhere; but one has a heart, the other doesn't. One makes for a joyful journey; as long as you follow it, you are one with it. The other will make you curse your life. One makes you strong; the other weakens you.

– Carlos Castaneda,
The Teachings of Don Juan

Related Chapters

6. It's Not Personal

To lose the self is to be enlightened by all things.
— Dogen

I throw a rock straight up in the air. Gravity pulls it straight down on my head. *Thunk!* The sore lump on my skull feels intimate, like a personal message: "Doug, don't ever do anything so stupid again."

Message received.

But it's not a private note. Gravity works the same in Chicago, Helsinki, and Buenos Aires as it does in my backyard. It follows the same principles on the moon, on Jupiter, across the galaxy, and across the universe. Gravity is a universal law intrinsic to the universe. To think it is personally concerned with my well-being or demise is narcissistic confusion.

I'm not helpless. If I understand gravity, I can throw a rock at a 45-degree angle. Or not throw it at all. It doesn't land on my head. I'm happier.

There are many laws that define the parameters of our lives. Some, like gravity, are simple and easy to understand. Most people objectively see the effects of gravity and don't take them personally. After falling off a porch, few people shake their fist at the sky and yell, "Gravity, stop picking on me!"

But some natural laws are subtle and complex. It's difficult to see how they operate. Not understanding them, we take them personally.

For example, more common than unwanted rocks dropping on my head are unwanted thoughts dropping into my mind. Subtle natural laws govern how this works. If I don't recognize the principles involved, I may see the thoughts as rude invaders of my space.

I began to understand this on a retreat in the desert a few years ago. One afternoon after a long, peaceful sitting, I went outside to do walking meditation. Thoughts began dropping in. They were old and repetitive – not even creative! I wished them away. They kept coming. I tried meditative techniques to get rid of them. They kept coming. "Why are you picking on me?" I muttered. They kept coming.

As if in response to my questions, an image of a brain appeared in my mind: an interconnected network of a hundred billion neurons. Over the years, I've thought about certain issues in certain ways. This fires related neural pathways. Repetition builds up these specific circuits. This is how the brain stores memories.

When I went outside, the breeze, birds, and sunlight stimulated the neural system. The extra energy flowing through the network lit up those old pathways. Subjectively I experienced these as familiar thoughts.

I chuckled. Even my thoughts were impersonal: by-products of biological laws generating neural paths.

If I get frustrated, that extra energy lights up more circuits. If I try to stop the thoughts, that exertion lights up more circuits – like trying not to think of a white horse.

Thoughts flow through the mind like waves flow over a pond. If I jump in to slap the waves down, that creates more disturbances. If I sit quietly by the pond, the waves run out of energy and a natural calm returns.

I'm not helpless. If I see how this works, I can regard the thoughts with a kindness and acceptance that put less stress into the system. If I relax, the circuits quiet down. In time they fade. Like the pond, the mind returns to its natural peace.

There are many other laws that govern how various states of mind and heart arise and pass away. The Buddha described these in detail in his Laws of Dependent Origination (*Paṭiccasamuppāda*): how everything arises because of causes and conditions. We have no control over what arises in the present. But our responses to this moment are part of the causes and conditions of future moments.

If we greet the present with strain and effort, it encourages tension in the future. If we greet the present with ease, we encourage the mind-heart to return to its natural equanimity. These are natural, impersonal laws of how the cosmos is put together. There is no reason for them. That's just how it is.

Wisdom meditation is a process of observing the mind-heart quietly and openly until we see how it works: how various attitudes and states arise, hang around, and pass away. The more we know how these laws operate, the less personal they seem. And the less personal they seem, the less tempted we are to rail against gravity or the chatter in the mind. We accept the way things work, and play within those dynamics. Rather than being upset about the lump on our head or the jingle in our mind, we laugh at our foolishness and stop throwing rocks straight up in the air or kvetching about the firing of a few synapses.

These laws aren't personal. They never were. And when we know this, they aren't a problem. Life feels lighter.

Every time I think of myself, I get depressed.
Ajahn Sumedho

Related Chapters

7. Contentment Without a Purpose or Secret Mission

Life has no purpose — it just is.

One way I can bolster a belief in an independent self-essence is to imagine that my life has a unique purpose: the universe has given me a secret mission to fulfill. If life feels flat, dull, or meaningless, I imagine I have lost touch with this purpose. In this mindset, I believe spiritual life is about discovering my purpose and devoting myself to it.

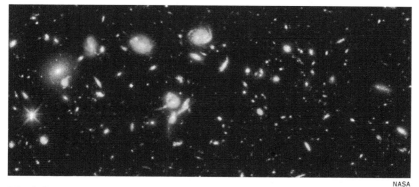

NASA

Hubble

When I find myself thinking this way, I like to reflect on a picture taken by the Hubble telescope. In the fall of 2003, scientists pointed the telescope's ultra-sensitive instruments at a seemingly empty spot of sky southwest of the constellation Orion. The spot spans an arc one-tenth the span of a full moon. For three months they collected readings from that tiny dot. They compiled the data into an image called the "Hubble Ultra-Deep Field."

Within that patch of space they found over ten thousand galaxies — not *stars* but ten thousand *galaxies* — that previously had been invisible to us. The average galaxy contains a hundred billion stars. Scientists now estimate the universe contains at least one hundred million million billion stars — that's a 1 followed by 23 zeros, or 100,000,000,000,000,000,000,000 stars.

How many of these stars have planets that might support complex life? Estimates run from one in five, to most of them. We might wonder, "What are the chances of intelligent life out there?" Close to 100 percent. "What are the chances that we humans are the most evolved species in the universe?" Close to zero.

To try to get my brain around that, I make the most conservative assumptions on these statistics and assume that only one in a million stars has life smarter than me. I look up at the sky at any area the size of the moon. That area probably contains at least three quarters of a billion species more advanced than me.

Arthur C. Clarke once said, "I'm sure the universe is full of intelligent life. It's just been too intelligent to come here."

So when I think the universe has given me a special mission, I sometimes lie down outside on a clear night and gaze into the sky: billions of galaxies and billions of billions of stars, and probably millions of millions of species smarter than me.

And here I am, lying on the edge of a tiny planet, circling a nondescript yellow star, in a life that lasts less than a blink of an eye compared to the thirteen billion years this universe has been unfolding. And I'm thinking the forces in the vastness of time and space have assigned me a special secret mission for my little squeak of a life? How narcissistic! That leaves this little, temporary self smiling.

Yes, I arise out of all of this. So there's probably a way I can live in harmony with all of it. But first I must see the universe as it truly is. To think the universe has singled me out from the seven billion people and hundreds of billions of creatures on this planet, amidst billions of billions of stars, is silly.

All paths lead nowhere.
– Carlos Castaneda

Related Chapters

8. Take Care of Awareness and It Will Take Care of You

*The Great Way is not difficult
for those who have no preference.*

– Sengstan

Walking through the fields along the American River, my mind ambled off into little vignettes about different people and situations. Some of the stories were embellished memories. Others were pure fiction. But they all had similar outlines: someone was treating me badly, and I was calling them out for it.

"Hmmm," I thought, "This is interesting."

I shifted my attention from the plot to the feeling tone of the thoughts. There was a sharp bitterness behind each story.

"Forgiveness is wiser than bitterness," I thought. I found a comfortable place to sit in the woods. I closed my eyes and began forgiveness meditation. The mind-heart resisted. It preferred bitterness to manufactured forgiveness. Hmmm.

I've come to trust the mind to know how to untangle itself. I didn't want to push it in a direction it didn't want to go. Instead I got out some writing paper and began to list people against whom I held a grudge. I didn't write about why. I stayed away from stories — I don't believe them anyway. Instead I relaxed and wrote about the feelings that arose.

Underneath the bitterness was hurt or loneliness or poignancy. I let go of the labels and softened into those tones and textures.

After doing this for a short time, I noticed I was smiling. There was still heartache or lonesomeness. But there was also a glowing well-being that left me beaming without realizing it. As I became more aware of that glowing in the back of my mind, it spread. Soon it was difficult to remember what had been upsetting or even who the difficult people were.

Back home an hour later, the glow still suffused my awareness. It was as if the mind-heart just wanted me to notice those negative *feelings without judging them. Simple awareness allowed them to release and natural buoyancy to surface.*

It's a lesson I seem to have to learn over and over. We don't have to fix the mind-heart, push it into a spiritual mold, or grab for the gusto or reach for the holy. We just relax into a guileless, kind, open awareness. The trick is to ignore the stories and open to the tones and textures without preference or opinion.

All we have to do is take care of awareness. Then awareness will take care of us.

> *If you wish to see the truth*
> *then hold no opinion for or against.*
> *The struggle of what one likes and what one dislikes*
> *is the disease of the mind.*
>
> — Sengstan
> *Hsin Hsin Ming: The Book of Nothing*
> translated by Richard B. Clarke

Related Chapters

9. Hissing and Purring

Rejoice in the lovable oddity of things.
– Carmen Bernos DeGastold

Bailey is a black-and-white, athletic, and clumsy cat. We met him in the animal shelter where he was leaping to a little platform high above the floor. He often overshot or landed on the edge and tumbled off. He didn't think these mishaps were a problem — he was interested in leaping more than landing.

We were touched by his rambunctious, sweet spirit and took him home to join our family.

Eight months later we returned to the shelter for a second cat to keep him company. We brought Lila home and closed her into a separate room. Bailey realized there was another creature in his house. He sat motionless outside her door and growled.

In a few days they were playfully batting under the door together. It was time to meet face-to-face. We opened the door.

He sat in the family room. She tiptoed in warily. He hissed.

I sat next to Bailey and scratched his ears. He closed his eyes, savored the massage, and continued to hiss. I stroked him gently from head to tail. He rolled over so I could rub his tummy. He purred deeply and continued to hiss.

Bailey's response seemed odd. Hissing expressed fear, anger, or wariness. Purring expressed comfort, ease, and contentment. They seemed incompatible. But to Bailey, hissing and purring at the same time was not a problem.

Looking at him through the lens of the Buddha's Laws of Dependent Origination,[13] Bailey had two opposing series of events operating at once.

---

[13] The traditional model of Dependent Origination lists twelve events. Each event is the cause of the next. Specifically: Ignorance (*avijjā*) gives rise to Formations (*saṅkhāra*) which give rise to Consciousness (*viññāṇa*) which gives rise to Mind-Body (*nāmarūpa*) which gives rise to the Six Sense Bases (*āyatana*) which give rise to Contact or Raw

On the one hand, the sensation (*phassa*) of having his ears scratched gave rise to a pleasant feeling tone (*vedanā*) that gave rise to the desire (*taṇhā*) for tummy rubbing. His mind latched onto (*upādāna*) this wanting and triggered his habitual tendency (*bhava*) to act (*jāti*) by rolling over and purring.

The Most Visible Links of Dependent Origination:	
phassa	raw sensation
vedanā	feeling tone
taṇhā	desire
upādāna	clinging
bhava	habitual tendencies
jāti	birth of action
jarāmaraṇa	grief, and despair

On the other hand, the sight (*phassa*) of a foreign kitty gave rise to the unpleasant feeling (*vedanā*) of fear and threat that triggered aversion (*taṇhā*). His mind grabbed (*upādāna*) this disliking and set off his habitual tendency (*bhava*) to act (*jāti*) by hissing.

Each string of events made sense to me. But I would have expected one to overpower the other, or both to cancel each other out. It was odd to see them both in full bloom in the same moment.

Actually, our neural physiology suggests this is perfectly normal. Part of our neural circuitry specializes in detecting pain. Another part specializes in detecting positive sensations. These two sets of neurons tend to run parallel to each other. There is no reason they cannot both fire at the same time. If something is intensely painful or intensely pleasurable, we tend to ignore the weaker signals. But we're wired in such a way that they can function simultaneously.

Sensation (*phassa*) which gives rise to Feeling Tone (*vedanā*) which gives rise to Craving (*taṇhā*) which gives rise to Clinging (*upādāna*) which gives rise to Habitual Tendencies (*bhava*) which give birth to Action (*jāti*) which give rise to Grief, Sorrow, and Suffering (*jarāmaraṇa*). In describing Bailey's response, some events are listed. For an in depth exploration of Dependent Origination see Chapter 4 of *Buddha's Map* [Kraft, 2013].

Like Bailey, our minds can hiss and purr at the same time. We can feel agitated and peaceful, sad and okay, confused and relaxed all at once. It needn't be a problem.

In meditation our job is not to get rid of the hissing. We don't have to fix unwholesome qualities. Wanting to do so adds more greed, aversion, and confusion to the mix.

Imagine if I had tried to stop Bailey from hissing. We adopted him from a rescue shelter. He was probably mistreated in his earliest years. He is sweet but spooks easily. If I had spoken to him sharply, "Be nice or leave!" or bopped him on the nose, I would have deepened his wariness and the effects of early trauma. This would have made it more difficult for him and Lila to become friends.

Greeting him with patience, kindness, and reassurance allowed his suspiciousness to surface without harm. And it allowed the two cats to negotiate their own relationship.

Similarly, we needn't judge the mind for hissing, growling, chatting, wandering, pushing, or pulling. Our job is to see it as it is. Treating it with friendliness and wisdom allows old wayward tendencies to naturally uproot themselves and fade in time.

The implications of this go beyond what neural science can easily explain. If we have both wholesome and unwholesome qualities in the mind-heart at the same time, which one wins?

If we grab hold of one or the other, that grabbing or pushing itself creates more tension and moves the mind-heart in an unwholesome direction. But if, like Bailey, we don't favor one state over the other and let them both co-exist without interfering, which one wins?

> *When wholesome and unwholesome qualities exist in the mind at the same time, the wholesome wins.*
> – Sayadaw U Tejaniya

Try it out. If we're upset but view the upset with open clear awareness, that wholesome quality softens the upset. If we're sad and view our sadness with kindness and dispassion, the kindness softens the heartache.

So in meditation or life we don't have to *get rid of* unwholesome qualities. All we have to do is *cultivate* wholesome qualities and they will take care of us.

The mind-heart unfolds at a natural pace that cannot be rushed but can be stopped.

Related Chapters

10. Wise View Is No Opinion

If you wish to see the truth,
hold no opinion for or against.

– Sengstan

Sammā diṭṭhi is the first aspect of the Buddha's Eightfold Path. The Jesuits, who did one of the first translations of Buddhist text from Pāli to English, rendered it "Right Understanding."

This resonated nicely with the Christian worldview that if we subscribe to the right statement of faith, we're guaranteed a bedroom in Heaven and freedom from the flames of Hell. There are many different Christian sects and many different statements of faith. So "Right Understanding" may sound like the Buddha's statement of faith — his beliefs about how life works.

But sammā diṭṭhi is not a faith statement. The term has also been rendered as "Harmonious Perspective" and "Wise View." The Buddha was not referring to a particular understanding, perspective, or view.

He saw that there is a universe out there run by natural laws. He also saw people holding multitudes of beliefs, philosophies, metaphysical understandings, concepts, convictions, ideas, values, and opinions about life and the universe. Too often they squabble over whose views are true. Yet reality is more multifaceted than any of these beliefs or opinions. Life is more interesting and complex than our poor brains can process. The Buddha said that trying to figure it out can drive us nuts -- we just don't have enough neurons to process it all. To hold to any particular understanding only deepens suffering.

So sammā diṭṭhi is not about what we understand but how we understand. It's not *what* we view but *how* we view it. It's a verb, not a noun. It's a process: wise viewing.

Anytime there is liking, disliking, fuzziness, or a sense of self, our view of life is distorted. We're looking through colored lenses.

Wise View is not an opinion. It's learning to view the world without the distortions of opinions and beliefs. It's about seeing with fresh eyes.

This side of enlightenment, none of us can do this perfectly. So the most important aspect of Wise View is learning to recognize the distortions in the mind so we can know them as personal views, release them, relax, smile, and see a little more clearly.

The good news is that we don't have to control what's in the mind-heart. That's a fool's errand. We just have to know what's going on as clearly as we can. The work is not about adopting a particular vision. The work is about seeing how craving and a sense of self distort our vision and clearing those distortions.

> *Some people debate maliciously.*
> *Others honestly.*
> *But the wise*
> *are silent,*
> *stand back from arguments,*
> *keep the mind*
> *open.*

— The Buddha
Sutta Nipata 4.3
translated by Lebkowicz,
Ditrich, and Pecenko

Related Chapters

11. Six Questions

Ground in the present.

As the elevator starts to rise, a man standing next to you glances at the book you're holding. The cover displays a picture of a statue of the Buddha. "I hear a lot about Buddhism these days," the man says casually. "What's it all about?"

The Buddha's ministry spanned four decades. As the elevator passes the second floor, you realize you've been asked to summarize what the Buddha taught and thought in twenty seconds. The question is simple yet genuine. What do you say?

When Siddhārtha Gautama, the Buddha, was confronted with a comparable situation, he didn't answer so well. The first person he encountered after his awakening was the young ascetic named Upaka who asked, "Who is your teacher? What do you teach?" The answer the Buddha gave was incomprehensible to Upaka, who walked away shaking his head (see pp. *xxix–xxx*).

If we too have difficulty coming up with a good Buddhist elevator speech, we are in good company.

Nevertheless, from time to time we may be asked sincerely to offer a short answer to the question, "What is Buddhism?" It's helpful to have a coherent response.

As I reflect on a Buddhist elevator speech, it seems that statements can be misleading. They sound like a catechism or a confession of faith. The core of Buddhism is not a proclamation of metaphysical truths but a method of inquiry. The scope of this inquiry might be conveyed better with questions rather than statements.

So here is my attempt to outline the scope of Buddhist interest in about twenty words formed into six questions:

How does life rub you the wrong way?
Where do you find contentment?
What are you?
What matters?
What's next?
What helps?

I don't know how well those questions would work as an elevator speech. But they do give a compass bearing on how we can engage the Buddha's path. So I'll close this section of the book by elaborating on these questions and how they arise out of the text.

How does life rub you the wrong way?

© Jon Toney, unsplash.com

The Buddha never said "Life *is* suffering." He said "Life *has* dukkha." It rubs us the wrong way. The Pāli word *dukkha* originally referred to the axle hole in the center of a wheel when the hole is off center or covered with sand or gravel: it grinds and rubs as it turns. The Buddha said life grinds and rubs us from time to time. He didn't define exactly what he meant by dukkha. Rather, his style was to offer illustrative examples:

> *Birth is dukkha; aging is dukkha; illness is dukkha; death is dukkha; grief, lamentation, bodily pain, mental pain and despair are dukkha; having to associate with what is displeasing is dukkha, separation from what is pleasing is dukkha; not getting what one wants, that too is dukkha.*
> – Dīgha Nikāya 22, Saṃyutta Nikāya 56.11,
> Majjhima Nikāya 9, 28, 141

Dukkha has a wide range of meanings, from a minor annoyance to a full catastrophe. Dropping peanut butter on my sandal is dukkha. Death of a loved one is dukkha. Ripping your sock is dukkha. Totaling our car is dukkha.

Dukkha is usually translated as "suffering" or "dissatisfaction." But saying peanut butter on my sandal or a tear in a sock is suffering is a little over the top. And saying death or totaling our car is dissatisfying, misses the depth of pain.

As mentioned in the introduction (pp. 4–6), the teacher/scholar Leigh Brasington suggests that the hippie slang "bummer" may come closest to conveying the breadth of meaning: "Life has bummers." "How do you get bummed out?"

"Bummer" also suggests that the problem is not the external trigger but our internal reaction:

"Bummer! I've got peanut butter on my sandal."

"Relax. It's only a sandal. Don't bum yourself out."

Most people come to Buddhism (or any spiritual practice) because they are bummed about some aspect of life. They suspect more is possible. The Buddha met people where they were by acknowledging dukkha. The first of his Four Ennobling Truths is "Life has dukkha/bummers" (see pp. 4).

Each of the four truths has a practice. The practice for dukkha is understanding. The Buddha said, "Dukkha must be understood." If we want to solve the problem of suffering, first we must understand how it works. If we are busy avoiding, denying, or fixing bummers, we may not really see what's going on. If we don't understand, we may react poorly rather than respond wisely.

So rather than turn our backs on bummers, we can instead turn toward them to see how they operate and feel (see pp. 3–14).

There is no need to analyze, theorize, psychologize, philosophize, or spiritualize suffering. The question is not "Why do we suffer?" It is also not a metaphysical question like, "Why do bad things happen to good people?" The question is about process: "How do we suffer?" It asks us to look directly into our own experience.

When we do this, we notice tension at the core of suffering/bummers. Tension can take many forms: resisting, holding on, pushing away, anger, trying to rise above, etc.

So the second Ennobling Truth says that the origin of getting bummed is tension (taṇhā, grasping, aversion, confusion). The practice the Buddha recommended is abandoning the tension. That is to say, relaxing and releasing.

Where do you find contentment?

© John Travis

When we relax the tension, we experience relief. So the third Ennobling Truth is *nirodha*, or the cessation of suffering (see pp. 9–13). Another word for this is "contentment." Whether or not we resolve the situation that triggers the difficulty, if we relax and find contentment, we're fine.

The practice the Buddha recommended for cessation is "to realize" — through direct experience we realize the relief of not wanting. We feel better not because we got something. We feel better when we no longer want it. The grasping has been abandoned. For example, as mentioned earlier (see p. 10–11), when we get the chocolate we've wanted, for a moment we no longer want it because we have it in our mouth. For a moment the wanting disappears. This contentment is not about the object craved — chocolate — it's about no longer craving.

If we recognize this, then rather than crave more sweets, we practice releasing the craving itself until this experience of release is realized — it "becomes real."

This contentment or satisfaction feels great. But it doesn't last. Old habits soon kick in again. We have a wonderful sitting or a wonderful walk in the woods or a lovely bit of chocolate. Then old neuroses trample our relief. Old habits of desire fire up.

We wonder, "What can I do to lessen these habitual tendencies?"

The Buddha's answer was the fourth Ennobling Truth, which is also known as the Eightfold Path. It's not a sequence of steps as much as an Eightfold Checklist we can use to examine our practice. Depending on temperament and experience, some beginners may get some value from studying the Checklist. But it's more effective for people who already have some understanding of how bummers arise, how to abandon tension, how to realize contentment, and still wonder how to make contentment last longer.

What are you?

The first aspect of the Eightfold Path is "Wise View." This means seeing life clearly as it is rather than seeing it through the lenses of yearning, fear, or confusion. The core of Wise View is seeing that life is an impersonal process: what happens to us isn't personal. In fact, there is no enduring self-essence. (See pp. 27–35.)

Like I said, the Eightfold Path is not for beginners. Imagine someone coming to the Buddha asking, "How do I get free of suffering?" and the Buddha responding, "Just get over yourself." They'd probably walk away baffled or indignant. So he started with the first three truths and practices.

Now imagine someone coming to the Buddha and saying, "I've been practicing what you taught and have gotten good results, but I keep relapsing." The Buddha would know the seeker is ready to go deeper. He'd say, "Life has bummers.

Everything breaks in the relative world. The disease of suffering is incurable. We can't cure it, but we can get rid of the patient. We can get you to take those painful sensations less personally — to not identify with them. If there is no one to suffer there is no suffering — just a flow of phenomena."

So the first aspect of the Eightfold Path asks "What are you? What is it that you take personally? What are the natural processes that you separate into self and other?"

The question isn't "Who are you?" assuming there is a self. It's "What are you?" or "What are these processes called 'self'?" The question arises naturally out of seeing how suffering and contentment arise and pass.

What matters?

As that sense of an enduring self dissolves into impersonal processes, the question arises, "Well, what matters in life anyway?" Standing in an open field on a starry night, we might stare into the vastness of time and space and feel how short and fragile life is and wonder, "What matters anyway?" (See pp. 37–39.)

We can only answer this question through direct experience. No one can do it for us. The Buddha offered hints about what matters when he spoke of wholesome qualities like friendliness, kindness, compassion, joy, peace, generosity of spirit, equanimity, etc.

These resonate with me. Given how quickly my life will fade from this planet, it seems that kindness is what matters most. (See pp. 27–32.)

But you can't take anybody's word for this — not mine nor the Buddha's. The only useful answers arise out of a deep and luminous mind-heart.

What's next?

Once we have even a tentative sense of what matters, it prompts the question, "What's next?" We don't have to work out the total path, but it helps to know what our next steps might be.

The next steps might be in items three, four, and five of the Eightfold Checklist. Together these are the ethical aspects of the Eight. I think of them as "cleaning up our act." They are:

Wise Speech: how we speak, write, email and otherwise communicate with one another and with ourselves;

Wise Action: how we interact nonverbally;

Wise Livelihood or lifestyle: how we take care of our needs for food, clothing, shelter, relationships, money, health care and all those other aspects of living in the world. (See pp. 225–238).

Another answer to the question "What's next?' might be cleaning up our meditation practice. The last three items on the Eightfold Checklist are about spiritual practice: wise effort, wise awareness or mindfulness, and collectedness or stability of mind. Together these are traditionally called "practice." I call them "getting our selves out of the way." (See the next section of this book.)

What helps?

When we have a sense of what's next, it is wise to ask, "What might help me take those next steps?" "What kind of support would be beneficial?"

Buddhism is famous for its meditation practice. So having a sense of what helps our practice is wise.

The Buddha said that one of the greatest supports on the spiritual path is the community of fellow seekers — the support of a saṅgha.

Depending on our inclinations, talents, and temperament there are many things that can help us from books to classes, retreats to

Six Questions
How does life rub you the wrong way?
Where do you find contentment?
What are you?
What matters
What's next?
What helps?

pilgrimages, solitary practices to communal gatherings.

"What helps?" is a good question to hold lightly in the back of the mind as our practice unfolds.

Finding a Compass

As we explore these six questions, we might find the Buddha's footprints on the path before us. They provide the compass bearings that he followed and encouraged us to follow on our spiritual quest.

Be kind. Pay attention. Relax.

Related Chapters

II
Getting Our Selves
Out of the Way

Best way to take a punch, no be there.
— Mr. Miyagi / Robert Mark Kamen[14]

© Adam Eurich

---

[14] Mr. Miyagi is a fictional character in the 1984 – 1994 movie franchise, *The Karate Kid*, created by *Robert Mark Kamen*.

12. Selflessness Grows out of Self-Care

Self-love and self-care are the seeds of selflessness.

Henry, our grandson, was teething during one of our visits. So we weren't surprised that he was fussier than usual. What continued to surprise me was how fluid his emotions were. One minute he was grinning ear to ear. The next minute his face crumbled into misery as he poked his sore gums. The next he both pouted and smiled as he looked at me over his wet hand. I was charmed.

© Nathan Kraft and Jess Gregg

I saw in him no sign of an ego or sense of self that is so ubiquitous in us adults. While he has memory, I saw no sign of reminiscing or anticipating. He lived utterly in the moment.

The ability to live in the present is a sign of spiritual freedom. But I saw no sign of freedom either. If anything, he was trapped by sensations: his well-being was bounced around by the feeling in his tummy, his gums, his state of rest, the state of his diaper, and the sights and sounds around him.

He is a relatively happy baby, thanks to his parents and his disposition. But inner freedom requires more than presence. As the Burmese meditation master Sayadaw U Tejaniya puts it, "Mindfulness alone is not enough." Freedom requires wisdom. And wisdom requires understanding how the mind-heart works and how the mind itself is an ever-changing illusion.

Before he can develop wisdom and selflessness, Henry needs a few more building blocks – object constancy, cause and effect, empathy, objectivity, deductive reasoning, collectedness, and so forth.

© Nathan Kraft and Jess Gregg

It's for emotionally mature adults to get over a sense of self. As Jack Engler wrote thirty years ago, "You have to be somebody before you can be nobody."

He's only four months old. And I'm delighted to watch him unfold at his own pace.

Along with wisdom, selflessness has a few other qualities. It is sweet, tender, friendly, joyful, clear, and spacious. He's coming along just fine in those departments.

I don't know if selflessness requires an indulgent grandpa. But just in case, I'm there.

We have to have a healthy sense of self before we can get rid of it.

Related Topics

13. Awareness Meters

The way is not in the sky. The way is in the heart.
— The Buddha, *The Dhammapada*

Vedanā

If we'd like to get our selves out of the way, deepen our meditation, or bring more clarity and vitality into our lives, relating skillfully to *vedanā* is very helpful. However, it isn't always obvious what vedanā is, much less how to relate to it wisely.

Vedanā is a *Pāli* term usually translated as "feeling" or "feeling tone." It is not emotion. Emotions are complex. Vedanā is simple, although it is one ingredient of emotion. *Vedanā is the level of discomfort or pleasantness in any experience.* That's all. It is modest, subtle, and often difficult to recognize in the clamor of thoughts and emotions. But with a little practice, we can get to know it well.

I first stumbled into its importance many years ago, though it took me decades to appreciate what I'd found. So I'll begin with that story. Then I'll unpack what vedanā is and its central role in the Buddha's teachings followed by a tool that helps us relate to it wisely. I'll also show how that tool can relate to other essential qualities of awareness.

First the story:

During my first year of college, my high school girlfriend jilted me. I understood her reasons, and still felt brokenhearted. As the sting subsided over several months, I began corresponding with a close friend. I wondered if something more was possible between us. As Spring break approached, I offered to take a six-hour bus ride up to New England and visit her at her college.

When I finally saw her, she said, "What are you doing here? I couldn't figure out why you were coming."

"Oops," I thought, "I misread this." My insides knotted in embarrassment. I wanted to run. But the bus home didn't leave until the following day. Awkward!

The next morning I gazed out the bus window as it rolled south. The melting snow revealed dirt and grime. The woods were leafless and gray. A melancholic fog shrouded the countryside. Nature mirrored my mood.

I began writing song lyrics about gray skies and tarnished snow. After a while I noticed I was feeling better. This surprised me. Writing helped me see my life with a little dispassion. The loneliness didn't abate. But my mood seemed manageable. I knew it would pass and I'd go on to live another day.

I thought, "What a wonderful tool! If I can express what's really going on inside, it takes the edge off."

The tool required stepping back from my emotions. But I wasn't pushing them away — quite the opposite. I was stepping back to see them clearly in a larger context. The feeling tones were fuzzy, so exact words weren't possible. Yet images and metaphors gave satisfying hints. That was enough.

What a lovely tool!

I had stumbled into something like the Six Rs (see p. 287–291). I didn't have that nomenclature or all six elements. But I had the essence of turning toward, relaxing into, and savoring whatever came up (see p. 3). This strange combination worked.

Neural Physiology

Recently I learned the neural physiology underpinning this phenomenon. The circuits that register raw pain feed into the lower brain — the reptile cortex. Signals of pleasantness go into the mid-brain — the limbic system. There is no self-awareness in these regions. Self-reflection arises in the higher brain — the neocortex.

The neocortex is home for labeling, conscious thought, ideas, poetry, stories, and concepts. However, the neocortex doesn't directly receive signals of pain or pleasure. Therefore, pain is preverbal and precognitive. It can fly below the radar screen of conscious awareness until signals are relayed to higher centers. And not all signals are sent "upstairs."

While I was composing lyrics, the locus of brain activity shifted to the neocortex, which doesn't register pain directly. This put some neural distance, if you will, between those difficult feelings and my reflections.

Many of us understand this instinctively. In rough times, we may look for mental distractions or intellectually analyze our situation. This creates some neural distance. However, ignoring physical or emotional stress has long-term problems. Denial doesn't allow us to integrate the difficulty or respond compassionately. The stress in the lower brain becomes a guerrilla cadre that roams around undetected as it looks for things to blow up. We may think we're fine until something triggers an outburst.

The trick is to engage the higher brain's wisdom and understanding without ignoring data in the more primitive, pain-receptive areas. Writing lyrics that reflected what I was feeling did that for me. Even if the poetry was bad, the intention to understand and express was sufficient.

This is a middle path between getting lost in the raw stress of the lower centers and getting lost in the stories, concepts, and analysis of the higher center. At the very least, we have to learn to tolerate difficult states long enough to see them clearly as they are.

The best tool I know for doing this is the six Rs: **Recognize** what's going on in its own terms; **Release** it or let it be as it is without trying to control it; **Relax** tension; **Re-Smile** or bring lighter states into the mix; **Return** to our base practice; and **Repeat** as often as needed.

Equanimity

The Buddha did not know neural physiology. That information wasn't available 2600 years ago. But he understood the phenomena itself with remarkable clarity. And he had a word for the result: equanimity (*upekkhā*).

Equanimity is not being oblivious to the delight and bummers that flow through our lives. It is seeing them so openly that they don't throw us off balance. With equanimity we know what's going on, but understand the larger, deeper, impersonal nature of life itself.

When equanimity is strong, the mind-heart becomes steady enough to see pain or pleasantness without immediately having to do something about it. We can see pain as pain and pleasantness as pleasantness without grabbing or holding them. I could sit on the bus and see my inner states without trying to change them. I was more interested in describing them than in fixing them. Though I didn't know the word "vedanā" at that time, the writing process helped me peacefully watch the textures of pain and pleasantness as they ebbed and flowed.

The Buddha's Teachings

Getting our selves out of the way is the theme of this section of this field guide. Observing vedanā with equanimity is key to seeing how the sense of self arises and gets in the way in the first place.

If vedanā is painful, the mind tends to move away from the uncomfortable feeling tone. If the vedanā is pleasant, the mind tends to move toward it. This leaning away or towards creates a sense of someone — a self — moving away or toward

© David Dawson

something — an object. Wanting and not wanting are different flavors of "craving" (taṇhā). In this case, rather than just an impersonal flow of phenomena, experience begins to split into self and other.

However, if the vedanā is relaxed, it

can dissolve and a sense of self does not congeal out of the flow of phenomena.

Vedanā appears in many other teachings of the Buddha. It is the seventh aspect of Dependent Origination (*paṭiccasamuppāda*) where raw sensory experience (*phassa*) can give rise to feeling tone (*vedanā*) and feeling tone can tighten into craving (*taṇhā*).

Vedanā is also the second of the five aggregates (*khandas* or clusters of experience) and the second of the Four Foundations of Mindfulness. In fact it is mentioned throughout the Buddha's discourses.

However, other than implying that vedanā is very important, the Buddha says little about it. For example, the "Discourse on the Four Foundations of Mindfulness" ("Satipaṭṭhāna Sutta," *Majjhima Nikāya*, 10), describes the other three foundations — body, mind, and dhammas — in detail over many pages. Meanwhile, the second foundation, vedanā, receives one short paragraph.

In the classical commentaries on the Buddha's teachings, vedanā is mentioned often but usually without comment. In contemporary Buddhist writings, there is little exploration of vedanā.

Perhaps because vedanā is subtle, preverbal, and preconceptual, it is hard to find words or concepts that are helpful. We're left to work it out for ourselves by exploring our own experience.

Vedanā Meter

One of my teachers, Tony Bernhard, came up with an elegant strategy for exploring vedanā. He calls the strategy a "mental app" which he named "The Vedanā Meter." Rather than installing the app on your smart phone, you install it

© David Dawson

in your mind. This is how it works:

You walk into the doctor's office and say, "I have this soreness in my arm." The doctor asks, "On a scale from zero to ten where zero is pain-free and ten is excruciating, how intense is the pain?"

After a moment's reflection, it's easy to give numbers: "In the morning, it's usually a two. In the evening it's a six. Right now it's four and a half." Those numbers are measures of uncomfortable vedanā.

We could also set up a pleasantness scale: "On a scale from zero to ten where zero is boring and ten is total delight, how is eating that cookie?" "... petting a kitten?" "... spring flowers?" "... your favorite music?"

A complete vedanā meter has both scales. It runs from the worst intensity you could experience without blacking out to the loveliest rush you could know without blissing out.

To create your vedanā meter, imagine such a scale in your mind. You can design it any way you like.

Tony's looks like a circular car speedometer. Zero on the left is the most painful. Ten on the right is the most wonderful. Five in the middle is neutral.

The first image in my mind was a horizontal bar that ran from -10 on the left (torture) to 0 in the middle (neutral) to +10 on the right (bliss). A needle moved back and forth on this scale.

-10	-8	-6	-4	-2	0	2	4	6	8	10

As I used the scale, the needle vanished and two shaded bars appeared. Each started in the middle and grew outward in one direction or the other depending on how painful or pleasant an experience was. Sometimes both bars grew in opposite directions at the same time. Some experiences were painful and pleasant all at once. (See "9. Hissing and Purring," p. 43.)

 Another yogi's vedanā meter resembled a stereo equalizer with different scales for different frequencies.

The mental images are just metaphors. So use whatever works most naturally for you.

Once your vedanā meter app is complete, you can calibrate it. To do this, bring to mind a range of painful and pleasant experiences and see how your meter responds. Remember, what's important is not what you *think* about the phenomenon but how pleasant or unpleasant it *feels*.

For example, see how your meter registers the following:

- Chocolate ice cream
- Child on a swing set
- A glass of milk
- A hug
- In-laws
- Your father

- Public speaking
- Dog poop
- Donald Trump
- Sun on your face
- Your 1st grade teacher
- Stubbing your toe

Once you're familiar with how your meter responds to a wide variety of experiences, you're ready to bring it into meditation and life. What does the meter register at this moment?

When I first tried out my app, it seemed pretty simple — perhaps even simplistic. But the results were unexpected.

To my surprise, I realized I'm basically happy most of the time. My meter is usually in the 3 or 4 range. As the day flows along, it sometimes dips to a -4 or -5. Sometimes it rises to a 6 or 7. But mostly it hovers in a moderately positive range.

This threw me a little. If you ask me at a random time how I'm doing, the first thoughts that pop into my mind are complaints. Those negative thoughts are the product of childhood conditioning a long time ago. Yet today, my thoughts still tend to say "I'm a -2 today" when my actual vedanā meter is usually more of a +3. I didn't realize how different my thought content could be from my mood.

Another surprise was how much I enjoy thinking. While meditating, I often view a thought sprint as an annoyance. But when I'm thinking, the meter can go up to a 6 or 7. The thought content can be negative while the process of thinking can be positive.

Seeing how pleasurable thinking can be has made it easier to not fight thoughts. I understand the mind's attraction to them. Rather than push them away, I can take in the pleasant vedanā and release the thought content. The underlying uplifting quality can be healing if I don't fight it. I don't have to get lost in the content of the thoughts. That can be released. I just rest in the pleasantness behind them and let it radiate outward.

Another observation I've had and heard from others is what happens when vedanā is in the painful range. If I see that feeling tone with dispassionate interest, the meter tends to move in a pleasant direction on its own. This is what happened to me when writing song lyrics on the bus so many years ago. Only now I know the actual lyrics didn't matter. It was the quiet, openhearted observation of my inner experience that allowed tension to release and relax so that the vedanā shift toward pleasantness.

From this I've come to appreciate that vedanā – the preverbal painful and pleasantness dimensions of everyday experience – may be so subtle as to be under-noticed. Yet it may have tantalizing insights to share if we learn to listen to its moods with an opening heart and a quieting mind.

Tanhā

Vedanā and *taṇhā* are closely related. They have different moods and styles, but often interact together. If we want to deepen our meditation, bring more peace and vitality into our lives, or simply get our selves out of the way, relating skillfully to taṇhā is very helpful. It's at least as important as vedanā.

Taṇhā is a Pāli word usually translated as "craving" or "desire." But it has a much wider range of meanings and strength than these common translations. *Taṇhā is the intensity of wanting, not wanting, or confusion in any experience.* It is felt as tension. Like vedanā, it is preverbal — something we can feel directly — and can be thought of as negative (aversion) or positive (desire). It can be powerfully positive like the craving of an addict for a fix. "Positive" doesn't mean "wholesome," only that it is a wanting to have something. It can be gently positive, like soft yearning. It can be gently negative like "no thank you." And it can be intensely negative like rage or terror.

Wanting Meter

Taṇhā is a good candidate for a mental app. Tony Bernhard calls it a "Wanting Meter." Rather than measuring painfulness or pleasantness, it measures the intensity of desire and aversion.

We can create a Wanting Meter in a manner similar to creating a Vedanā Meter: produce a mental image of a scale that runs from gentle indifference to powerful desire to do something. Then add numbers to the scale. That's it.

The Wanting Meter may not need to be pre-calibrated. We pre-calibrated the Vedanā Meter by thinking of various painful and pleasant sensations and seeing how the Vedanā Meter responded to each.

But the intensity of taṇhā is not tied as directly to raw sensations. For me, chocolate often produces pleasant vedanā. Sometimes I crave chocolate; other times I can take it or leave it. The pleasantness of chocolate may stay the same but the strength of wanting can vary widely. An insulting remark might trigger hatred or mild annoyance. Thoughts might be fueled by a powerful craving to solve a problem or by a faint wondering. Since the intensity of desire or aversion for a specific object can vary, pre-calibrating our Wanting Meter is less effective or necessary. We can simply start using it.

Vedanā and Tanhā in Dependent Origination

As we use the Wanting Meter, we can see how close taṇhā and vedanā are to each other. The Buddha describes this in his Laws of Dependent Origination (*paṭiccasamuppāda*). So I'll give a quick summary of how they work together and with other states.

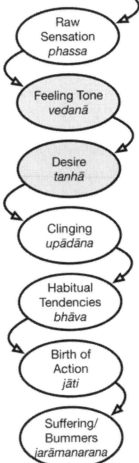

Dependent Origination is like a line of dominos, where each domino falls to knock over a bigger domino. Each domino is an inner event. As described earlier, raw sensation (phassa) can give rise to feeling tone (vedanā). If vedanā is seen clearly and the tension around it is relaxed, the mind-heart becomes peaceful. Otherwise, vedanā can give rise to wanting or not wanting (taṇhā).

If the tension in taṇhā is seen and relaxed, the mind returns to its naturally peaceful state. Otherwise, taṇhā can give rise to clinging (upādāna).

Up to this point, each domino is preverbal and preconceptual. But with upādāna, the mind shrink-wraps around the experience and gives it a name or label. Clinging is always experienced as a thought. The first mental concepts have formed. Awareness shifts away from the preverbal experiences of vedanā and taṇhā and clings to the thoughts and concepts.

If the clinging is seen and relaxed, the mind-heart returns to it's underlying equanimity. But these dominos are big and have a lot of momentum. Clinging can trigger thoughts, ideas, emotions and other habitual tendencies (bhava). Habitual tendencies may spur us into action. If wisdom is not strong, those actions can get us into trouble and we suffer. Bummer.

Fortunately, it's not necessary to memorize this string of events. But they do have some implications that can be very helpful:

1. Desire is not Action

The Wanting Meter is not about action. It's about desire for or against. Actions come later in the series. Paying attention to what we do does nothing with the desire beneath it.

Thinking is considered a mental action in Buddhism. If we want a peaceful mind, stopping the action of thinking doesn't really help. It's the desire underneath that fuels the thoughts and actions.

Understanding this has been very helpful for me. When a lot of thoughts come up in meditation, rather than trying to stop the thoughts, I just check the Wanting Meter. If the desire to think is very faint, it's easy to relax the taṇhā. Then the thoughts just run out of gas and quiet down naturally.

If the desire to think is powerful, then I just see that desire as it is. This shifts the attention away from the content of the thought back to the tension that is fueling it. As I recognize the tension in the desire, I can relax it with the Six Rs. If there is a lot of fuel (desire), it may go on for a while, but I'm doing nothing to add more fuel. Eventually the thoughts run out of gas and quiet down.

2. Vedanā is not Tanhā

Though vedanā and taṇhā rub elbows all the time, they are different phenomena. They even have different underlying neurochemistry. The strength of pain or pleasantness is related to the levels dopamine. The strength of desire or aversion is related to the levels of opioids. A different biological process supports each. The Vedanā Meter does not dictate what the Wanting Meter will say and vice versa. They are related but not the same. Seeing each phenomenon on its own is very helpful.

3. Getting Out of the Way

As each domino falls on the next, the sense of a separate self can get stronger. Vedanā sends up the first shoots. Taṇhā sends down the first roots. Clinging (upādāna) sends out leaves by adding a label and concept for the self: "I want this" or "I don't like that." Attention shifts to the labels and concepts that are assumed to be true. The phenomena that give rise to the sense of self are not directly seen as we get entangled in the storyline.

If we'd like to get ourselves out of the way, we can't do it effectively once the thoughts and concepts have taken over. We're just arguing philosophy rather than directly experiencing phenomena.

But if we can recognize and release the vedanā or taṇhā, the sense of a separate self does not come up. There is just a flow of impersonal phenomena.

4. Vedanā and Tanhā are Weak Links

The Laws of Dependent Origination articulate a series of events that lead to bummers.

If we'd like to reduce our suffering, the most effective place to do this is not with the bummers themselves but with the smaller dominos that lead up to them.

The Buddha said that the weakest link in this chain is taṇhā. The events before taṇhā can be so faint that they are hard to see. The events after taṇhā can have so much momentum that they are hard to stop or see beyond.

But taṇhā is strong enough to be seen and still small enough to be relatively easy to relax.

The Wanting Meter is very helpful in seeing taṇhā objectively. It exposes the strength of aversion and desire. We can feel and see it directly as an impersonal phenomenon.

This allows more ease to flow through our life.

Everything Goes

The meters are images or mental constructs. As such they are relatively coarse. When the mind is busy or coarse, the meters can be helpful in tuning awareness of vedanā and taṇhā.

However, when awareness is light and refined and we're adept at recognizing vedanā and taṇhā, the meters may be too crude to be helpful. At this "higher altitude," mentally constructing the meters may just get in the way of seeing what we already see. So they can be dropped.

All meditation tools are like this. They are rafts to get to the far shore or greater awareness. Once on that shore, there is no need to put them on our back and carry them up the mountain. Instead we just release tension.

Related Chapters

14. Freeing the Cows: Observing, not Controlling

> *The best way to control a cow*
> *is to put it in a large pasture.*
>
> — Suzuki Roshi,
> *Zen Mind, Beginners Mind*

Sitting on the side of a mountain in northern New Mexico, I gazed across the high desert plain far below. The horizon was at least 75 miles away. Twenty miles to the west, a thunderhead rose thousands of feet. A dense shadow beneath it indicated heavy rain. Lightning arced a thousand feet from the cloud to the ground. Meanwhile, to the northwest, the sun was setting in a peaceful, clear sky.

I love the high desert. Natural forces are revealed in their power and glory. I am so small there that I observe rather than try to control nature. I'm left feeling peaceful and content.

The Buddha put more faith in awareness of the mind than in trying to control it. Attempting to stop the storms within is as futile and unnecessary as trying to stop a thunderstorm. We don't have the power. Mental whirlwinds arise out of tension. Trying to stop them puts more tension into them.

But if we put more faith in awareness, it allows us to mentally step back to get a wider view. It is like shifting our attention from the clouds to the sky that contains them. We pay less attention to the contents of the mind and more to the awareness that knows.

No matter how big the storm, the sky is always vaster. And it is always peaceful. In meditation this means becoming aware of awareness itself — becoming aware of that which knows. Pure awareness relaxes the mind.

The Buddha's path is this middle way between fighting and indulging the storms. We observe without interfering. We pay attention to the feeling in the mind without attending to its stories. Eventually we notice the awareness itself.

Suzuki Roshi said it using a different metaphor: "The best way to control a cow is to put it in a large pasture." We let the cows roam where they will without running after them. Rather than control the mind-heart, we learn to observe the awareness itself.

Meanwhile, on the side of the mountain, the thunderhead rained itself out. As the evening stars appeared the last wisps of clouds dissolved into the clear sky.

Related Chapters

15. Unhealthy Desire vs. Healthy Wisdom

Desire grasps. Wisdom observes.

"I want a new iPhone." "I'd like you to back off!" "I didn't like my last meditation." "Let's get some ice cream." Desire comes in many flavors: desire, aversion, yearning, preference, greed, lust, annoyance, anger, hatred, like, dislike, confusion, and more.

© Adam Eurich

Desire gets a lot of bad press — for good reason. It creates tension. We can feel it in those statements. Tension creates distortion, and distortion can lead to suffering. Wanting a new gadget or a piece of chocolate may seem like "sweet anticipation" as we imagine fulfilling the desire in the future. But in the present, desire doesn't feel so good.

Tension and distortion is obvious in strong desires, hatred, or addiction. But even quiet yearning colors our feeling, perception, and decision-making.

What if we had no desire at all?

Serenity

The 2005 science fiction movie *Serenity* plays with this question:

Hundreds of years in the future, humans are terraforming planets to support human life. On the distant planet Miranda, a colony introduces Pax G23 into the air filtration system. Pax is a new drug designed to suppress aggression and make people happy.

Communication from the colony stops. The authorities assume there has been an invasion or natural disaster, or that the Pax has backfired.

Through a series of adventures, the movie's lead characters arrive on Miranda. They find everyone dead. There are no signs of invasion, natural disaster, poisoning, or violence. A woman has apparently died while leaning against a library window. A man lies smiling and dead on the floor of a public building. Others died sitting in chairs or lying in the grass. Corpses are everywhere.

Eventually they figure out that Pax had worked too well. It had removed aggression and any emotion that might lead to aggression: hatred, anger, desire, greed, wanting, yearning, caring, hunger. The people became so peaceful, they stopped working, socializing, eating, or even moving — they just sat down and died.

In normal, everyday life, the complete absence of desire would be a complete disaster. Like the people on Miranda under Pax G23, we'd have no motivation to turn off the stove, feed the children, come out of the rain, or get out of bed in the morning. We'd waste away and die.

Yet the Buddha discovered that the roots of suffering are desire and its fraternal twins aversion and delusion.

To chart a middle way, the Buddha distinguished between neurotic desire (*taṇhā*) and healthy desire (*chanda*). When I first heard of these, I assumed the difference was their objects: taṇhā goes after unhealthy objects like money, sex, or power, while chanda goes after healthy things like meditation, inner peace, organic vegetables, and kindness. Wanting wholesome things must not cause tension or distortion.

At least that's what I thought at the time. However, it's possible to pursue peace in ways that make us restless. It's possible to pursue enlightenment in ways that make us miserable.

The difference between taṇhā and chanda is not their objects but the desire itself. Neurotic desire wants what it wants. It focuses on the object and getting it as quickly as possible. On the other hand, healthy desire focuses on the process — how various qualities like peace, joy, and happiness arise. It tries to cultivate the conditions that allow those qualities to arise naturally. It is more attentive to process than result.

To say this differently, greed and wisdom operate fundamentally differently. Taṇhā is motivated by greed, hatred, or delusion. It centers on outcome. Chanda is motivated by wisdom. It centers on the path to get there without preferring a specific outcome.

The monotheistic traditions put it this way: "Do the best you can and dedicate the fruits of your labor to God." Buddhism doesn't have theistic language, so it says, "Do the best you can, and be content that the outcome is determined by natural laws."

When healthy desire doesn't get what it wants, it is delighted to have more data to understand those natural laws. It is more interested in becoming wiser about how life works than in any specific outcome.

Perhaps we'd like organic vegetables. Greed just wants them. Wisdom figures out how to get to the farmers' market. If the market is closed, greed is unhappy. But wisdom is content that it has learned something. It knows it is not in control of the world. It is glad to discover more about how the market works so it can try a better strategy.

Or perhaps we realize we'd be happier if the mind was quieter. Greed grasps for the quiet any way it can. Grasping creates more disturbances. It doesn't work. Greed is unhappy.

Wisdom may also realize we'd be happier with a quiet mind and heart. Rather than grab for quiet, wisdom tries to create the conditions in which inner quiet is more likely to arise naturally. Wisdom doesn't know everything. It makes mistakes. It may try telling the mind to shut up. When that fails, wisdom thinks, "Oh, that didn't work." It learns from mistakes. Like a good scientist, it's happy for the negative results so it can try something else: "Maybe I'll just relax and see what effect that has."

Taṇhā is about having or not having. Wisdom is about causes and conditions. Healthy desire is fun and uplifting no matter what the outcome. Healthy meditation feels good. If it doesn't, there is taṇhā that can be Six-R'ed.

Eventually All Desire Goes

Even though some healthy desire (chanda) may be helpful in everyday life, as meditation deepens, all urges fade into dispassion. We remain interested enough to notice what's happening. We can act from wisdom but have no attachment to a particular outcome. The slightest leaning in one direction or another is enough to keep us from the highest well-being.

The gentle push and pull of chanda and wisdom are like a fire stick. In the burning ghats along the Ganges River in India, bodies of deceased people are placed on a funeral pyre — a neatly arranged pile of sticks. Before the wood is ignited, the fire master pulls out a stick he will use to stir the fire.

The pyre burns hottest in the middle. So the fuel and parts of the body in the center are consumed first. As the center gradually burns lower, the person tending the flame uses the fire stick to push any remaining body parts and fuel into the center. This insures that everything is consumed before the center burns out.

Then, when the body has been completely incinerated and only a few coals remain, the fire stick is tossed in. In the end, it too is consumed and disappears.

Chanda and wisdom are like a fire stick used to tend our fires when they burn hot. But in the end, all desires must go — all must be released and relaxed. With full liberation, nothing remains, not even ashes.

Wisdom discerns when it is skillful to cultivate healthy desire and when it is time to toss it into the flames.

Related Chapters

16. Self-Torture 101

The comparing mind is a hurting mind.

Don't make yourself miserable. This sounds like strange advice. Who wants to make themselves miserable? None of us. Yet we do it all the time.

Dan Greenburg wrote a book called *"How to Make Yourself Miserable: A Vital Training Manual."*[15] It's in the style of a self-help guide, complete with exercises.

One exercise is to measure everything on our body including such details as the thickness of our eyebrows, the radius of our chin, and the angle of our nose. The book provides a list of "normal" measurements for a man and a woman. We are instructed to compare these standards with our own or with those of a prospective lovemate. Deviations from the standards are considered defects.

Another exercise asks us to make a list of our accomplishments. Then we're told that Einstein formulated his theory of relativity at age twenty-six; Mozart composed his first symphony and three sets of sonatas by the age of eight; Kuwaiti civil servant Abdullah al-Salim receives a salary of $7 million a week. Every two hours and forty minutes he earns the equivalent of the average American lifetime income. The instructions are to dwell on the difference between our accomplishments and those of these "ordinary" people.

The book includes sections on "Basics of Self-Torture" and "Twenty-Six Masochistic Activities of Beginners," with suggestions like "Make a list of all the things you nearly had but somehow blew." "After leaving a room full of people, try to imagine what they might be saying about you." "Make a list of

---

[15] Dan Greenburg with Marcia Jacobs, *How to Make Yourself Miserable* (New York: Random House, 1966, 1987).

all the great things you can't do anymore." "Schedule your next nonessential drive downtown during peak traffic hour."

The book is funny because it details nonsensical ways most of us secretly compare and judge ourselves. Doing these quietly under the radar makes us miserable. Seeing them out in the open makes us laugh at how silly we can be.

These same habits leak into meditation as we compare our practice to some standard, evaluate our accomplishments against those around us, try to figure out which jhāna we're in, and worry about whether our practice is good enough.

The mind is designed to make these assessments. They are part of an evolutionary survival mechanism and are natural to us. Judging ourselves for having these kinds of thoughts can make us miserable. Yet seeing them clearly can make us laugh.

I think laughter is better. So it helps to Six-R even the most reasonable comparisons.

And better yet, if we see through the delusion of an essential, enduring self, then there is no one to judge. There is no self to be made miserable. There is only the freedom of open awareness.

Related Chapters

17. We Get What We Put Our Energy Into

Wisdom says I am nothing. Love says I am everything.
Between the two my life flows.
— Sri Nisargadatta

During my college undergraduate years, I spent two summers working for a child psychiatrist. I ran a day camp for groups of his patients. It was my first supervised clinical training.

I grew fond of many of the kids. So I asked the psychiatrist if it was okay for me to tell them I loved them.

He looked at me quietly and quizzically. "Words are just claims," he said. "They don't mean much to these kids. Their parents lie to them all the time — they say one thing but do something else.

"If you're mean to them and tell them you love them, they'll throw the words back in your face.

"But you're kind. If you tell them you love them, they'll cautiously believe you. In fact, since you treat them well, they know you care about them even if you say nothing."

His words stuck with me. Naively, I had thought psychotherapy was about words. But he was saying that for kids, what I said had less impact than what I did.

The same principle holds for adults. Ralph Waldo Emerson said, "Your actions speak so loudly I cannot hear what you are saying."

This also applies to how we relate to ourselves in meditation and elsewhere. The principle is: we get what we put our energy into. Words have less energy than actions. They are relatively ghost-like. How we treat ourselves or relate to the mind-heart has a lot of energy. It has a stronger impact.

The Buddha said the same thing using a different metaphor: we get what we feed. So we must be aware of what we are nurturing. This advice helps only if we understand what nourishes the feelings in the mind-heart — that is, what energizes them — and what is little more than a wisp of wind.

For example, let's say I'm angry. I tell myself all the ways I'm being mistreated. This feeds the anger by putting more energy into it. I become a mess inside.

Now, let's say I'm angry and I give myself an affirmation: "I am peace and happiness." I use the affirmation to suppress the anger. My thoughts are about peace, but my action suppresses. Anger is an aversive state. Suppression is an aversive action. I'm using aversion against aversion. This is like yelling at an intimidated child, "Be peaceful and happy!" It's not soothing. The words "peaceful and happy" have very little energy. But the vocal tone and the aversion of aversion have a lot of energy. So I get more uptight until I lose control in an angry outburst. Or conversely, I may quietly seethe or become depressed. While I give lip service to peace, I'm putting energy into aversion. That is what I feed. And that is what I get in return.

Now, let's say I'm angry and my mind is generating stories about what a misunderstood martyr I am. I don't try to stop the stories. They are just words without much inherent energy. I don't indulge them or push them away. I recognize them but let them run without giving them more attention. Instead, I bring awareness to the feeling of anger itself. It's tense and uncomfortable. I don't try to get rid of the tension or discomfort. I just bring open awareness to it. As the mind-heart becomes more intimate with the tension, it naturally relaxes. Or I can gently invite the tension to soften, if need be. But I don't push anything away.

It feels like relaxing into the tension and discomfort.

In this way, I'm bringing awareness and acceptance to what is actually going on. These are practical expressions of wisdom and kindness (see p. 219–220). I am putting energy into wholesome qualities like awareness, wisdom, acceptance, and kindness. They don't change the moment. But in the long run, these qualities are being fed and strengthened.

We don't have to get rid of uncomfortable qualities. We just bring in wholesome ones, and the mind-heart takes it from there. That is how we get what we put our energy into.

Related Chapters

18. Feelings Aren't Thoughts

See below the surface of things.

I heard my wife calling me from several rooms away. Her voice was calm and steady. But something in the timbre raised the hair on the back of my neck. I rushed to her. She was holding our youngest son. "He's having a seizure," she said.

My body went numb. My mind began to race. It might take five or ten minutes for an ambulance to get here. I turned to my mother-in-law who was watching, "Get a blanket and call the doctor." I told my wife, "Carry him to the car. I'll get the keys." In less than a minute we were on the way to the hospital.

I was not aware of feeling anything. My mind was clear and focused. Feelings didn't matter compared to getting my son safely into medical care.

Many hours later, after I was certain he was in good hands, my mind began to slow down. Then I began to actually feel fear, worry, and other deep emotions. That allowed me to shake and cry rather than keep the tension locked up inside under a barrage of thought.

It is easy to see how this human ability to suppress emotions and concentrate on solving a problem was bred into us by evolutionary forces. When threatened, focused, fast, clear thinking gave us a survival edge. Rather than trying several alternate strategies physically and seeing which was most effective, we could "try them out" in our minds more quickly.

This ability to try things in our minds is generalized rather than specific. Our brain didn't evolve to suppress feelings about giant cave bears or sons with seizures. It evolved the ability to suppress feelings under stress.

The stress of modern living can trigger the ability easily. Even in meditation, when uncomfortable feelings arise, the mind can switch into thinking and suppress feeling. If we are in danger as we sit on a zafu, this is entirely appropriate. But we're rarely in danger while meditating. Nevertheless, uncomfortable feelings can cause the mind to shift attention into trying to think our way through them. But it just does not work.

Meditative wisdom requires seeing how the mind-heart operates, including when we're uncomfortable.

The Buddha said we need to experience sensations as sensations, perceptions as perceptions, feeling as feeling, thought as thought, and awareness as awareness. They are all valuable. But each needs to be seen on its own terms.

Too often meditators will give a long explanation of what they are feeling and why. This is trying to experience emotions through thought. It's like looking at feelings through a spyglass from a distant hill rather than up close.

Sensation, perception, feeling, thought, and awareness are different realms. Deep meditation requires that we experience each of them up close and in its own realm.

As meditation goes deeper, there is more and more equanimity. From the outside it may look as if we're feeling less. It's not true — we actually feel more. But when we allow feelings to be feelings and thoughts to be thoughts, we can see sensations and emotions without being thrown off balance by them. This allows the feelings to run through us without disturbing our calm.

This equanimity begins by feeling feelings as feelings and not confusing them with thoughts.

Related Chapters

19. Deliberate Ignorance

*Truth comes as a conqueror only to those who have lost
the art of receiving a friend.*
— Rabindranath Tagore

When unpleasantness arises, some yogis recognize that
pushing it away is aversion, an unwholesome attitude. So rather
than shove the unpleasant aside, they try to shake it off, wiggle
free of it, or just not pay attention to it. This avoids the pitfall of
aversion and stumbles into the pitfall of ignoring. Trying to
shake something off is deliberate ignorance — self-imposed
delusion. It's like saying, "I don't like feeling sad, so I'll just
ignore it." The mind-heart may believe that an unwholesome
quality has been avoided.

Wisdom practice is based on seeing things clearly as they
are and accepting them as they are. Deliberately trying to push
something away creates tension (taṇhā) as much as liking and
disliking. Aversion has been compounded with ignorance.

The Buddha suggested a different strategy:

*A person understands mind affected by desire as mind affected by
desire, and mind unaffected by desire as mind unaffected by desire.
One understands mind affected by aversion as mind affected by
aversion, and mind unaffected by aversion as mind unaffected by
aversion. One understands mind affected by delusion as mind
affected by delusion, and mind unaffected by delusion as mind
unaffected by delusion." ("Satipaṭṭhāna Sutta," Majjhima Nikāya
10.34)*

Notice there is no attempt to get rid of or avoid any state.
The only effort is to see clearly what's actually going on.

If we find ourselves stuck in an unpleasant state, we can
notice if we've developed aversion to the state. Being angry at
anger, feeling lonely about loneliness, or worrying about worry
doesn't help. Instead we can let the feeling be. Give it space to
run by simply noticing the aversion to the state. Recognize the
disliking and Six-R any tension within it.

As we release, relax, and smile, the aversion will begin to run out of gas. Seeing the aversion clearly brings wholesome attention to unwholesome attitudes. Our job is not to get rid of the unwholesome; it is to see it through wholesome attitudes of acceptance and clarity. This brings wisdom and mindfulness that will dissolve any unwholesome qualities.

So if we get caught in unwholesome attitudes, it doesn't help to try to shake them off. Or to take them personally. Our job is to see how the mind feels — that is, to be aware of the attitude of the awareness. Awareness and wisdom will take care of the rest.

Related Chapters

20. Don't Scapegoat Distractions

Distractions are innocent.

"Bhante, I Six-R'ed it many times — but it keeps coming back."

He sighed patiently, "The Six Rs are not about getting rid of anything."

"Oh right," I thought. "I knew that. At least I thought I did. This must be the slipperiest fish of all."

© Adam Eurich

When I began teaching the Six Rs, I'd say: "This is hard to remember: the Six Rs are not about getting rid of anything."

Yet during interviews and classes, yogis worried, "I Six-R'ed it, but it won't leave me alone."

It is easy to forget that the Six Rs are not about getting rid of anything. Yet, they can be very effective in dissolving tension, hindrances, distractions, defilements, and other difficulties *when used skillfully.* It's a paradox.

Using them skillfully without force means not trying to make something go away. We Recognize what's going on (without trying to get rid of it). We Release it and let it be what it is (without trying to get rid of it). We Relax the tension and tightness inside (without trying to get rid of the feeling or the storyline). We Smile (which helps us take the distraction less personally without trying to get rid of it). And we Return to sending out mettā (without trying to control or change anything).

This is the essence of Wise Effort — effort without strain; letting things be without trying to fix, improve, change, or demolish anything.

Tension (taṇhā) is the fuel that powers defilements and hindrances. As we Six-R, we stop putting fuel in the tank. If the tank is full, the engine keeps going for a while. The defilement may not cease immediately. We may have to patiently repeat the Six R process. But if we stop putting gas in the tank, it eventually runs out and the unwholesome qualities fade.

The mind is a learning machine. As we use the Six Rs, the mind learns that they release hindrances. Soon, the mind not only recognizes their efficacy, it expects the Six Rs to get rid of the "problem." Residual greed and aversion don't like these states. They think, "The Six Rs work. I'll use them to whack that wandering thought, suck the air out of that crummy feeling, or squash this annoying memory. I'll use it to fill me up with the peace and well-being that I dearly want."

At this point, the Six Rs are being driven by liking and disliking. They've been co-opted by the tension they are supposed to release.

When the Six Rs aren't working, usually it's for one of two reasons. One is that one of the Rs has been left out inadvertently. The solution is to bring them all in for a tune-up. (See "35. Six Rs Tune-Up," p. 159.)

The other reason is they have been co-opted by desire or aversion. The Six Rs themselves are being driven by tension. Few meditators like distractions. By definition they take our attention where we'd rather not go. When the mind isn't clear, it easily scapegoats the object that captured awareness. But the problem is not the distraction, it's how we relate to it.

The solution is to Six-R the new tension that crept up the basement stairs. As we do this, both the original hindrance and the new one begin to fade.

The Six Rs are effective because they release the fuel that drives distractions without adding more fuel to them. *Done skillfully*, they are effective at getting rid of unwholesome qualities, but only when we don't mind whether they stay or not. As soon as the subtlest wanting or not wanting sneaks in, their effectiveness diminishes.

When this happens, it's important to stop scapegoating the hindrance and start relating to it wisely. The Six Rs are not about getting rid of anything. They are about how we relate to everything.

The Six Rs are not about getting rid of anything. They are about how we relate to everything.

Related Chapters

21. Meditation Is About the Mind, Not the Object

If you are never aware of awareness, your practice won't go very far.

– Sayadaw U Tejaniya

When anything arises in the field of awareness, there are three elements: (1) the object being seen, heard, felt, tasted, smelled, or thought about; (2) the awareness that knows these objects; and (3) the attitudes of the mind-heart that filter awareness. These attitudes are lenses we look through. If the attitude is strong, it distorts perceptions and thinking. If the attitude is weak, it's like looking through a light haze. If the attitude is clear and relaxed, it's like viewing the countryside on a bright clear day.

At any given moment, we have no control over what arises in the field of awareness or thinking. However, the attitude with which we view what's arisen has an influence on the next moment.

The attitude through which we view experience or thought is like a cloud or clear sky. It has a powerful effect on how clearly we know what is going on.

The Buddha found that when we can see clearly, that is enough to awaken us. We don't have to control what we see. We only have to clear away the distortions.

The easiest way to see these potential distortions is to note how the mind-heart feels. Is it light, heavy, thick, thin, clear, foggy, jumpy, relaxed, filled with emotions? Once we Recognize the quality of awareness, we can use the rest of the Six Rs to allow the distortion to dissipate.

Remember that meditation is about awareness, not the object of awareness. It is about clearing awareness of distortions. We attend to the mind-heart, not the object.

The Buddha said this succinctly in the "Satipaṭṭhāna Sutta: The Foundations of Mindfulness" stanzas 34:

How does one contemplate awareness as awareness?

Notice that the Buddha is not encouraging us to see the awareness as thought or to think about or analyze awareness. He wants us to see the awareness on its own terms: awareness as awareness. In other places he recommends seeing feeling as feeling, thinking as thinking, and perception as perception.

But in this passage, we're looking at the mind. In this case, mind is a synonym for awareness.

Some scholars translate this phrase as "mind as mind" rather than "awareness as awareness." But in English, "mind" has many connotations. "Awareness" gives a clearer sense of what the Buddha was talking about.

The passage continues:

When awareness is affected by desire, one knows it has desire. When it doesn't have desire, one knows it has none.

When awareness is affected by aversion, one knows it has aversion. When it doesn't have aversion, one knows it has none.

When awareness is distorted by delusion, one knows it is deluded. When it doesn't have delusion, one knows it is not.

When awareness is contracted with sloth and torpor, one knows the mind is contracted. When it is not contracted one knows it is not.

When awareness is scattered by restlessness, one knows it is scattered. When it is not scattered, one knows it is not.

When awareness is exalted by a lower jhāna, one knows it is exalted. When it is unexalted, one knows it is not.

When awareness is in a surpassed state of a higher jhāna, one knows it is in a surpassed state. When it is not surpassed, one knows it is not.

When awareness is collected and stable, one knows is it collected. When it is not collected, one knows it is not.

When awareness is liberated, one knows it is liberated. When it is unliberated, one knows it is not.

Notice there is no concern for the object that may be giving rise to desire, aversion, delusion, restlessness, or anything else. It is sufficient to notice the awareness itself.

After all, meditation is about awareness — not the breath, a mantra, a kōan, or any other object of awareness.

Related Chapters

22. Attitude of Mind Is Key; Content Is Irrelevant

How we see is more important than what we see.

I trained in Thailand under the meditation master Ajahn Tong. In the beginning, I tried to explain my distracting thoughts to him; I said I was thinking about my family or job or something that had happened in the *wat* (monastery). He usually interrupted me, smiled, and said, "There's no need to apologize."

At first I took this as a cultural misunderstanding. I wasn't confessing. I was trying to tell him something important. Gradually I realized that the content of my thoughts was never important. He was interested in the attitude of the mind itself — was it restless, agitated, groggy, clear, frightened, joyful, or serene? The content was irrelevant. If the attitude shifts, the content takes care of itself.

If the content of thought could wake us up, we'd be living in a very different world. But alas, that is not the case. We need a different strategy. As Ajahn Tong suggested, we need to recognize the attitudes in the mind-heart.

One of the easiest ways to make this shift is to ask, "How does the mind feel?" The question does not ask us to analyze. It simply instructs the mind-heart where to look and what is most helpful to notice.

When a distraction captures awareness, the distraction itself is not important. How the awareness feels is very important. So we ignore the content of the distraction and what we think about it. Instead, we pay attention to how the mind-heart feels.

If the distraction is an animal sound, questions like "What made that sound?" "What's it doing?" and "I wonder if it has babies with it?" can lead down long roads of speculation. This does nothing to cultivate wholesome awareness. But noticing how the mind-heart feels (startled, curious, restless, frightened, entertained, ...) is the road to peace.

If the distraction is the memory of a sarcastic comment from a friend, speculation about where our friend was coming from or what we might say as a clever retort does not bring forth contentment. Instead, we can notice the quality of awareness itself: is it angry, defensive, hurt, grumpy, or aggressive?

If the distraction is remembering a distant summer afternoon, the content of the memory can ramble on forever to no good purpose. So we ignore it. Instead we notice the feeling tone in the mind-heart. It might be light, wispy, longing, happy, restless, or dreamy. If we can identify the feeling tone, that allows awareness to release, relax, smile, and return to sending out wholesome qualities.

If the distraction is a recent political escapade, thoughts about who are scoundrels and who are saviors is not a wise place to begin. It is better to ignore the analysis for the moment and attend to the mood of the mind-heart. Is it permeated with fear, dread, vengeance, compassion, or clarity? Whatever qualities are present, noticing them with kindness and clarity help the mind-heart become less reactive and more responsive and wise.

When a distraction arises, asking, "How does the mind feel?" "What's its mood?" or "What's the texture of awareness?" can be helpful. These types of questions don't stimulate speculation. They just allow the mind to recognize its own attitude. This is the first step of the Six Rs. Releasing, relaxing, re-smiling, returning, and repeating follow naturally.

Related Chapters

23. Don't Stand up in the Hammock

There is no freedom for the self – only freedom from a self.

As the mind moves into the higher jhānas, it becomes peaceful and serene. Remaining tensions are subtle and difficult to see. However, the mind-heart always knows what's going on. We just have to learn to hear its quiet intuition.

One way to do this is to ask simple, open-ended questions like, "What do I need to see?" or "What meditation instructions would be most helpful?"

Once the mind knows the question, we release it and go back to our regular practice. The Friends (Quakers) call this "holding a question." We don't hold onto the query, but let it float easily in the background. Sometimes an insight arises in a short while or in a few days.

On one retreat, my practice plateaued. So I asked, "What guidance would be most helpful?" Soon three suggestions arose:

"Observe how the mind creates itself out of nothing."

"Let it (the mind-heart) dissolve naturally."

"Don't stand up in the hammock."

The first two instructions were clear. The third was amusing. But I didn't understand what not standing in a hammock meant. As I practiced with the first two, the meaning of the third became apparent: the mind is not its contents. Trying to juggle, manage, and sort out the

© Mike Martin

contents is like trying to stand in a hammock – it's hard to do, unnecessary, and more likely to lead to suffering than freedom.

To unpack this, consider this. The eye is not what it sees. The ear is not what it hears. The hand is not what it holds. The mind is not what it thinks, feels, or believes. Yet the mind often identifies with its experiences. It's an odd phenomenon. It's as if the eye sees a bush and thinks, "I am a bush." Only rather than identifying with an external object like a plant or a stone, the mind is more likely to identify with an internal "object" like a thought, opinion, belief, or preference. It tightens around an inner object.

An essential ingredient for a sense of self is tension. Without tension there is just a mellow flow of phenomena. With tension, experiences start to stick in the mind rather than arise and pass on. The Buddha described the process this way: "This is me, this is mine, this is who I am."

One Buddhist word for mind is "citta" (pronounced "cheetah"). Citta is defined as "that which knows and that which thinks." The mind is considered to be the knower and the thinker. Knowing and thinking arise and pass all the time.

By identifying with what is known rather than with the knower, the thoughts rather than the thinker, the contents of experience rather than the experiencer, the mind is creating a self out of nothing. Knowing arises out of nothing. Thinking arises out of nothing. All phenomena arise out of nothing. Perhaps we are the experiencer, but we are not the experience.

Meditation is learning to observe how the mind operates — seeing its processes. It helps to not pay attention to what the mind notices. When the mind gets drawn into the *content* of experience it often misses *how* it experiences. Knowing this, we may try to push the contents away. However, that is just aversion — more tension. Not so helpful.

To observe how the mind works, we can shift attention from the contents to the mood of the mind (as described in chapter 21). Does it feel open, tense, thick, light, dull, clear, angry, expansive, contracted, easy going, or up tight?

The mood of the mind is midway between the content and awareness. If we notice the mood, we are paying more attention to the awareness itself and how it operates. We see the *processes* of awareness not just the *topics*.

Shifting attention to the process in this way helps to de-personalize the mind-heart. As we observe the process objectively, all that content seems secondary to the awareness that notices the content.

As the tension relaxes, phenomena such as thoughts or ideas don't stick as much. They flow through. They become something we observe rather than something we are: "This is not me. This is not mine. This is not who I am."

That is how the self softens and dissolves naturally.

Trying to free the self is an oxymoron. There is no freedom for *our* self. The self is part of the trap. There is only freedom from *a* self as it dissolves naturally back into the flow of phenomena.

The Buddha's teaching about self and non-self can be confusing if we approach it as a philosophical or intellectual problem to be puzzled out. Like standing in a hammock, the puzzling creates tension. The tension increases the subjective sense of self that he was challenging.

However, his teaching was not meant as a metaphysical principle. It was intended to be a practical guide to awareness. He suggested relaxing into the metaphorical hammock and observing openly, clearly, and gently. Then we see no self – just a flow of experience.

Humor also helps. As we laugh we take our self less personally.

Related Topics

24. The Trap of Getting Free

Wherever you go, there you are.
— Buckaroo Banzai / Earl MacRauch[16]

What is the most common phrase used in Hollywood movies? Several decades ago researchers combed through hundreds of scripts to tabulate an answer to the question. They found the most popular phrase was "Let's get outta here!"

Doesn't that sound American? Wanting to be where we're not? It was the pioneer solution to difficulty: "Let's move West. Let's get outta here." Today we see this in the politics of saying "no:" no taxes; no incumbents; less government; "I don't like him / her," etc.

The phrase intimates that we can escape oppressive conditions if we just get outta here. It whispers the promise of freedom elsewhere. Yet the attitude itself can become a trap. Paradoxically, believing spiritual freedom is somewhere other than where we are makes freedom more elusive.

Star Trek

An episode in the original *Star Trek* television series allegorized this predicament. The series featured Captain Kirk, a human, and Mr. Spock, his science officer who was half human and half Vulcan. Vulcans were devoted to logic. They used mental discipline to augment intellect and suppress emotions.

One episode opened with the discovery of a new planet near a distant star. The planet was covered with buildings, roads, and advanced technologies. But the inhabitants were missing for no apparent reason.

---

[16] Buckaroo Banzai is a fictional character in the 1984 film *The Adventures of Buckaroo Banzai Across the 8th Dimension,* written by Earl MacRauch. Jon Kabat-Zinn used the phrase as the title of his 1994 book published by Hyperion Books.

Kirk and Spock went down to the planet's surface to see if they could solve this riddle. As they explored, they inadvertently triggered an alien mechanism that surrounded them with a force field. When they relaxed, the field grew weak and transparent. If they pushed against it, it got a little stronger. If they threw themselves against it, it became dense and powerful. The more they fought it, the stronger it got.

Finally they realized their prison was only as strong as their effort to be free of it. If they just saw that they were free, they could walk out of the field without effort. If they had any doubt – even a flicker of concern – that was enough to power the force field and keep them trapped.

Kirk couldn't get out. He intellectually understood that they were free. But he still desired to get away from the alien apparatus. He thought he would be a little freer "over there." That hedging was enough to keep him trapped. Spock, with his greater intellectual discipline, could see that they were free and harbored no doubts. He simply walked through the field.

This is a wonderful allegory for our situation. We are free, we are enlightened, we are awakened … use whatever metaphor you like. The only place we can experience this well-being is in the moment, since the present is the only place we actually experience anything. But if we think we would be freer, happier or more peaceful in a future moment after doing some more "spiritual growth," then we feel less free, happy, or peaceful in this moment. We are trying to get outta here — or "get outta now." We feel bound relative to what we think we could be. Like Kirk, we are trapped by the belief that we are trapped.

It is a ghastly/wonderful paradox. Before we can feel liberated, we have to feel liberated. In order to be free, we have to know that we are already free.

Woody Allen once said, "I don't believe in heaven, but I'm going to take a change of underwear just in case." We say, "Ah yes, I know I'm a Buddha, but I need to change myself a little just in case."

Since we equivocate, we need help. We don't need help changing anything that's real. Reality is not the problem. But we do need help in seeing reality more clearly. That is why meditation is so important.

Our educational system at its best teaches us to think clearly. But it does little to help us see what's really here before we decide what to do about it.

This Star Trek allegory illustrates the paradox of the spiritual path. The path seems to take us somewhere. But as Buckaroo Banzai put it, "Wherever you go, there you are." The one thing we can never escape is our mind. We take it with us. "Wherever we go, there it is."

Practice

All this shows up in our meditation practice sooner or later.

During a dhamma talk, a long-time practitioner, Laura Rosenthal, said she had to keep re-learning "the only mind I get to practice with is this mind, not someone else's better mind." On a recent retreat she had an "aha" moment: "Whose mind did I think I was practicing with anyway?"

We all laughed. She had articulated a dynamic that hovered quietly in the shadows of our minds as well. We too often prefer a mind-heart different than the one we have. If we see that wish clearly, we can smile at its naiveté.

Reality is what it is. We cannot escape it. Wherever we go, there it is. Reality has no opinion about what it should or shouldn't be. It is not anthropomorphic. It simply is what it is.

Paradoxically, within the bounds of reality, we are already completely free. We feel trapped when we pay more attention to our opinions about what

© Adam Eurich

reality should be than to what reality really is.

When we feel trapped, it is as if we are imprisoned in a house. There are at least three ways we can approach that feeling. The first is to work with the emotions themselves: the anxiousness, anger, worry, despair, and so forth and see if we can soothe them. It's like moving the furniture around in the house. We make it more comfortable but remain confined. It helps a little.

Another approach is to look for a door or window to get out. This seems more promising. But unless we truly understand the nature of the house we are caught in, running out the door or jumping out the window leaves us, bewilderingly, in another house.

A third approach is to just see the nature of the house that confines us. The Buddha discovered that if we can just see clearly, the house is seen for what it is — a delusion. We are already free. Like Spock, we can just walk away. And wherever we go, there we are: free.

These three approaches are not mutually exclusive. But without the last approach, we will remain less than completely free.

Stephen Levine once said that most people approach meditation making a bargain: we'll put up with the time and effort required if we get some peace and clarity in return. It's like a monetary exchange. We want something for something.

But real freedom comes only with dispassion. Dispassion means we're more interested in what's going on than in our opinions about it. We aren't meditating to get anything. We are content with whatever arises.

Then we are free.

Related Chapters

25. Alfred Hitchcock Moments

When awareness is strong enough to know something is amiss but not strong enough to know what to do about it, there's no need to fix it. Let mindfulness deepen naturally.

Alfred Hitchcock was the master of suspense. His secret was to make the audience aware of a disaster that was about to happen. For example, a deranged guy breaks into a house and hides in the stairwell with a knife. A young woman returns home, unaware of the intruder. She walks toward the stairs as he crouches to leap. The second before he strikes, the phone rings and she turns aside, oblivious of the danger she avoided for the moment. But as she talks on the phone, the guy sneaks toward her. And so the suspense is agonizingly dragged out.

In meditation, an old argument may come to mind. If awareness is weak, the mind may be drawn into rehashing the squabble. But if mindfulness and wisdom are strong, the mind sees the futility of going that way and is not tempted. It releases the memory and relaxes into equanimity.

But there are Hitchcock moments in between when awareness is strong enough to see what's going on but not strong enough to release it and relax. If we try to force the mind to stop, that force puts more tension into the system and gets it stirred up further. If we indulge the arguing, we train the mind to behave in unwholesome ways.

A middle way is to recognize that there is nothing to fix. We allow the mind to have its argument, but we don't get involved in the content. We recognize the feeling tone of the mind-heart — we notice its attitudes. Then we release the attitudes by letting them be just what they are without holding onto them or pushing them away. And we relax any tension we notice in the mind or body.

What made the Hitchcock movies so compelling was his ability to get his viewers entangled in the plot. Once caught in the storyline, it's almost impossible to release and relax. The same is true of the mind's movies.

So rather than try to push the storyline away — which adds aversion to the mind — we can let the drama continue but shift awareness to the feelings and moods of the mind. As we observe these, we can release, relax, and smile. Then when the mind-heart is more relaxed, we gently go back to the object of meditation.

We can't forcefully purify the mind-heart of these distractions and unwholesome qualities. Instead, we Six-R. Over time this strengthens mindfulness. And with mindfulness comes wisdom. We see the process as an impersonal one. It is the job of mindfulness and wisdom to dissolve the tension of unwholesome qualities. And when they are strong enough, they will do so effortlessly.

Related Chapters

26. Hindrances Like the Back Door

Hindrances never come in the front door.
—Sayadaw U Tejaniya

Hindrances never walk in the front door. They always slip in the back door, sneak through the sliding door from the porch, or squeeze through the rat hole in the wall. We don't see them coming.

Awareness dissolves tension. Hindrances survive on tension. Therefore, they won't arise when awareness is strong and clear. They wait for mindfulness to take a little nap.

Years ago I became curious about the nature of thoughts — what they

© Oumanima Ben Chebtit, unsplash.com

actually were. I easily noted thought content — the ideas, stories, complaints, explanations, and narratives. But it was harder to see the thought itself. If thoughts had been ice cream, it was as if I only noticed the flavor of the thoughts — vanilla, strawberry, mango – but not the ice cream itself that carried those flavors. I wanted to see the substance of the thought, not just its flavor.

At that time, I could sit for short periods without thoughts arising. So, in those quiet spaces, I decided to watch carefully and catch a thought as it arose. Then I might be able to see its nature. It was as if I were sitting in a theater. The curtains were open but the stage was empty. I sat quietly waiting for actors to come onto the stage.

For the first time in my life, I had stretches of twenty, thirty, or forty minutes without a single thought. Prior to this I had always wanted to be rid of thoughts. Now that I wanted to see them, they went on strike!

Then my attention would flit to the theater's Exit sign, the ceiling, or the seat next to me. When I looked back at the stage, it was filled with actors chattering away. Thoughts arose only when I wasn't paying attention.

Hindrances do not arise when we are aware of what's going on. They can only slip into our blind spots. When awareness is relaxed and open in all directions, hindrances cannot arise at all.

Hindrances run in gangs.
– Sayadaw U Tejaniya

Related Chapters

27. Kindness Toward Tension

Kindness wins in the long run.

Many flavors of Christianity say that human nature is fundamentally corrupted: original sin. Since we are flawed, we need Divine intervention to save us from ourselves.

Buddhism says that human nature is fundamentally enlightened: original purity. Defilements (*kilesas*) may cloud the mind and heart, and twist our perception, feeling, and thinking. But they don't corrupt our original nature — they just obscure it.

The solution is not to change who we are but to free ourselves from the influence of defilements. The root of all defilements is *taṇhā*: a preverbal and preconceptual tightening commonly experienced as liking, disliking, or confusion.

Taṇhā is like a rat: it is very good at hiding, and it can live on very few calories. Taṇhā is hard to find and it doesn't take much tension to keep it going.

Mammalian rats hide by slipping into tiny cracks and crevices. However, there are no crevices in the mind. We experience the mind as a field of awareness. Pure awareness is unobstructed by hills, trees, rocks, or cavities.

So taṇhā "hides" by diverting attention away from itself. When the mind-heart tightens, it looks to the world around it to find a cause. Or it looks for mind objects like concepts, ideas, beliefs, and stories. Attention rarely goes to the nonconceptual taṇhā itself. Taṇhā remains in plain view, but we miss it because we're busy looking at the content of our perceptions or thoughts. And it only takes a small amount of tension to lure our attention away from our primary object of meditation.

Don't get me wrong. I'm not literally suggesting taṇhā is a rat. Taṇhā is an evolutionary adaptation that has served us for millions of years.

Imagine walking through an ancient forest. We catch a hint of food. Taṇhā creates a tension that shifts our attention to scanning the environment. Or we hear a faint crunch of leaves under the feet of a stalking predator. Taṇhā focuses outward to scan for danger. That is a good thing in these situations.

Taṇhā is not perfect. It just shifts our attention to something in the environment and leaves it to us to figure out what it is and what to do. We get false positives — we startle at seeing a snakelike stick in the grass. The anxiety doesn't feel great — but we can still pass our DNA along.

However, if we are so mellow that we mistake a poisonous snake for a stick, we might be killed and our DNA taken out of the gene pool.

Taṇhā is better at picking up negatives than positives. Today taṇhā remains a deeply wired, automatic instinct. Modern communication technology sends us bad news from around the world. Taṇhā can get hyper-stimulated. It doesn't feel good, but it doesn't prevent us from procreating. Without taṇhā, the human species would have become extinct a long time ago.

Rather than viewing taṇhā as an annoying nuisance, it's more accurate to view it as a loyal friend trying to serve us even when we treat it poorly. It may be unwise and hyperactive, but its heart is in the right place.

This also doesn't mean that we can't get free from the effects of taṇhā. The Six Rs can be very effective. It just means that it's unwise to blame taṇhā for doing its job or blame ourselves for the tension. It's a natural, biological process best regarded with kindness and treated with wisdom.

Kindness is bigger than ourselves.

Related Chapters

28. Hindrances As Invitation Only Guests

Nothing arrives in the mind-heart without an invitation.

I awoke in the middle of the night, rolled over, and snuggled back down into the pillow. Then I remembered an offensive remark from a lunch conversation. "I don't want to think about it now." I yawned and closed my eyes. Then I thought of a clever retort. "I'll send him an email. But not now." My intention was to sleep. But forty-five minutes later I was still rehashing the old conversation and rehearsing a new one.

Anyone who has ever meditated for more than three minutes is familiar with this phenomenon. We close our eyes to meditate, intending peace and tranquility. Instead we find the inner landscape populated with fantasies, to-do lists, reruns of old songs, and other colorful characters.

These intrusions seem like burglars who snuck into the house in the dark of night, or like unshaven guests who arrived for dinner unannounced. "I didn't invite them," we say.

But we did. Nothing pops into our minds without an invitation. During solitary moments in the night, quiet moments of meditation, peaceful moments walking through the fields, or dull moments driving down the freeway, these distractions come at our beckoning. Perhaps the summons didn't come from the self we identify as "me." But a subpoena was issued from the psychophysical energy system in which we live. "Distractions" show up because some part of us wanted them.

If we don't remember enticing these guests or we don't recognize our signature on their letters of introduction, then their appearances are opportunities to explore parts of our energy system we've lost touch with. It's a chance to peer into the dusty corners of the psyche's closet beneath the stairs.

There are several kinds of invitations — misguided energy, crossed intentions, self-concepts, and more. But they all require complicity. We'll explore these more in coming chapters.

Related Chapters

29. Crossed Intentions

We rarely do anything with a single intention.

My plan was to spend a few hours at my desk writing. Sometimes the words flow very easily. More often they don't. I thrash through several drafts. I wish I could imagine a whole chapter in my mind and, like Mozart, transcribe it onto paper. But I'm not Mozart. I work things out by writing a lot of awkward text, recognizing the problems, and starting again. The process can be uncomfortable. But when it works, the reward is worth it. So this morning my plan was to keep at it for at least an hour.

Fifteen minutes later my head was in the refrigerator trying to decide between the yogurt and the cheese. Or maybe ice cream would be better.

I paused. "How'd I get here?" Mentally I traced the path from my desk to the family room to the kitchen to the refrigerator. But the memory was dreamlike. My awareness had been weak. I was barely conscious of discarding my determined plan and seeking a distraction.

This episode illustrates crossed intentions: wanting focused time for writing was at odds with wanting relief from the discomfort of writing. In service of getting some writing done, I tried to ignore the stress.

Unfortunately, ignoring a discomfort doesn't get rid of it. The discomfort just operates like a guerrilla band that launches a surprise attack.

This phenomenon is familiar to meditators. We call it a "hindrance." Many hindrances arise from crossed intentions. Consider:

Sitting on the cushion, we go over and over a recent fight with our boss. "Go away," we tell the thoughts, "I don't want to fight him now." But secretly we'd like to rehearse a few zingers so that next time, we can win. We have mixed intentions.

Maybe a sexual fantasy pops up. We protest, "I don't want this messing up my meditation." Yeah, right! Part of us rather enjoys it.

One of the reasons hindrances show up is because of mixed intentions. Hindrances may keep coming back until we see them clearly and Six-R them. Hindrances show us a distortion in our system that needs wise attention.

In our daily life, hindrances might appear as procrastination, loss of willpower, distractibility, discouragement, loss of self-esteem, or self-defeating behavior.

All of these create suffering. It's natural to want to resist them, push them aside, or try to override them with counter-intentions. It doesn't work in the long run. New Year's resolutions have a poor track record.

Rather than deepening our resolve to ignore what we don't like, it's wiser to deepen awareness. We can't control something and be fully aware of it at the same time.

So if we're dogged by a recurrent hindrance, we can ask gently if there is a crossed intention: we can pause for a few moments and notice the motivation in the distraction. We can feel it out or notice the emotional undercurrents. If we can see these, then we can Six-R them.

This side of enlightenment, we all have mixed intentions. Wisdom grows from seeing them as they are.

Related Chapters

30. Covert Intentions and Self

Self-image generates intentions.

Intention is a kind of "leaning toward." Like *taṇhā* (aka unwholesome desire, liking, disliking, ignoring) and *chanda* (wholesome desire), it can be obvious or subtle. In fact, the distinction between intention and desire is blurry. Our self-image can be laced with hidden intentions.

While I was meditating one morning, my mind kept wandering off to the tasks I was facing that day. I called these wanderings hindrances that disrupted my intention to cultivate well-being rather than prattle. But with clearer awareness, I noticed the mind wanted to think about the problems of the day. It worried over facing a tough situation without a plan. It enjoyed untangling a good problem.

My storefront intention was to meditate peacefully. But in the back room, the mind took pleasure in explaining things and found relief in solving difficulties.

Explaining and problem-solving are so familiar to me that they seem to be "just part of who I am." Some intentions are rooted in self-image. They get absorbed and obscured in a sense of self. "I like music, ice cream, walks along the river, and meditating." I don't think of these as intentions. But they lead me in certain directions and shape how I think, speak, and act.

Self-image sounds static, but it's not. It influences our thoughts and movements. And our thoughts and movements influence it.

Intentions range from the obvious to the obscure. The obvious ones use willpower, such as a resolution to eat less and exercise more. The subtle ones are cloaked in self-image and habit (like eating more and exercising less). When we are acting out of habit, we don't think about our motivation. It just feels like "who I am."

But just because an intention is difficult to see doesn't mean it is weak! *Habit is stronger than will.* Self-image is stronger than will. Willpower can move us along for a while. But self-image and all its clandestine motivations and habits can wear willpower down until we revert back to that old, familiar, ingrained self-image.

In reality, the mind-heart is just a field of awareness. Experiences arise in it. Some of these we call "me." Others we call "not-me." But these labels are just mental constructs that pretend to segregate perceptions.

When we sit down to meditate, many intentions can poke up their heads to puncture the field of awareness: peace, serenity, revenge, kindness, ill will, and more. The natural mind makes little distinction between overt and covert intentions. Intent is intent. As the mind-heart opens and softens, all those mixed intentions may float to the surface.

As they do, we can Recognize how self-image leans in one direction or another. Then we can Release the self-image, Relax the tension, and smile.

© Paul Morris, unsplash.com

Related Chapters

31. Recognizing Two Species of Intentions

What's the mood of the mind-heart right now?

The Buddha departed from the Jains, Brahmans, and other contemporaries. He placed less emphasis on action and more on the leanings in the mind urging those actions. From the perspective of future suffering, what we do is less important than the intentions behind what we do.

Future

To understand what the Buddha was talking about, it helps to distinguish between two different species of intentions: intentions directed toward the future and intentions that arise spontaneously in the present.

Conventional intentions focus on the future: "I intend to go to the post office and stop at the grocery store for cat food on the way home." They are a plan or strategy to be executed in the future. They have a goal. And they imply an agent — a self — to remember and implement the plan later. "Next time I see that guy I'm going to let him know what I think." Sometimes they require will or determination. "Every morning I'm going to meditate for an hour." "During the next sitting I will not let my mind wander." They don't have to be doable or wise. (Good luck controlling the mind.)

Present

The Buddha was a be-here-now kind of guy, less interested in future plans and more interested in what arises spontaneously in the present.

In Pāli, the language of the suttas, *sankappa* is one of the words for intention. *Sañña* is the word for perception. In

Buddhism, perception refers to mentally labeling phenomena. For example, we see a blotch of green. The mind goes through its catalog of green objects and comes up with "leaf." That's perception.

The Buddha said that sañña and saṅkappa are conjoined. Perception and intention arise together.

When I first heard this, it didn't make sense to me. When I see a leaf, I don't necessarily plot what I intend to do with it. Maybe the intentions the Buddha talked about were not plans or strategies.

So I investigated. You can do this by closing your eyes, opening your sensitivities, and having someone slowly read you the list of words below. They are labels for things you could perceive. See how each affects the mind-heart. Or you can slowly scan the list, pausing to feel the effect of each:

Sunset
Blizzard
Velociraptor
Kitten
Flock of geese high in the sky
Cow dung
Mother-in-law
Donald Trump
9/11

Can you feel images, moods, emotions, and memories shift as the mind realigns around each label? They lean in one direction or another in response to each word.

The Buddha called these forces and tugs "intentions."

Vast Space

The mind is a vast space that includes thoughts, images, words, feelings, emotions, ideas, memories, beliefs, plans, strategies, dreams, wishes, and choices. It can contain anger, kindness, fear, delusion, compassion, peace, agitation, wisdom, and more. Flowing through all these are intentions. They are subtle forces that organize factors in the mind and point them in one direction or another or, possibly, collide with each other and create confusion.

Saṅkappa has also been translated as "directionality of mind." Intentions don't necessarily have a goal. But they have a direction or orientation. They are difficult to see until they are activated. They are inclinations that get energized.

Did you notice that no one creates the intentions? They just arise on their own with each perception. Slowly scan the following list and notice how the mind responds to each item:

Purple
God
Sin
Punk rock
Lavender
Chocolate
Anthill
Lynching
Ocean
Mountain

Intentions can be as subtle as the urge to breathe. They precede everything we do, say, or think. They permeate our system. They are the juice that keeps our system going. They are everywhere. When we pick up a cup, turn on a light, or scratch our nose, the action is preceded by an intention. Its effect may be obvious but the intention itself can be softer than a whisper.

Here's another example that distinguishes future intentions from present intentions.

We can plan to open the door. This is a conventional intention about the future. It's easy to recognize this intention.

On the other hand, we can plan to go outside. As we approach the door we will probably open it using the same motions as if we were thinking about opening the door. The intention to turn the doorknob may be below the threshold of awareness — the mind was fixed on the backyard, not the door.

Nevertheless, something in the mind causes the hand to grasp and turn the knob. That force is a present intention.

Attitude

The first aspect of the Eightfold Path, *sammā diṭṭhi*, is usually translated as "Wise View." The second aspect, *sammā saṅkappa*, is usually translated as "Right Intention." Sayadaw U Tejaniya translates it as "Wise Attitude." He says we cannot conjure up Wise Attitude, but if we perceive reality correctly, this perception gives rise to a Wise Attitude. In other words, Wise View triggers wholesome attitudes, inclinations, or intentions. Nobody creates the intentions — they arise spontaneously from how we see.

We do have some control over how we respond to intentions. And how we respond influences the likelihood that that those intentions will arise in the future. However, in the moment, they just happen. We can only embrace them or restrain from acting on them.

Neuroscience

Neuroscience supports the Buddha's understanding of intentions. Before I raise my arm, a neural signal goes from one part of the brain to the motor cortex. The motor cortex relays the signal to the arm muscles. As that signal is being passed along, I become aware of the intention, "I think I'll raise my arm."

Very sensitive scientific instruments consistently demonstrate that I become aware of that intention to raise my arm *after* the first signal is sent but *before* it reaches the motor cortex. In other words, the sequence is: an intention arises, a split second later I become aware of it, a split second later the arm rises. Notice that the intention is in the pipeline before I'm conscious of it.

However, I can sense the intention before the action actually takes place. I can't prevent the intention but I can prevent the action.

One of my teachers, Tony Bernhard, says, "We don't have free will. But we do have free won't."

This is why precepts are framed as restraints. (See "Appendix D. Precepts," p. 299–312.) We may undertake a precept to refrain from speaking or acting with ill will. But we don't undertake a precept to refrain from feeling ill will. It is not possible to prevent ill will from arising, but it is possible to not act on it.

There is no Buddhist precept to tell the truth. But there is a precept to refrain from lying. A guy says, "Doug, we'd love to have you over for dinner on Saturday. Are you free?" I'd rather not spend an evening with him. My mind starts creating alibis. I take seriously the precept to refrain from lying. It makes me more sensitive to noticing the urge to lie. So I catch it early, Six-R the tension that triggered the alibis, and keep my mouth closed while I consider my options.

If I feel threatened, my arms and fists may tighten. That tightening is a biological fight-or-flight reflex. But if I've vowed to not harm, I'm more likely to notice the intention to strike before I act. I can Six-R and back off.

Strength

Both future and present intentions can be strong or weak. The strength of an intention is the likelihood that it will prevail when pitted against a conflicting intention. It's rare that we do anything with a single motive. When we have multiple intentions that conflict, the strongest wins.

I walk into the kitchen thinking, "I'm going to get an apple," and walk out eating a cookie. It's not until I finish the last bite that I remember, "Oh, I was going to get something healthy."

The intention for the apple was loud and clear. But seeing the cookie jar triggered my sweet tooth. A powerful yet subtle intention can be like a guerrilla fighter who blows up a building and leaves before we see his face.

I wake up in the morning and think, "Ah good. It's time to meditate." Instead I lie gazing out the window for a while.

One night I crawled into bed thinking, "I'll play one game of solitaire on my iPad before going to sleep." My overt intention was firm: one game.

I played six.

This happened often enough that I became fascinated by the phenomena. Like a field anthropologist observing strange animal behavior, I was more interested in understanding what was happening than controlling it.

At first, I couldn't see the intention to play another game. I could have exerted more will power, but that would have overridden the intention without actually seeing it. I wanted to observe it directly.

So I relaxed and tried to get out of the way.

I began to notice that as I finished a game, a little whisper arose: "One more." It was nearly inaudible yet firm. In the middle of the next game if I thought, "I could stop now," an urge arose: "We'll finish this one first."

These intentions had nothing to do with the future or a goal for the future. They were entirely in the moment: "start another," "keep going."

There had to be some intention to keep me playing, otherwise I would have stopped. Once I could see the urges arise, I knew what to look for.

And sure enough, I began to feel a soft tug, as if from a steel hand in a velvet glove. There were flickering images in the background. One was of me winning a computer solitaire tournament. Another was of me as an aspiring holy man who found solitaire tournaments embarrassingly silly and wanted to blot them all out.

As the Olympic solitaire player and the holy man struggled against each other, awareness receded into a haze.

However, I was able to see enough to Six-R the images and intentions. Six-R'ing is not about getting rid of anything. Six-R'ing is not about aversion. I just Recognized the images on their own terms. I Released them and let them be as they were without going into the storylines. Then it was possible to Relax the tension in the intentions, Smile a bit, and Return to sending out well-being.

This allowed for the card player and the holy man to recede and for wisdom to come forward and take over. As awareness grew stronger, I could at last see the subtle intentions in the present.

Identification

The first quality of an intention is whether it orients toward the future or resides in the present. The second quality is its strength. A third quality is identification. We tend to identify with loud, future-oriented intentions. We think, "This is me wanting that." If a present intention is stronger, we may see it as a hindrance or distraction.

I thought that I was the one wanting the apple and that the hindrance wanted the cookie. At first, I identified with the intention to play one game and saw the other intention as a problem to be fixed. But they were both just intentions — inclinations in the mind.

We sit down wanting to meditate peacefully, but the mind is more interested in a recent argument with a coworker. It devises splendid rejoinders. We identify with the overt intentions to meditate and view the quarrelsome thoughts as illegal immigrants.

But they all arise in the same mind-space. They are all mind-stuff. The split into me and not me, self and hindrance, is artificial. It's an illusion.

Mood, Tone, and Texture

Biology and life experience wire inclinations into us. They may be dormant until some energy lights them up and makes them knowable as present intentions. They only exist in the present.

We experience them as attitudes in the mind. We all have luminous, clear awareness. This pure awareness looks through the attitudes in the mind to see sights, sounds, thoughts, and other objects. The attitudes color and potentially distort what we see. If we are depressed, that inclines the mind in one direction. If our attitude is elated, it inclines the mind another way.

As we've seen, these attitudes are what the Buddha called intentions. They organize the factors in the mind in one way or another.

You won't find these present intentions in thoughts. Conventional future-oriented intentions — plans and strategies — can be found in thoughts. But present intentions are preverbal and preconceptual. They are even pre-awareness — they arise and send out neural signals before we know they are there.

However, you can notice them in the moods, tones, textures, feelings, and attitudes in the mind.

If that attitude has tightness, judgment, discouragement, or other unwholesome qualities, here's the good news: We can't change the present moment. It arose before we knew it. Trying to change the present is like trying to change the past. So we are off the hook. We didn't create it. It just arose out of causes and conditions. It arose mechanically from the internal and external environment. So be kind to yourself.

Here's more good news: We can influence how we respond. And how we respond affects future moments. If the mind is tight, angry, and upset and we respond out of tension and self-criticism, those reactions create the environment for future unwholesome states. However, if we respond with qualities like clarity ("Oh, look at this lovely mess. Far out."), acceptance ("It is what it is"), ease (soften any tension), uplift (good humor and smiles), kindness (radiate friendliness or peacefulness), and patience, then these uplifting qualities are more likely in the future.

The Six Rs are a very wholesome way to respond to whatever arises. They won't change the present one bit. It has already arrived. In fact, by the time we know what's present, it is already a split second in the past.

But the Six Rs are a response that inclines the mind-heart in a wholesome direction in the future. They are a wise way to be with what is.

Chirp

Simple perception can have a powerful effect on present and even future-oriented intentions:

Joseph Goldstein tells of a couple moving into a new house. The first morning in this house, they woke up to the sounds of birds chirping in their basement. They heard them on and off through the day. They must have had a family of birds nesting down there.

They were delighted. It felt like a blessing to have these woodland creatures take up residence with them. They decided to stay out of the basement lest they scare them off before the babies were grown.

However, a few days later, they had to go down to the basement to tend to something. The husband tiptoed down as unobtrusively as he could. He quietly looked around for the birds or their nest.

He saw nothing.

Then he heard a loud chirp. He turned around. He wasn't looking at a bird at all. He was looking at a smoke detector. It chirped again.

Everything changed. The squawking of the defective smoke detector was so annoying that they called an electrician to come out as soon as possible and fix the darn thing.

Related Chapters

32. Uprooting Hidden Intentions

Hindrances can't survive in the light of clear awareness.
— Sayadaw U Tejaniya

Many years ago I noticed that my wandering thoughts were often in the form of explaining something to somebody. In one sense this was no surprise. Evolution gave the mind the job of knowing what's going on. It's natural for it to comment lightly on experience. Usually these comments come with a little tension. In meditation, as long as we're aware of sending out uplifted qualities, these comments can be ignored.

Still, it was interesting that the mode of my comments was usually explanatory. Perhaps I became a preacher and psychotherapist because my mind likes to explain. Or perhaps it likes to explain because, as a preacher and psychotherapist, my mind developed the habit.

So rather than just ignore the comments, I ignored the content and felt the tone of them. The tone wasn't so light. It felt earnest, even urgent.

I wondered, "Am I experiencing what the Buddha meant by subtle intentions?" It fit his description: I never saw the explanations coming. They arose on their own. They were in the present. They directed the mind in a specific direction.

As I felt the tones and textures of the thoughts and the voice speaking them, the earnestness turned to loneliness. It was sharp and painful. The mind said, "Let's not go there." But my mind has a deep habit of turning toward anything with a charge. So it relaxed into the loneliness.

The mind felt young, like a little boy hoping to get people to understand what he was saying so they'd understand him. There was a lot of emotional isolation in my early years. The affect of my family members was often flat and colorless. In old photos my eyes look forlorn.

I softened into the loneliness. It spread out and became poignant, spacious, and okay. Quiet smiles arose. Gradually everything faded into nothing — just a luminous quiet with no thoughts left: I was in the jhāna of neither-perception-nor-non-perception.

And the next day the explaining was back.

Over the years this inclination toward explaining had become deeply embedded in my wiring. It doesn't happen all the time. But when the mind has a little extra energy, the old habits come to life. The Buddha called them "subtle intentions" (*cetanā*) and "subtle hindrances" (*anusaya*).

I wish that inclination wasn't there. I wish I could meditate with a different mind. It's a cute and naïve wish; I smile when I see it. After all, the mind I have to work with is the mind I have.

Paradoxically, skillful acceptance of these leanings and inclinations allow them to surface, relax, spread out, and gradually dissolve on their own. To uproot them, we have to see them, let them be, relax into them, smile, and softly radiate kindness or peace — in other words, use the Six Rs.

In the quiet recesses of our minds, there are lots of subtle leanings and inclinations that push the awareness in one direction or another. Maybe your mind explains, plans, wonders, or muses. Maybe not. Each of us has different inclinations. But the process of uprooting them through seeing and accepting is similar for all of us.

Present and Future Intentions

In the last chapter we noted that conventional intentions are premeditated plans for the future, while subtle intentions are non-premeditated attitudes that arise spontaneously out of the internal and external environments and shape the mind-heart. We don't see subtle intentions coming because they exist only in the present. We don't have control over them in the moment, though we can do things to influence their likelihood of appearing in the future. The tendency in my mind toward earnest explaining is an example.

The Buddha was more interested in these subtle, present intentions than in future goal-oriented planning. As we'll see, there is a relationship between subtle intentions and hindrances. This relationship suggests various strategies for uprooting unwholesome subtle intentions and hindrances. This is a major theme in meditation: how to relax inner tension and dissipate unwholesome inclinations so the mind's natural buoyancy and clarity can be revealed.

Dynamics

To work wisely and skillfully with intentions and hindrances, it helps to understand their basic dynamics. So we'll start there.

Intentions begin in tension. As the word suggests, inside every intention is tension. If we have strong emotions like fear, anger, excitement, or yearning, the tension is obvious and orients us toward the future. If the intention is subtle it is not so obvious and quietly colors the present. As we saw in the last chapter, the perception or mere thought of a sunset, cow dung, a flock of geese, or torture can lean the mind in one way or another (see pp. 131–132). These leanings contain subtle tension.

If the tension is relaxed, it dissolves. If it isn't, it may become an inclination. This inclination may then trigger physical, verbal, or mental action. Repeated action can become a habit. A habit can become an identification. We think "I am a person who ..." or "I'm someone who doesn't ..." Inclinations, habits, and identifications have tension in them. If they are not softened, they may trigger further intentions.

The basic flow is that tension begets intention, which begets inclination, which begets habit, which begets identification or sense of self – we take it personally rather than objectively. Inclination, habit, and identification beget more intentions. And so forth.

Some intentions, inclinations, and habits are helpful. Sending mettā as we walk down the street or Six-R'ing when we feel upset are wonderful habits to cultivate. Some habits give rise to happiness. But other habits — like being quick tempered, conflict avoidant, or easily discouraged — aren't helpful. These habits give rise to bummers.

When intentions are helpful, we may not notice them. When they aren't, we might call the result hindrances.

We're tempted to ignore the intentions and try to chop down the hindrances if we don't like them. But acting out this aversion is as effective as putting out a fire with gasoline. Aversion is unwholesome and fuels hindrances.

On the other hand, indulging the hindrances feeds their growth as well.

So how can we work with the difficult ones?

Roots

Hindrances and the intentions that drive them are like plants. If we like the plant, we call it a flower. If we don't like it, we call it a weed. But the plant itself is neutral — it's just a plant.

If we don't like the plant, then the stems and flowers are hindrances, and the roots are intentions that support them. Some roots go deep. Some are shallow. Some have lots of stored energy. Some have little.

If we cut the plant off at ground level and it has shallow roots, it will probably die.

However, dandelions can send roots down ten or fifteen feet. If we cut them off at ground level, they will grow back. Nevertheless, if we keep cutting off each shoot before it can produce leaves, eventually the plant will run out of energy and die.

But some hindrances run so deep that they can't be successfully cut off at the surface. We have to dig out the roots.

A few years ago I spent several weeks with Palestinians in the West Bank. Among many other things, I learned about olive trees. They can live hundreds, even thousands of years in that arid climate. When it's too dry, they appear to die. But they are only dormant. Ten or twenty years later when moisture returns, they will start sending out new leaves.

Plants vary from species to species. So do hindrances. If we diligently cut hindrances at the surface by Six-R'ing, some will fade immediately. Others, like dandelions, keep sending up shoots. If we keep Six-R'ing them, they eventually fade. For others like olive trees, Six-R'ing only sends them into dormancy. Years later they may spring back to life. To truly uproot them, we must go "below ground" and take out the root intentions. We have to relax and open awareness enough to see the inclinations and intentions that feed them.

@ Lukasz Maznica, unsplash.com

Eight Tips

Here are eight tips for uprooting persistent hindrances, some of which have been discussed in previous chapters:

1. Feelings, not Thoughts

When dealing with a hindrance or just meditating, ignore the content of the thoughts, explanations, stories, judgments, or musings. Instead simply observe how they feel: light, curious, interested, bored, tired, peaceful ... Notice the attitudes in the mind.

This will allow mindfulness to become subtle enough to recognize those pre-thought intentions as they arise.

If you can't see the intentions, don't worry. As awareness grows, you will see them. And the best way to strengthen awareness is to Six-R anything that hijacks awareness. Six-R'ing allows the tension to dissipate and natural clarity to arise like the sun coming out from behind a cloud.

2. Crossed Intentions

Watch for crossed intentions. We may tell ourselves that we don't like our meditation disturbed by ruminating over an old fight with a colleague. But some part of our system wants to win the fight. The mind intends to ruminate until it figures out how to win the fight.

Rather than scapegoat the hindrance, see if something in the mind invited it. Once you see that, you can Six-R it.

3. Secondary Hindrances

Look for secondary hindrances. If, for example, the mind is consistently restless for a while, the mind may begin to dislike the disturbance. The primary hindrance is restlessness. The secondary hindrance is aversion to restlessness.

It's easier to notice the primary than the secondary. But once you see the secondary, you can Six-R it. That allows both of them to soften and evaporate.

4. Subtle Intentions

Look for hidden intentions. Subtle intentions are difficult to see coming because they are dormant until a spark of energy brings them to life. However, once an intention below the surface is active — as in my solitaire games — it is easier to recognize. Once we get to know its subtlety, it's easier to see. We can Six-R and gradually extract it, root and all. But it takes time.

5. Dispassion

Cultivate dispassion. Dispassion doesn't care whether the hindrance stays or leaves. It's like the good scientist who is more interested in seeing what data his experiments reveal than whether the data supports his pet hypothesis or not. Similarly, dispassion is interested in seeing the hidden intention without caring if it remains or departs.

This relaxed, accepting attitude makes it easier to feel the intentions below the ground. As awareness grows, it will gradually uproot them for us.

Deliberately trying to uproot deep hindrances creates tension. So we relax. Open. Soften. This way we take care of awareness and awareness takes care of us.

6. Impersonal Observation

Anytime something feels personal, Six-R the feeling.

Deep-rooted hindrances often become entangled with our identity — the very sense of who we are. If they are uprooted, we can feel like we're coming apart. Sometimes that is joyful. Often it's unnerving and causes us to tighten some more. If so, we can Six-R even the sense of self. At the very least this helps to see the impersonal nature of the hindrance.

7. Labels, Language, & Nīvarana

Pay attention to the language and labels you use in thinking and talking about hindrances, and the attitudes they generate.

The Buddha noted that perception and intention arise together. Perception is a process of labeling a phenomenon. How we label our experience generates an inclination or intention.

The Pāli word *nīvarana* is often translated as hindrance. The label "hindrance" sounds negative: it's an obstacle in our way. We generally don't like them.

But nīvarana actually means "covering" or "veil." It veils something important. It tells us, "There's some tension or distortion here that needs good awareness." A wise attitude is less about trying to get rid of veils and more about peeking underneath to see what's there. Under the veil we see precisely where some good attention is needed.

In this way, nīvarana are like messengers. They have some important news to impart. If we listen to them deeply — see the inclinations and intentions driving them — then the messengers are helpful. They are friends, even guides showing us where to explore. (See "33. Hindrances Want to Retire," 151.)

The Burmese meditation master, Sayadaw U Tejaniya, encourages people not to use personalizing language. Rather than say, "My mind is full of wandering thoughts," say more objectively, "there are wandering thoughts in the mind." At first this may seem counterintuitive. But think about it. If I have a pencil and call it "my pencil," this means that I have control over it. I get to take it with me. If someone else walks off with it, that is stealing, because it's supposed to be mine to control.

If the mind were ours, then we'd be in control. We could say, "No more anger," "No more depression," "No more agitation," and these states would be gone. But we don't have that control. If we had control of our bodies we could say, "Fat be gone," "No more gray hair," "20-20 vision," and that's what would happen. But we don't have that kind of control. We have a little influence, but no real control. The body is not truly ours.

Nevertheless, the mind and body don't behave at random either. There are laws that govern their operation. Things happen in the mind and body when the conditions are right for them to happen. So if we are skillful, we can behave in ways that influence the mind or body in one direction or another. But we don't have control.

When we drop the language of hindrances and ownership, we will come into a wiser attitude toward this mind-body system. Rather than saying, "I hurt," "I'm comfortable," "I want some food," "I'm at peace," or "I'm overrun by hindrances," we say, "There is pain in the body," "There is comfort in the body," "There is wanting in the mind," "There is peace in the mind," or "There's a lot of stuff going on in the mind."

This is a wiser, clearer, more objective view. It tends to generate Wise Attitude and Wise Intentions. And we are less identified with critical thoughts. We become a little kinder.

8. Intentions and Hindrances

When I became interested in subtle intentions, many teachers told me they were too subtle to see. I don't believe this is the case. They are subtle, to be sure. But seeing them and uprooting them is more about developing skillful techniques than superpowers. If we know what to look for and how to relax with a kind, accepting, dispassionate awareness, the subtle intentions reveal themselves and can be softened.

Try to be mindful and let things take their natural course. Then your mind will become quieter and quieter in any surroundings. It will become still like a clear forest pool. Then all kinds of wonderful and rare animals will come to drink at the pool. You will see clearly the nature of all things in the world.

– Achaan Chaa
quoted by Jack Kornfield and Paul Reiter,
in *A Still Forest Pool*

Related Chapters

33. Hindrances Want to Retire

Hindrances want to retire. They just don't know how.

One summer during a retreat, restlessness seeped into my meditation. I didn't like it. So I Six-R'ed to get rid of it. I wasn't cognizant of the aversion. So there was restlessness, aversion to restlessness, and confusion about the whole dynamic. Hindrances tend to run in packs. My meditation went downhill.

Then I became aware of the aversion under my nose. I saw the meanness I was directing at the restlessness. I Six-R'ed the aversion — not to get rid of it (that would be aversion to aversion), but to release it, let it be, see it more clearly, and get to know how it really feels. I softened and observed kindly and openly. I wanted to see and understand. I was asking the restlessness, "What do you want?"

The restlessness wasn't trying to give me a hard time. It wanted exactly what I wanted: for it to disappear. Restlessness was the result of too much energy. Physically it wanted to fidget, squirm, race around, and burn off that excess vim so it could relax. Emotionally, restlessness manifested as worry or anxiety. These too expended energy, but not as fast as physical movement might have. Mentally, restlessness manifested as thinking, thinking, thinking. This also burned calories, but less efficiently.

The problem was that fidgeting stimulated fidgeting, emotions stirred up emotions, and thinking triggered thinking. If I got caught up in restless stories, I was off into a fantasy and forgot to relax. The stress didn't have the space to unwind itself.

Still, restlessness was doing its best to get rid of that hyper-energy. Its heart was facing the right direction. Rather than fight it, blame it, or blame myself, I could bring the wisdom it lacked. I could Six-R. When I did this, we became partners. Restlessness burnt off what it could. I relaxed as much as I could. I smiled to keep it light and impersonal and repeated as needed.

Gradually the confusion cleared, the aversion faded, and the restlessness melted into peacefulness.

Five Hindrances

I was struck by the realization that restlessness wanted to get rid of itself — it wanted to retire from a job it didn't like. It just didn't know how.

I wondered about other hindrances. Traditionally there are five: the one we were just talking about, restlessness (too much energy), sloth and torpor (too little energy), desire (wanting something we don't have), aversion (not wanting something we do have), and confusion (not seeing clearly).

As those arose in meditation, rather than see them as hooligans or incorrigible children, I gently and kindly looked into their nature.

Each hindrance had its own flavor and dynamic. But underneath, each wanted out. And each needed some guidance to do that. Consider:

Sloth and Torpor are the opposite of restlessness. They suffer from too little energy. Sloth is a loss of motivation. Torpor is a groggy, drowsy quality of mind. Both want a sabbatical if not full retirement and don't know how to get there.

Sloth and torpor can arise from physical fatigue. In this case, the nap they long for may restore depleted reserves and bring energy levels back up to normal.

Sloth and torpor can also arise from sluggish mental states. Sluggishness has tension that's hard to see because the mind is dull and thick. Still, it wants to relax. Its heart is in the right place.

If I blindly push against this lethargy, the situation gets worse. But if I look kindly and deeply into sluggishness, the tension becomes obvious. I can help it soften and relax with the

Six Rs. With this, the mind-heart becomes clear and mellow and energy levels balance out.

Desire is another traditional hindrance that seems very different from restlessness or sloth and torpor. On the surface, desire just wants what it wants. If I've wanted a particular lovely piece of music for a long time, when I get that the desire vanishes because now I have it. The discomfort of wanting then fades into the lovely feeling of not wanting (see pp. 10–11).

We routinely confuse getting what we want with not wanting. So after satisfying a desire, rather than letting it rest, we think, "Oh that was lovely. I want more." What we really need then is not-wanting. But in our confusion, we go for another drink. And another. And another — until we're bloated.

Desire wants to retire, but ends up looking for something else to desire. It's up to us to see its deeper longing and help it ease up.

Aversion is the opposite of desire — wanting to be rid of something that we have or could have. When aversion is strong, it turns into anger or hatred. This powerful energy can be difficult to work with. So let's look at an example.

Imagine that we see an adult yelling at a small child. The child looks frightened. But the adult seems not to notice and keeps pouring out invectives. Our face flushes as anger rises inside. The anger "wants" to yell at the abuser to back off.

On the surface, this anger feels natural and appropriate. It is a response to hurt and injustice. Let's look below the surface.

Below our anger there is usually hurt. In this case, it may not be obvious. But with quiet reflection, we notice heartache — an empathetic resonance with the child. We feel the fear and hurt she must be feeling.

Underneath hurt, there is almost always alienation or feeling cut off from the flow of life. We don't want to be part of a world in which small children get hurt unfairly. Yet it happens every day. We often come to feel disconnected from this part of reality.

On the surface, our anger "wants" to flare at the attacker. At the very least, it wants to protect the child. This urge can be forceful.

But underneath, the anger wants to soothe the child and itself and to reconnect with the flow of life.

If we feel and understand all this intuitively, the situation is still complex. But we have a chance to sort it out and respond from a wiser understanding.

The surge of anger encourages us to do something. If all we are aware of is the anger, we might attack the attacker. But if we feel the deeper hurt and alienation, we may be able to direct the anger into protecting the child without lashing out. And our heart might remain open enough to watch for hurt and alienation in the abuser to see if there is some way to connect with that person as well.

If this is possible, then our anger gets what it truly wants: protecting the child from harm and isolation and giving the abuser a chance to feel less hurt, frustrated, and alone. If this happens, the anger truly dissipates in a deep and gratifying way. And even if such a complete resolution is not possible, the situation is more likely to move in a way that's life affirming rather than in a way that perpetuates violence and ignorance. We're more likely to find a way to keep our heart open while still maintaining good boundaries and being firm where we need to be. This allows the mind-heart to find a natural peacefulness while engaged in the world or while meditating.

Doubt is the last of the five hindrances. It is sometimes called confusion or "ignorance" — not seeing things as clearly as they are. More than the other hindrances, doubt wants to make itself go away. We don't like feeling doubtful or confused. Doubt and confusion have their own brand of discomfort.

Being doubtful and seeing it clearly allows the mind to relax and become more confident. Being confused and knowing we're confused is the beginning of clarity – confusion starts to sort itself out. Rather than struggle against doubt or confusion, it is wiser to relax, open, and simply know doubt as doubt and confusion as confusion. This is where wisdom begins.

Confusion plays a role in all the hindrances. Without delusion, none of the hindrances could survive. They'd all go into retirement.

So seeing things clearly and wisely as they are is a powerful way to relate to any hindrance or distortion.

Impersonal

And speaking of confusion, in this discussion I personified hindrances — talked about them as if they had intentions and personalities, aspirations and fears of their own. But clearly they don't. Hindrances are dumb, biological reflexes, wired into us, and shaped by experiences. Restlessness doesn't "want" to burn off excess energy in the sense of reflecting on its best interest and deciding what to do about it. Rather, restlessness is a complex biopsychological pattern that, left unimpeded, tends to burn off extra energy. Torpor doesn't try to talk us into revitalizing our energy by getting a nap or releasing a sluggish mental blockage. But it is a natural biopsychological complex that motivates us to do just that. And so forth.

Nevertheless, we do tend to personify our inner experience and relate to these complex reflexes with annoyance, exasperation, or aversion as if they were naughty or willful. That is an unwholesome reaction to natural processes. It puts unwholesome energy into our system and distorts it.

On the other hand, when we relate to hindrances with kindness, clarity, and the Six Rs as if they were benevolent though confused allies, a kind, pure, wholesome energy flows into our system. It helps us see the nature of the hindrances and our own deeper reality. Clear, undistorted seeing is wisdom. Wise-seeing helps hindrances unwind naturally until they rest in peace. We then can experience equanimity and dispassion.

Related Chapters

34. The Six Rs Are Self-Correcting

The process is more important than the result.

Wisdom-based meditation is ultimately about the qualities of the mind-heart. If we do not notice the qualities, our meditation will not go very far. If awareness stays exclusively with an object like the breath or a mantra and does not broaden to become aware of the awareness, the progress of our meditation can plateau.

However, if we are not able to see the awareness itself because mindfulness is too weak, we need not be concerned. With a little practice, mindfulness will emerge on its own. Pushing or straining to see what we don't see adds greed and tension to the practice. It doesn't help.

If we want to learn how to knit, we don't have to strain. We get a few instructions and just knit in a relaxed way. We make mistakes. We learn from the mistakes. We practice — we simply get better.

The same principle applies to learning to see the qualities of the mind.

When the mind's attention is drawn away by a distraction, we can spend a few moments with the Recognize step of the Six Rs, to see if we notice the qualities of the mind-heart at that moment. If the content of the distraction is too strong or awareness is too weak, we won't be able to see those qualities. However, we will have encouraged the mind-heart to notice them. That is enough. As awareness grows, the mind will begin to notice them more and more. We don't have to force it. Force is never needed.

The Six Rs are self-correcting. We only have to recognize what is apparent. The rest will take care of itself with time and patience.

Related Chapters

35. Six Rs Tune-Up

Take care of awareness.

The Six Rs are six actions: things we can do. They are not six states or qualities of the mind-heart. That is a good thing, because we have no control over the states and qualities that arise in any given moment. If there is sadness in the heart, we can't make the heart feel happy in that instant. If there is anxiety in the mind, we can't force that anxiety out of existence. Trying to change what has already arisen is like trying to change the past. Good luck with that!

However, if we respond wisely to what is present, we increase the odds of wholesome qualities arising in the future. We can Recognize sadness. We can Release it in the sense of not trying to hold onto it or push it away. We can Relax any tension inside us. And so on.

In other words, the Six R actions are not really about changing anything that's present. They are about responding wisely to reality.

As we practice the Rs, they start to blend together. To Recognize something clearly, we Release it and mentally step back to get a wider view. As we Release, we tend to Relax the tension inside. As we Relax, we smile (or Re-Smile) and lighter states tend to arise. As the lighter states arise, it is time to Return to sending out kindness or other lighter qualities.

As the Rs blend together, they begin to feel more like one motion — one action that includes them all. We call this "rolling the Rs." It is helpful and makes the practice feel simpler and easier.

However, as the Rs roll together, one or two may quietly slip away. We may Recognize, Relax, Re-Smile, Return, and

Repeat without realizing we left out the Release step. Or we might leave out the Relax step.

The Six Rs truly are one motion that includes all of them. If one is left out, they don't work as well. In fact, when the Six Rs stop working, the most common reason is that one R was left out.

One solution is to bring the Six Rs in every few thousand miles for a tune-up. A tune-up consists of slowing the Rs down and separating them back into six distinct actions for a short while. As we do it, it becomes clear if we've left something out. We add that back. Once the Rs are working properly, we can take them back "on the road."

Pure Awareness

Such tune-ups are also important because they help the mind-heart attune to pure awareness. Pure awareness does not become apparent until the higher jhānas or beyond, though some yogis have glimpses of it in earlier practice.

Pure awareness is awareness with no object other than awareness itself. It is a taste of the enlightened mind-heart with no distortion. It is clear, has no agenda, and is deeply relaxed, uplifted, luminous, and patient. It's not a collection of separate qualities but a simple, unified field of all those qualities.

Notice that these qualities of pure awareness resonate with the Six Rs:

• Recognize — pure awareness is clear and sees things just as they are without intervening concepts or ideas. It simply recognizes what is.

• Release — pure awareness has no agenda. It is not trying to twist or mold the mind-heart into anything it is not. It releases any tendency to push or hold.

• Relax — pure awareness is deeply relaxed.

• Re-Smile — pure awareness is uplifted. When we smile quietly, the mind naturally lightens and brightens.

• Return to radiating mettā — pure awareness is luminous and naturally radiates wholesome qualities.

• Repeat — pure awareness is patient. It has nowhere to go, no schedule to meet, no mountain to climb. It is content to be as it is. And if a distortion arises, the mind-heart is content to Six-R patiently to get back to its natural state.

There is nothing we can do to cultivate pure awareness because it is already with us all the time. Since it has no tension to draw our attention, it is easy to overlook it.

While we can't create pure awareness, we can Six-R the tensions that conceal it. Since each of the Rs resonates with a quality of pure awareness, they are subtle reminders of what is already here.

As we become more familiar with pure awareness, it becomes the object of meditation. We let attention rest there. When fluctuations arise, we Six-R them as one motion.

Keeping the Six Rs finely tuned not only helps us respond wisely to distractions, it also quietly and subtly nudges the mind-heart into pure awareness. In pure awareness, there is no grasping, preferring or suffering.

Related Chapters

36. Goodness and Meanness

Don't brood over the faults of others.

– Atiśa

Josie and the Turkey

I love the woodlands and meadows that stretch along the American River near our home. One afternoon I was sitting in a grove of trees writing. I looked up and noticed a wild turkey in a clearing about a hundred feet to my right. Her movements were angular and aggressive as she paced back and forth. After a minute she settled into high grass, sank down, and disappeared. Her head then rose up like a suspicious periscope looking this way and that. Then it slid down out of sight.

A few moments later, a big, white, happy-go-lucky dog with a red mouth came loping up a path. He was oblivious of the turkey hiding in the grass. Suddenly the turkey leapt straight into the air and came down toward the dog, talons extended.

Surprised by the ambush, the dog backed up half a pace. His back legs tripped, causing him to sit on his rump. He outweighed the turkey at least five to one. So his ears perked up and his eyes lit up as if to say, "Oh boy, look what I found!" He leapt at the turkey. The bird was faster out of the starting block and got a ten-foot lead: the chase was on. As they came up to full running speed, the dog was a little faster. He was closing the gap between them. My stomach clenched.

"Josie!" a big voice yelled through the woods. Back near the clearing a man stood with hands on hips. "Josie! Get back here, Josie!"

Josie was too excited to notice, much less heed the command. Her teeth were a few inches from her quarry.

The turkey spread her wings and flew a few feet above the ground. The dog continued the chase, but the turkey was faster in the air. When she had a ten-foot lead, she came out of flight and started running again!

Josie closed in.

A shrill whistle pierced the woods. "Josie! Leave that turkey alone! Get back here!"

Josie slowed a little, veered off the chase, and circled back toward his master.

The turkey changed course as well, pursuing the dog, trying to peck his butt!

The dog stopped dead in his tracks and spun around toward the bird. They were face to face. The bird's head was low. Her eyes squinted as she all but scratched the ground menacingly. The dog was bright-eyed with delight. He leapt at the bird. The chase was on again.

The whistle shrilled again, but Josie was engrossed. This time, when the turkey took flight, she rose higher and landed in a tree. Josie stopped below the bird and looked up silently and wistfully.

Another harsh whistle: "Get back here, Josie!"

Josie's shoulders slumped as if to say, "Aw shucks. I was so close," and he ambled back to his master. The two of them turned their backs on the scene and wandered away down the path together.

From my vantage point, I couldn't actually see the turkey in the tree. So I returned to my writing thinking, "That has to be the meanest, stupidest bird I've ever seen. No wonder they call them turkeys!"

Five minutes later I looked up. The turkey was back in the clearing. Now her motions were graceful and gentle. I noticed some peculiar leaves or feathers blowing around her ankles. When I looked more closely I saw they were tiny chicks. They could not have been more than a day old.

Suddenly the bird was transformed from a stupid, mean turkey into a smart, courageous mama whose instinctual love had caused her to risk her life to distract the dog and protect her babies.

My heart went out to her in admiration.

Beneath the Surface

Of course, the bird had not transformed. The mama with her babies was the same creature who had taunted the dog earlier. I just hadn't known the whole story. Nothing real had changed; it was my opinion that was transformed.

True mindfulness is not a stone skipping across the surface of a pond. It settles into the depths. In Pāli, another word for this is *sampajañña*. Sampajañña means seeing what's going on in the moment and seeing the larger context *at the same time*. Often translated as "clear comprehension," it's like a wide-angle lens that sees both depth and breadth.

I had misjudged the bird because I hadn't seen beneath the surface. When I did, I saw goodness in her. It was a reminder that when I can't see goodness in a person (or a bird), then I haven't seen very deeply.

Goodness

I received a lot of training in seeing hidden goodness in the mid-1980s as I developed a counseling center for street kids. I worked with adolescents at high risk of drug abuse and delinquency. For example, Randy was a young man who pounded steel spikes through a baseball bat and used it to chase police. Most of my kids were not that extreme, but I got to know a lot of mean turkeys.

I learned that I had to be able to see goodness in each kid or I'd be of no help. Many had been abused and mistreated. They were very good at sniffing out insincerity. I didn't have to like them, but I did have to love them genuinely. And to love them authentically, I had to see light beneath their dark exteriors.

The first time I met Randy, his stance was tall and proud despite his short stature. His jaw was rigid and his eyes were cold. He was frightening. But as I relaxed, I noticed a touch of fear hidden in the corners of his eyes. I sensed a little boy trying desperately to protect himself. I saw a lost, innocent child — a sweetness beneath the crusty exterior.

Mettā, the Pāli term for kindness or friendliness, is described as the outflowing of the heart in response to the goodness in someone. As long as I could see that goodness, I could feel kindness toward Randy and relate to the goodness in him.

At the same time, it was important that I not be naïve. Despite Randy's innocent core, he was capable of considerable damage. The turkey in the woods was a courageous, kind, loving, mother who would have pecked Josie's eyes out without remorse if she'd had the chance.

There is the light of goodness in all of us. And in the wrong circumstances, we're all capable of meanness.

Meanness

I saw my own meanness one day driving down the highway. A car hurried up the entrance ramp. Rather than yielding as I "knew he was supposed to," he pushed into my lane. I braked and swerved slightly. When I recovered, I blew my horn. He flashed me a rude gesture and sped down the freeway.

When my composure returned, I looked at my motives for honking. I'd like to say I wanted to remind him of good driving skills or to keep us both safe. But honestly, I wanted him to feel bad for being an inconsiderate jerk. I wanted him to suffer.

My operational definition of "evil" is "wanting someone to suffer." By my own standards, my action was evil. That's sobering. I can justify and rationalize what I did. I can see the goodness in me. But I don't want to be naïve. So I have to know my own potential to harm and to wish harm on others.

This side of enlightenment, in the right (or wrong) circumstances, we all have the potential to cause damage intentionally.

Back in the counseling center, if I couldn't genuinely love an adolescent, I had no kindness to offer. And if I couldn't see their capacity to harm, I had no wisdom to offer. They needed both kindness and accessible wisdom.

I never found a kid in whom I couldn't see a glow somewhere. I couldn't help all of them. Some were damaged beyond the time, talent, and resources available to me. But given a little time, I could always see a glow beneath the surface.

Eventually I left the counseling center. I took this practice of looking for that inner glow in others into my work as a private psychotherapist and a minister. I tested it. I never found a client or congregant in whom I could not see that goodness. There are some I would not want to see in public office or positions of power. There are some I'd want to keep away from sharp objects. There are some in whom the potential for violence was all too accessible. But if I could get to know someone, I could always see that light of goodness somewhere below the surface.

Time, patience, ease, and steadiness

The world needs more kindness and wisdom. Our lives need more kindness and wisdom. Our meditation practices can help cultivate them if we don't skip over the surface lightly. It takes time, patience, ease, and relaxed steadiness to see depths within and around us.

One way to carry meditation out into the world is to look for that spark of goodness in everyone. We all have the potential to awaken. We all were once a child and an infant. There is innocence and a light in each being. And at the same time, under the right conditions most of us can feel the urge to peck someone's eyes out. We needn't be naïve. To hold both of those realities at once helps relax the judging mind and awaken the discerning mind. We can let go of trying to think we are good or bad. If we do that, the old self fades into irrelevance. Kindness and wisdom remain.

Kindness without wisdom is not kind. Wisdom without kindness is not wise.

Related Chapters

37. Gifts and Vulnerabilities

Our gifts and vulnerabilities are intertwined.

Angulimāla

Ahimsaka was the son of the royal chaplain of King Pasenadi's court. The King was a steadfast supporter of the Buddha. Astrologers noted that Ahimsaka was born under the "robber star" (Sirius) and believed he was vulnerable to becoming a robber or criminal.

So his parents named him "Ahimsaka" which means "harmless" in hopes this would inspire that ideal in him. They raised him with care and kindness. He grew up strong, intelligent, well-behaved, and diligent in his studies.

He was so diligent that his parents sent him to the famous university of Takkaskila. A renowned teacher accepted him, and he excelled in his studies. He served his teacher so faithfully and humbly that he became the teacher's favorite. The teacher's family gave him meals.

Other students grew envious and plotted to drive a wedge between Ahimsaka and the teacher. They quietly hinted that Ahimsaka was disloyal and plotting to push the teacher out.

At first the teacher dismissed the innuendos. But in time the poisonous suspicion took root in his heart, and he schemed to get rid of Ahimsaka.

Since Ahimsaka's studies were nearly completed, the teacher said that his final duty was to honor the teacher with a gift.

"Certainly, master!" he said. "What shall I give you?"

"You must give me a thousand fingers of the right hand." He figured Ahimsaka would be caught or killed in this task.

"O, how can I do that, master! My family never uses violence."

His teacher was firm: "You must give your education proper homage, or it will bear no fruit." Eventually Ahimsaka was persuaded of what he must do.

He gathered weapons and retreated into the wild Jālini forest in his home province of Kosala. He took up residence in a high cliff that offered a clear view of the road below. When he saw a traveler, he hurried down, killed him, and took a finger. He hung the fingers in a tree where birds ate the flesh away. To protect the bones from rotting, he threaded them into a necklace that he wore around his neck.

News of the gory crimes spread. No one knew his identity, so they called him "Angulimāla" which means "Finger Garland."

People stopped traveling through the Jālini forest, so Angulimāla ventured closer to the villages to find victims. Like modern refugees fleeing a war zone, the villagers abandoned their homes and sought the protection of cities.

Thus King Pasenadi learned of the one-man reign of terror and gathered a regiment of soldiers to hunt him down.

The Buddha learned as well and, intuitively sensing goodness in him, went to visit Angulimāla. By now he had killed 999 people.

(Picking up the story in the "Angulimāla Sutta" found in *Majjhima Nikāya* 86[17]:)

Angulimāla saw the Blessed One coming from afar and thought: "Isn't it amazing! Isn't it astounding! Groups of ten, twenty, thirty, and forty men have gone along this road, and have fallen into my hands. Yet now this contemplative comes attacking, as it were, alone and without a companion. I think I'll kill him."

Angulimāla took up his sword and shield, buckled on his bow and quiver, and ran with all his might to catch the Buddha, who walked at a normal pace. Yet he could not catch him.

Angulimāla thought: "Isn't it amazing! Isn't it astounding! I could catch a swift elephant, a swift horse, a swift chariot, a swift deer and seize them. But I can't catch this recluse walking at a normal pace."

So he stopped and called out, "Stop, recluse! Stop!"

The Buddha said, "I have stopped, Angulimāla. You stop too."

Angulimāla asked, "What do you mean? How have you stopped? How have I not stopped?"

The Buddha said, "Angulimāla, once and for all I have cast off violence toward all living beings. That's how I have stopped. You

---

[17] This passage has been rendered from the translations of Bhikkhu Bodhi and Thanissaro Bhikkhu and shortened for readability.

are unrestrained toward beings. That's how you have not stopped."

Aṅgulimāla reflected, "At long last a revered great seer has come to the forest for my sake. I will renounce evil forever."

He hurled his sword and weapons into a gaping chasm. He paid homage at the Sublime One's feet, and right then and there requested the going forth [so he could become a monk and disciple of the Buddha].

The Buddha said, "Come, monk."

With these simple words, Aṅgulimāla became a monk.

I suspect this conversation between the Buddha and Aṅgulimāla was more detailed than what has survived in the records. But we can see the flow of events.

Aṅgulimāla walked back to Sāvatthī with the Buddha and began training. This included meditation and daily alms rounds for his food. On his rounds, people were frightened and gave him little. Some threw clods and sticks at him. He often came back to the monastery cut and bleeding. But he continued the daily rounds because that was what was expected of a monk.

One day, on alms round, he saw a woman in difficult and painful labor. He was deeply moved by her suffering, and he shared his concern with the Buddha. The Buddha said, "You should help her."

Aṅgulimāla sent word that he was coming. Her family set up a curtain and a chair so he could sit in the room with the woman without seeing her.

In his presence, her difficulties subsided, the birthing went smoothly and woman and infant were healthy.

Word of the miracle spread. Other women in labor sought his help. As more were helped, attitudes toward him changed. He received food on his rounds, though a few still hurled stones. He bore these injuries with a peaceful mind and heart.

In time he became fully enlightened. Eventually he retired into the forest and lived serenely. We don't know much about his later years except for a few verses he spoke, such as:

*Who once did live in negligence
and then is negligent no more,
he illuminates this world
like the moon freed from a cloud.*

*Who checks the evil deeds he did
by doing wholesome deeds instead,
he illuminates this world
like the moon freed from a cloud*

*The youthful monk who devotes
his efforts to the Buddha's teaching,
he illuminates this world
like the moon freed from a cloud.*

— *Majjhima Nikāya* 86.18

Today in Buddhist lands, most children know Angulimāla's dramatic story. Pregnant women look upon him as a patron saint whose blessing ensures a successful delivery and brings children joyfully into the world.

Discouragement and Hope

As Angulimāla trained under the Buddha, he probably had moments of joy, peace, spaciousness, and deep relief. But I doubt it was all sweetness and light. He had given up violence, but the momentum of his crimes probably carried forward for some time. His bodily injuries were small compared to the horrific images arising in his mind-heart. He must have had moments of great discouragement.

When we sit down to meditate, we may have moments of joy, equanimity, and spaciousness. Insights into old habits give relief. We get a genuine taste of freedom

Then the meditation falls apart. The mind flies around the room like a party balloon that slipped out of our hands before we could tie off the valve. It goes *"phewwwww"* as it circles insanely around the room, smashes into a wall, and drops to the floor like a total failure.

While I was training in Thailand, I wrote in my journal, "My mind has checked out every other book from the Library of Congress and is reading them all at once."

This practice can be discouraging. We may think, "I don't have it." "It's beyond me." "I can get a little glimpse, but I'm no yogi." "I don't have the talent for this."

In this context, I share the story of Angulimāla for several reasons.

First, in the span of a few years, he went from killing 999 people to becoming an arahant, a fully enlightened being. Unless we have killed more than 999 people in the last few years, there is plenty of hope for us.

There is nothing essential keeping us from going as far as we might ever want to go. This sutta says, "Look how far we can go astray and still find full peaceful awakening."

This story reassures us that distractions are normal and not fatal.

There are many stresses in our lives. We have all done bad things intentionally and unintentionally. We stumble over and over. It's not surprising that disturbing states arise within us. This practice is about seeing the truth, not shielding us from it.

The story suggests that we can manage our difficulties. Probably none of us have gone over to the dark side as fully as Angulimāla. He awoke nonetheless. We can too.

The problem is not who we are. The problem may be who we *think* we are. It may be what we *fear* we are or *hope* we aren't. But it's not about the essence of *who* we are.

We don't take refuge in who we *think* we are. We take refuge in our *potential to awaken* whether we understand it or not. We don't take refuge in how we think life works. We take refuge in *the natural laws of how the mind works* whether we understand or not.

Gifts and Vulnerabilities

The main reason I share the story is that it suggests a relationship between our greatest gifts and our greatest vulnerabilities. Ahimsaka's greatest gift was healing: his serenity was so catching that women in difficult labor calmed down. Children who might otherwise have died were brought more easily into the world.

Angulimāla's greatest vulnerability was being gullible enough to be talked into killing innocent people: he violently took life out of the world. Ahimsaka / Angulimāla was a healer and a killer.

This suggests that our greatest gifts and our greatest vulnerabilities may be fraternal twins. Any religion, spirituality, or philosophy of life with any depth recognizes that the human heart has a tremendous capacity for kindness, compassion, generosity, and courage. We also have the potential to do great damage to ourselves and others.

Within each of is us an Ahimsaka and an Angulimāla, an Anakan Skywalker and a Darth Vader, angels and demons, Buddha nature and Mara (deluded) nature. We can help and we can harm. We all both help and harm.

We could call our greatest strengths and weaknesses Dhamma gifts and Dhamma vulnerabilities. These go beyond ordinary talents and frailties. Ordinary gifts might be music, writing, cooking, fixing machines, programming computers, or painting. Ordinary vulnerabilities might be having a short temper, being impulsive, being easily discouraged, or avoiding conflict. These are the stuff of personality and ordinary psychology.

Dhamma Gifts

But Dhamma gifts are deeper. They are the ways we connect with the core of life. They are the ways we touch a source of well-being that is undisturbed by the surface of life. They are the ways in which we are already enlightened.

All of us have one or two divine gifts. They may be so close to us that we don't recognize them. They may have been so ignored in our childhood that they don't seem real. They may be so denied that we have become cynical about them. But they are there.

For example, some of you have the gift of **Oneness**. You sense how everything is a part of everything else. Maybe the only place this surfaces is in your love of nature. When you're in the wilderness or a field, something deep inside you relaxes. Your armor — the ways you contain yourself — begins to melt. You feel more a part of everything.

Like Ahimsaka's concern for women in labor, some of you have the gift of **Compassion**. You're drawn to serve the suffering and oppressed. You aren't trying to relieve guilt or to be a do-gooder. You just feel more alive and whole when your heart flows into helping.

Some of you have Ahimsaka's gift of **Serenity**. You see the perfection in everything as it already is or as it is unfolding. Your capacity to look at suffering and remain serene is a gift of peace to yourself and comfort to those around you. They feel calmed and healed by your presence.

Some of you have the gift of **Lawfulness** and you sense the universal simplicity behind the surface complexity. Some of you have the gift of **Joy**. Some have the gift of **Faith**. Some have the gift of **Generosity**. Some have the gift of **Innocence and Openness**.

There are probably ten to fifteen relatively distinct Dhamma gifts. Each is related to all the others, so all of us know all of them a little. We can relate to every one. But I'd suggest that each of us has one or two of these gifts in great abundance. Our gifts may not be the same as Ahimsaka's, but we have one or two that shine while others are dimmer in the background.

Dhamma Vulnerabilities

If that were all there was to our story, we'd be living in a heavenly realm: life would be sweet, wonderful, blissful, clear, and delightful. Like Ahimsaka's later years, life would be groovy.

But life is more interesting than that. There is a dark side to each gift. Like Ahimsaka, we are gifted and confused. We have flaws, weaknesses, and blind spots.

Consider: There are many obstacles in life — detours, barricades, washed out bridges, potholes, and fallen trees. Life impinges on us through insults, thoughtless people, stubbed toes, blocked opportunities, and disappointments.

Though we may run into the same obstacles, each of us has different responses. To recognize our Dhamma vulnerabilities, we have only to recognize which obstacles get to us most readily.

Social rejection, for example, rolls off one person like water off a duck's back while another gets soaked and drowns. Under pressure, one person is serene, another frantic, another lethargic, another worried about safety. When impeded, one person feels oppressed, another invigorated, another abandoned, and another resentful. Some people are more prone to melancholy, others to anxiety. Some jump the gun again and again while others can't get off the dime.

Have you ever been in difficulty and wondered, "How'd I get here? Why does this keep happening to me? I know this pothole so well. How'd I fall into it again?" You were probably caught in one of your deepest vulnerabilities. Dhamma vulnerabilities are ways we get thrown off balance over and over.

If you take only one thing away from this chapter, I hope it's the willingness to explore the possibility that our deepest gifts may be tied to our deepest vulnerabilities. Our greatest strengths may give rise to our greatest weaknesses.

For example, if you have the gift of **Oneness**, when thrown off balance you are more vulnerable than others to feeling isolated, alone, and separated from the goodness of life. Because your sensitivity to feeling interconnected is so strong, when the connection is cut off, you more easily feel cut off from all of life.

If you have the gift of **Serenity**, when thrown off balance, you may feel jumpy or moody. Your mind may race. Your sensitivity makes it easier to slide into peaceful states without even knowing what you are doing. The same sensitivity makes you more receptive to agitation. And since tranquility comes so easily, normal states may seem so much coarser to you in comparison.

If you have the gift of **Compassion** and run into a roadblock, you may feel frustrated, angry, or irritable. Passion makes up 70 percent of the word "compassion." Because of the strength of your compassion, when it is thwarted, it can flare outwardly into anger or inwardly into seething or grumbling.

To see your Dhamma gifts and vulnerabilities, contemplate a few questions:

What is the beauty in me? What are my Dhamma gifts? How do I most easily connect with the highest in life?

After a while, shift to these questions:

How do I hide my beauty? What are my Dhamma vulnerabilities? What quirks and weaknesses blind me?

Non-Dual Nature

It is all too easy to think of Ahimsaka and Angulimāla as two separate entities who serially inhabit one body. But the Buddha didn't see it that way. Ahimsaka and Angulimāla were in fact the same being. Under different conditions, different responses arose, but not different people.

Our gifts and vulnerabilities do not arise out of separate angels and demons within us. We are unified in truth even if our delusions say otherwise.

So if you feel assaulted by hindrances and just want to be free of them, the most effective way may be to see that they are nīvaraṇa: masks disguising a deeper truth. Don't get caught in the storylines of the hindrances. Release and Relax and see beneath the surface. If all you see is Angulimāla, then you aren't seeing the whole picture. Don't try to get rid of Angulimāla. Instead Recognize, Release, Soften, Smile, and send out mettā.

The Buddha never said that we have an Anakan Skywalker and a Darth Vader within. But he did counsel developing Wise View: seeing everything that arises with dispassionate interest.

We humans are sensitive creatures. We are animals who stood up to expose the softness of our bellies to the world. If we treat our sensitivities with fear and rejection, that does not change the present moment one bit. But it does condition the future to have more fear and rejection. Our sensitivities then feel like a curse.

However, if we greet our present experience with kindness, our sensitivities become a blessing. The natural luminosity beneath and within comes to the surface more and more easily.

To repeat the passage from Carlos Castaneda's *The Teachings of Don Juan*:

> *Does this path have a heart? If it does, the path is good; if it doesn't it is of no use. Both paths lead nowhere; but one has a heart, the other doesn't. One makes for a joyful journey; as long as you follow it, you are one with it. The other will make you curse your life. One makes you strong; the other weakens you.*

Related Chapters

38. All Techniques Fail

Don't expect a standing ovation.

– Atiśa

Imagine we had lived our entire lives deep in a cavern. If we knew enough about stars, planets, and the way light can separate while traveling through different mediums, we might deduce that the sky was blue — the blue end of the light spectrum would be reflected back toward space, giving the sky its color. If we were very confident in our calculations, we might believe this very strongly.

If we then traveled out the mouth of the cave and looked up at a clear sky, we'd no longer *believe* the sky was blue. We'd *know* it was. Our calculations might explain the phenomenon, but our direct experience would leave a deeper impression than an equation. Direct knowing trumps believing.

Meditation is based on knowing, not on believing. When we experience the way suffering subsides in the light of pure awareness, then belief in meditation techniques becomes irrelevant. We know.

There are no meditative techniques that can create that experience. It is already here. We just don't know where to find it. We don't know where to look for the mouth of the cave.

At their best, some meditative practices are skillful means to inspire, nudge, or trick the mind into stepping outside itself. So all techniques can fail because they aren't the experience itself.

Sometimes they fail because they are lousy techniques not suited to our temperament. And sometimes they fail even if they are well suited. Any technique repeated over and over can become stale — something we repeat by rote with weak intentions or a fuzzy attitude.

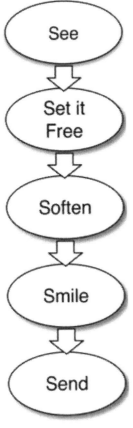

I've found awareness jhāna practice and the Six Rs to be some of the most effective techniques I know.[18] Yet at times they don't work so well, because I've fallen into a rut and my awareness is weak.

At these times it helps to adopt a similar though different technique to give a fresh perspective. Here are two that I've used to replace the Six Rs for short periods of time.

Five Ss and a P

Words don't have absolute meanings. Different words have different connotations for different people. So my sangha and I created another set of letters that might serve as a parallel reminder to the Six Rs. We call them "Five Ss and a P." They are described in detail in Appendix A (p. 287).

DROPSS

Before Bhante Vimalaraṁsi and his students composed the Six Rs, he used a technique called "DROPSS" which is an acronym for "Don't Resist or Push. Soften and Smile."

---

[18] The awareness jhānas and the six Rs are described in detail in my book *Budhha's Map*. The Six Rs are also outlined in Appendix A. The Six Rs and Five Ss Overview, p. 271.

It's not as full as the Six Rs, but it is a close cousin. It gives direct encouragement to notice resistance and to drop it. Sometimes the word "relax" in the Six Rs can sound a little abstract. When yogis ask me what it means to relax, I say, "Soften." Most get it immediately.

I don't recommend replacing the Six Rs with DROPSS. But if the Rs get stale, spending a few moments with DROPSS can remind us what the Rs are about.

Take a Break

And sometimes we can get into a subtle (or not so subtle) habit of pushing a little too hard. We have expectations of how the meditation should be rather than observing the mind-heart as it is. The mind and heart grow weary from such effort. At these times, stopping formal practice and going for a walk or just taking a break can help refresh the mind, give more perspective, and enliven the practice. If we feel caught in a rut, we can step out of it for a while!

Related Chapters

III.
Glowing Like a Candle

Be everywhere and nowhere.

39. Candles and Flashlights

Let the mind glow.

When I was nine years old, I entered a cave for the first time. While my family and I were on vacation, a park ranger led us three-quarters of a mile into a mountain. We reached a chamber where spotlights illuminated benches and railings. The rest of the chamber disappeared into darkness. "Take a seat or hold onto a rail," the ranger advised. "I'm going to turn the lights out."

She did. I waited for my eyes to adjust to the dark. They didn't because there was no light to adjust to.

After a few moments, she turned on a powerful four-cell flashlight that lit a tiny circle on the ceiling. I saw the texture of the rock. Then she shined it on a crack in a wall. She moved the light to three or four other places. The intensity of the beam was impressive. But I only saw tiny fragments of the cavern. The effect was not satisfying.

Then she turned the flashlight off and lit a single candle. The modest flame glowed in all directions, filling the entire cavern with a soft glow: I could see the people, stalactites and stalagmites, rock formations, a river flowing through, and the expanse of the cavern. It was beautiful and inspiring.

Different styles of meditation have different objectives: some develop the mind-heart like a flashlight beam, some like a candle flame.

The Buddha's first teachers trained him to focus like a narrow beam of light. He entered states of rapture and tranquility. He mastered one-pointedness beyond any of his contemporaries. But when he relaxed, old neuroses popped back up like a bamboo raft that had been held underwater. "This doesn't work," he realized. "One-pointedness produces peacefulness. But it doesn't last."

Rather than focus like a laser, he let his mind glow like a candle flame. After a few weeks of this, he woke up. An open, receptive awareness brought him freedom, ease, and wisdom. And these qualities didn't leave him for the remainder of his life.

Focus

The ability to zero in can be useful in getting things done, solving problems, and coping with emergencies. We use this ability to examine the cupboards and refrigerator and make a shopping list that ensures we get what we need. We use it to figure out why the toilet isn't working and find a solution.

But sometimes we want more from life than shopping efficiently or fixing a broken toilet. We want to thrive, not just manage a difficulty; we want to know the breadth of life, not just how to analyze details; we want to see the expanse of the cavern, not just the cracks in the wall. For this we need a mind-heart that is more like a flame glowing in all directions.

Flickering

The Buddha was a master teacher of this wise and open receptivity.

It requires patience. At first the mind flickers. It sputters on and off and dances around dimly, like a small flame in a breeze. We're tempted to clamp down on the mind, to hold it still, to force it to sit down and shut up. These efforts are counterproductive. They bring a little peace for a short time. But in the long run, forcing the mind to do anything is exhausting and agitating, like running around flapping our arms. Rather than scurrying hither and yon, we can watch the flame with peaceful interest.

As we relax, the breezes subside and the flame becomes steady and bright. In deep meditation, it becomes luminous — brighter than the brightest beam of light, but gentle and radiant. Everything becomes self-illuminating. We notice not just the objects of awareness but awareness itself and the consciousness around the objects. How does it feel? Is it tight or loose, clear or foggy, light or heavy? None of these qualities are good or bad.

They just happen to be here for now. We notice without judgment or preference.

This is awareness of awareness. This is the heart of advanced meditation. This is the path to true awakening.

Inner Glow

Awareness of awareness is difficult in the beginning because the mind is designed to look outside itself. Awareness is not as tangible as a mantra or the feel of the breath rising and falling. So some people begin meditating with an external object or a tangible sensation. But as awareness gets stronger, it naturally turns to see itself. We start to be aware of awareness.

As meditation deepens, we find that the quiet mind is not a cold void. As thinking shuts down, it is not like stepping into a gigantic deep freeze with the lights turned off.

The quiet mind sees clearly without judging. In human terms we call this "love" — seeing what is and accepting things as they are.

The quiet mind is also intelligent. Without distracting thoughts, it sees more keenly.

The quiet mind is luminous: a candle flame illuminating a vast space. As we experience this more intimately, it seems strangely familiar — like an old friend we knew a long time ago. We suspect it's been here all along, quietly and unpretentiously infusing everything.

When the busy, active, swirling aspects of the mind reassert themselves, the quiet glow seems to fade. But we know it's still there. It's been here all along. We know it will always be here.

And knowing this makes all the difference.

> *We shall not cease from exploration*
> *And the end of all exploring*
> *Will be to arrive where we started*
> *And know the place for the first time.*
>
> — T.S. Eliot

Related Chapters

40. Attunement, Not Attainment

The universal is found in the particular, not the general.

The lotus seed settles deep into the muck at the bottom of the pond and sends roots into the darkness below. It also sends a stalk up through the murky water toward the light. Unlike a lily that floats, the lotus rises out of the water holding its leaves above the surface of the world. The bud unfolds into a pink  flower that soaks up the sunlight. Soon the petals wilt and the colors fade. The remaining pod droops and drops its seeds.

 They settle into the mud at the bottom.

Another seed goes through the same cycle in the same pond. But it settles in deeper water. The nutrients are richer there, so it doesn't have to send out as many roots. However, it takes longer for the stalk to reach the surface. Its orange blossom opens a day later than the first. It rains on this day. It takes a little longer for the flower to open fully. The first one has gone to seed while the second is still coming into its prime.

This cycle has been going on for a long, long time: seed to roots to stalk to bud to blossom to pod to seeds.

The lotus doesn't notice if its roots grow far to find

nourishment or if it gets what it needs close by. It doesn't care if its flower opens sooner or later. It doesn't mind that its flower wilts. Unconscious wisdom allows it to be wherever it is in its cycle. Indeed, without a complex nervous system, the lotus cannot self-reflect. It just is.

We humans reflect. Evolution gave us minds that search and seek and try to find the best way to be. Our minds generate preferences, opinions, and judgments. We find it more difficult to just be.

We may look at the lotus and dislike its murky depths: too cold and gooey. However, when the blossom opens we get out the camera — that's the part we want to remember. When the flower wilts, we put the camera away.

We have our own cycles. Our consciousness arises from murky confusion into radiant awareness that fades into nothingness.

The Buddha offered a map of how our consciousness unfolds. His map includes instructions as to how to be with the various phases of meditation that we encounter as we follow the map. The instructions suggest when to send kindness to a friend and when to send it to all beings. They suggest when to ignore partial distractions that don't grab all our attention and when to Six-R everything. They suggest when to use a gentle effort and when to just get ourselves out of the way. They suggest when to investigate and when to just be.

The Buddha described this path by outlining stages (jhānas). It is easy to look at these stages through our preferring-comparing-liking mind and see them as states to attain. But that misunderstands the Buddha's intentions.

This path is about attunement, not attainment. It's not about getting anywhere. It's about stripping away tensions and distortions that prevent us from being fully where we are. The jhānas describe phases we can reach and make suggestions on how to relax more deeply into these various phases. This helps us find the wisdom that attunes to wherever we are.

The Buddha describes the jhānas in general terms. Yet everything unfolds in its particular way. No two lotus flowers are exactly alike. If they were, the pond would be monotonous. Each flower's beauty comes through its uniqueness.

The same is true of us.

I gave a Dhamma talk the other day. The average person listening was 54.3 years old, had brown eyes with a touch of hazel, stood 5 feet 9 inches tall, had 2.3 children and 0.7 grandchildren, and had been meditating for 3 years and 21 days. Seventy-two percent were female.

But no one fit this profile exactly: we were all different.

If we all went to see the same movie, some would enjoy it, others not so much. Some would be drawn into the plot; some would be fascinated by the characters; some would be taken by the cinematography. We would see the same images and hear the same sound track, yet our inner experiences would be very different.

This is a good thing. If we were clones, the world would be monotonous.

There is a beauty, vitality, and aliveness that can shine through everyone. But they manifest differently in each of us. A person is beautiful not because they are a generic man or woman but because they are uniquely who they are. *The universal is found in the particular, not in the general.* When we attune deeply to ourselves, when we are what we are, a universal vibrancy emerges. When we try to be just like someone else — even a Buddha — we become murky and cloudy.

The Buddha's path is about opening to what is present right now — attuning to the unique way the universal vibrancy manifests through us. The best way to use the Buddha's guidance is to allow it to point us in the right direction. Then we settle down and attune to what we actually experience.

When two guitars are tuned together, playing a string on one causes a string on the other to vibrate. The sound waves traveling through the air help the strings resonate together.

This meditation is about attuning and resonating.

Attunement is a lesson I learn and forget and relearn over and over again. If a lousy mood shows up, I may say, "Well Doug, you're in bad shape. You better fix yourself before somebody notices." I can struggle and push and try to "improve" myself.

Or I can bring an open and soft awareness to the crummy mood: just notice clearly what's there without creating a story about it. I can resonate deeply with this phase of the cycle. The lotus doesn't complain about the murky depths or the dropping pod. It's just a phase.

This gentle openness doesn't make the mood go away. But since I'm not wrestling with it, I don't engage it. If I don't engage it, I don't identify with it. It's just a mood: nothing to condemn or judge. Clear awareness is light and buoyant even when viewing something dark and murky. And then a smile arises from nowhere.

This practice is less about doing and more about being. It's less about getting somewhere than about being where we already are. It's less about improving ourselves and more about loving what is. It's less about fixing and more about seeing. It's less like making a floral arrangement and more like opening to the beauty of the wild.

It has nothing to do with attaining and everything to do with first attuning to ourselves and then attuning to life itself, just as it is in this particular moment.

Everyone's trying to get from A to Z.
I'm just trying to get from A to A.
                                        – Larry Rosenberg

Related Chapters

41. Whatever Arises in the Mind Is Not a Problem

The contents of the mind are not a problem.

When ease and dispassionate interest infuse awareness, we see everything that arises as the impersonal result of natural processes. This is what the Buddha meant by "Wise View."

When worry, fear, aversion, anger, melancholy, confusion, or greed pervade awareness, everything that arises seems like a problem: *my* problem. The real problem is not the thought, image, or feeling. It is the Unwise View: awareness distorted by unwholesome qualities.

However, when the mind is truly stable, open, kind, and objective, nothing can harm it. This is true even in extreme situations:

On the fifth day of a ten-day retreat, I sat peacefully in the Dhamma hall of the Insight Meditation Society in Barre, Massachusetts. A mental image arose gently of me pushing a long knife into my wife's back. I had not been thinking about her or about violence. It seemed to arise out of nowhere.

I did not greet this image with dispassionate interest, peaceful clarity, or Wise View. I freaked out: "Oh no! Are there violent urges hiding in my unconscious? Do I have a criminal psyche pretending to be a pacifist?"

I forced my attention back to the breath and held it there with white-knuckled intensity until the gong ended the meditation period.

At the beginning of the next sitting I coached myself, "Don't let an image of me stabbing Erika with a jagged knife arise in my mind."

This coaching didn't work.

Finally I got it: I can't hide from my mind. Everywhere I go, it follows. "If I have a hidden homicidal tendency, there's nowhere I can run from it. Trying to be a serene yogi will not change reality. If there's an urge to kill in me, I'd best get to know it lest it jump out of the shadows in a weak moment."

Despite the anxiety, I turned toward it rather than away. I relaxed and opened, but not because I suddenly had faith in my Buddha nature. I did so because I wanted to see the unblemished truth of who or what I was more than my preconceived ideas. I truly wanted to know what was going on.

I stopped fighting the image. It evaporated like a mist in the morning sunlight. I could barely remember what the turmoil had been. My body softened and a subtle smile arose.

In that spaciousness I realized what had happened. I had been holding onto a self-image of being a good boy. This was a mental habit I learned in childhood. Working as a minister reinforced it. That good boy found the jagged-knife image unacceptable, and he panicked. Once the fear got going, it became self-sustaining.

To get a clearer view of what was inside, I had to release all previous ideas of who or what I was. When I let go of the good boy, his evil twin evaporated too. The huge charge wasn't from an urge to kill, it was from aversion to the image itself. As I relaxed into the image with open acceptance, it had no substance. It simply vanished.

That was over forty years ago. Imagine if I'd kept trying to push that image out of my head for all these decades. The denial and rejections would have fed that tension until it became a massive lump of fear held at arms' length.

This is an example of Wise View in action. Rather than trying to control the thoughts, images, feelings, or attitudes that arise within us, we Recognize and Release them so we can see and understand more fully what is going on. We notice the tension (taṇhā) and abandon it by Relaxing back into our deeper nature. That brings the uplifted mood of cessation. If it's slow in coming, we can encourage it with a soft Smile. As the lighter mood fades, we Return to our practice of sending out kindness and peacefulness, and we Repeat it as often as needed. This develops the path the Buddha describes.

The actions of the Six Rs are embedded in Wise View. It's a way of relaxing into life as it truly is. We take refuge in the potential to awaken and the natural laws of how the mind really works. And when we do this fully, nothing that arises is a problem.

Related Chapters

42. Mistakes As Teachers

There are no mistakes, only lessons.
– Sayadaw U Tejaniya

"Well, Bhante," I smiled. "I think I found a new way to fall off the horse."

This became a standing joke between Bhante and me. "I find every possible way to meditate wrong. When they have all failed and the only option left is the right way, I give it a try."

I used to bemoan how long it took me to figure out how to meditate effectively. I would marvel at some of my students who breezed through and mastered various teachings and techniques so gracefully. I wondered, "How'd they learn that so quickly?"

Now I've come to accept that each of us progresses in our own way. I have an incorrigible curiosity that runs me off cliffs and into trees and ditches. I no longer even hope to stay on the road very long — I just hope I'll fall off each side an equal number of times. That seems to be my path. I don't think we get to choose our path. It's more like our path chooses us. We are who we are.

Sayadaw U Tejaniya says, "There are no mistakes, only lessons." I've been blessed with many, many lessons. And I do see them as blessings. There are few blind alleys my students walk into that I haven't explored already. I can speak from personal experience about so many different potholes and wrong turns. I've learned them well.

So when I offer students directions and they seem unsure, I say, "I'm a great believer in empirical trials. Try it various ways. Don't worry about making mistakes. For some of us it's the fastest way to learn."

"However," I caution, "pay attention to the results from those empirical trials. Learn from them. Some of us have to try things on to learn deeply. That's fine. If you do learn, 'mistakes' are just lessons. If you don't learn, then mistakes are discouraging mistakes."

Sisyphus's torment was not in rolling the boulder up the hill. It was in not learning. After the boulder rolled back down the first, third, or fortieth time, he still rolled it back up the same way the next day.

I'm a great believer in mistakes. We can learn deeply from them. If we do, they are blessings.

Related Chapters

43. The Earworm's Gift

Notice process.

"*Listen to my story about a man named Jed, a poor mountaineer barely kept his family fed …*" In my early meditation training, this theme song from  *The Beverly Hillbillies* often took residence in my head. I had never watched more than one or two episodes of the TV show. But on retreat, the tune got caught in a brain loop. In later years, a favorite line from a Paul Simon song or other music did the same thing.

"Earworm" refers to a catchy piece of music that repeats itself in the mind. Most meditators are more familiar with the phenomena than they'd like. The tune can be as lovely as Rumi or as embarrassingly inane as the Beverly Hillbillies.

Yogis often find earworms vexing. But in recent years I've found them to be wonderful meditation coaches because they show where mindfulness is needed. The problem with earworms can be summed up in three to four words: "I (don't) like it." Breaking the phrase down gives some insight into earworms and how they can be helpful.

"I …"

Earworms can feel quite personal. They waltz into "my space." The sense of self strengthens as if there is someone (me) engaged with something (the song). If the sense of self relaxes, there is no one for the song to entice, and the melody tends to fade.

"... (don't) like ..."

Aversion often surrounds earworms. Aversion latches onto what it doesn't like. If there is somebody we don't like, they will show up in the mind more often than a neutral person. The same with earworms.

Subtle attraction sometimes surrounds earworms. Attraction latches onto a song that offers welcomed entertainment. But more often people feel disliking around earworms.

Aversion and attraction both have tension. When we struggle with earworms, there is often both aversion and attraction working at cross-purposes. The mind thinks, "I don't like it" and "I like it."

Tension fuels all hindrances. With earworms, disliking and liking give the hindrance a full tank of gas.

"... it."

It's easy to see an earworm as an "it" — as a thing rather than a process. But music is clearly a process that plays out in time.

Process

When I started applying the Six Rs to earworms, I began to see how the song arose. First, there was a sound in the mind. That sound reminded the mind of a melody. The mind brought up the next phrase from memory. That memory triggered the next phrase. And so on. The mind was creating the song by anticipating what it liked or didn't like! The song was not a foreign invader, but a memory juiced by attraction, aversion, or both.

So rather than push the song away, I just relaxed into it. I accepted its presence without fuss. If it grabbed the mind's attention, I let it. All I did was relax using the Six Rs.

What happened next was fascinating. The mind became more attentive to the present and less anticipatory of what might come next. It became more interested in seeing what was there and softening into it. As liking and disliking faded, the song slowed down. The next phrase came up more leisurely since the mind wasn't as irritated or grasping. Each sound stretched out longer and longer until there was just a single tone. As the mind relaxed into that tone, it slowly faded into deep equanimity.

To say this differently, the mind treats irritation as a threat. Evolution programmed the brain to pay attention to threats. (Those whose brains didn't were more likely to be eaten or killed.) As long as I related to the earworm as a distraction threatening my meditation, the mind did its job of trying to get rid of it. There was a self fighting an invader. Such drama!

And if the mind was enticed at the same time, the drama increased that much more.

However, when I treated the sounds as impersonal, the tension of liking or not liking drained away. As I accepted coexisting with the sounds, the sense of self softened. In time, the earworm ran out of energy and fell silent.

And the mind remained behind, clear, bright, spacious, and peaceful with a lingering sense of gratitude for how skillfully the earworm brought the mind-heart into the luminous present.

Earworms teach awareness if we let them.

Related Chapters

44. Wisdom and Knowing Many Things at Once

The mind knows more than we know it knows.

I trained for years in one-pointed concentration. To do this I focused on a single object: the sensations of the breath. If other things floated into awareness, they were distractions. They were not okay and needed to be eliminated.

However, wisdom meditation is not based on one-pointed concentration. It wants to know how the mind operates, how it moves, how different aspects of it relate to one another. This requires an awareness that knows many things at once.

If we practice one-pointed concentration, we might train the mind to blot out everything but the breath or the mantra. If we get good at it, we blot out irritation, malaise, fear, and other disturbances in deference to our favored focus. This leaves the mind-heart in a blissful state.

But there's a cost. We are acting against the nature of the mind. It takes a lot of effort and strain to pull off one-pointedness. And the state doesn't last. When the mind relaxes, all those suppressed feelings erupt. This is what the Buddha discovered.[19]

So he advocated a different kind of training that does not try to control what the mind sees and knows. What the Buddha advocated exerts no preference, no priorities, no agenda. He advocated pure awareness without any inclinations.

As awareness gets stronger and subtler, we notice many things at the same time. This may not be a sign that mindfulness is weakening. It may be a sign that it is getting stronger — it's noticing more.

---

[19] For example in the "Mahāsaccaka Sutta: The Greater Discourse to Saccaka," *Majjhima Nikāya* 36.

Right now as you read these words you can also be aware of your body posture, the temperature of the air on your skin, the touch of your fingers on the page, the light around you, sounds in the background, the feeling of your breathing, the sensation around your eyes, and much more.

Relaxing makes this easier to do. If we tighten up, it is more difficult to know all these at once. Tension makes the mind less aware. But when we relax, a quiet, open awareness knows multiple things.

It may even know more than we know we know. We might walk through a crowded room. As we come out the other side, someone asks, "Is Jane in there?"

"I don't know." We pause and reflect for a moment. "Oh yes, she was over on the left by the wall." The mind knew — even if, for a moment, we didn't know it knew.

There is an important caveat. If we meditate without giving the mind anything to do, its habits of wandering are likely to step in. To begin meditation, it's helpful to give the mind a simple job to do in the foreground and let everything else slip into the background. This strategy should not be confused with one-pointed concentration.

For example, in the "Discourse on Mindfulness of Breathing" ("Ānāpānasati Sutta," *Majjhima Nikāya*, Sutta 118), the Buddha suggests that one job we can give the mind is awareness of breathing. He describes the practice in detail, starting with preliminary advice: find a quiet place, sit down comfortably, be mindful, and know the quality of the breathing. The language about breathing starts in verse 18:

> *Breathing in long, he understands he is breathing in long.*
> *Breathing out long, he understands he is breathing out long.*
> *Breathing in short, he understands he is breathing in short.*
> *Breathing out short, he understands he is breathing out short.*

Notice that he says nothing about controlling the breath. The Buddha doesn't say breathe in long or short. He just says understand when the breathing is long or short. In the literary style of the suttas, "long" and "short" are examples of some of the qualities we might notice. They are not meant to be an exhaustive list. These instructions say, "understand the qualities of the breath as they arise."

The verb is "understand." Some scholars translate it as "discern" or "be sensitive to" or "observe." No scholars translate the verb as "focus in on" or "pay attention and exclude everything else." There is nothing in the text to suggest one-pointed concentration.

Do you understand that you are breathing? That's all the Buddha is saying. To use the breath in meditation, we start by knowing the qualities of the breath as they are.

Now we move to the meditation itself. The last half of verse 18 moves from preliminary to core instructions. This is marked by the key phrase, "he trains thus":

He trains thus: "I shall breathe in experiencing the whole body;" he trains thus: "I shall breathe out experiencing the whole body." He trains thus: "I shall breathe in tranquilizing the bodily formation;" he trains thus: "I shall breathe out tranquilizing the bodily formation."

Notice there are multiple objects: the breath and the whole body experienced through lots of sensations. "Tranquilizing" means "bringing tranquility to" or more simply, "relaxing." "Bodily formations" means "tension in the body."

So the Buddha's breath meditation begins by being aware of the whole body on each in-breath and out-breath and by relaxing any tension we notice.

As we practice this way, at some point we will notice feelings of joy and happiness. They arise from a relaxed, open awareness. These are included in our awareness. The next instructions are in verse 19:

He trains thus: "I shall breathe in experiencing joy;" he trains thus: "I shall breathe out experiencing joy." He trains thus: "I shall breathe in experiencing happiness;" he trains thus: "I shall breathe out experiencing happiness."

We are starting to move up through the awareness jhānas from joy to happiness. These are described extensively in my book *Buddha's Map*[20]. For now, the point is that even in the sutta where the Buddha talks in the greatest detail about breath awareness, he is not talking about one-pointed concentration. He is talking about a mind-heart that can and does know many things at once. We naturally multiprocess.

Related Chapters

---

[20] Doug Kraft, *Buddha's Map: His Original Teachings on Awakening, Ease, and Insight in the Heart of Meditation*, (Carmichael, California, Easing Awake Books, 2017), Chapter 11, pp. 145-157.

45. Natural Multiprocessing

The mind does many things at once.

Many years ago I learned that, according to the Buddhist psychology, the mind only does one thing at a time. It can do them so quickly that it seems like multiprocessing. But it finishes one task before going on to the next.

It's like a single-processor computer. In computer games, several images seem to cross the screen at once. But the computer updates them one image at a time. It switches from one to the next more quickly than we can perceive. So the rapid sequence looks simultaneous.

The brain is often referred to as a computer, and a computer is sometimes called a brain. So all this made sense to me.

And it was wrong. It's in the nature of the mind to multiprocess. It's how it's designed.

In my early years of meditation training, I noticed songs in my mind. At the end of the first verse, my attention might move elsewhere. A short while later I noticed the song was in the middle of the third verse. It continued even when I wasn't noticing. The mind's nature is to do many things at once.

In the early texts, the Buddha says nothing about the mind doing only one thing at a time. The *Abhidhamma* (the text describing Buddhist psychology) and other later commentaries articulated this doctrine of "one at a time." But it isn't mentioned in the early texts that are probably closer to what the Buddha said.

The brain is not a single-processor computer. If anything, it's a network of computers, each capable of doing its own business while communicating with others. The brain is a vast network of a hundred billion neurons and millions of billions of connections. The synapses don't fire one at a time. Entire clusters of neurons don't fall silent waiting for other clusters to finish. They easily operate in parallel.

Walking through the woods the other day, I was reflecting on this. Meanwhile I was aware of the path before me, the unevenness of the ground, the cool air on my arms, the waning daylight, a slight hunger in my belly, the sounds of birds, a ringing in my ear, the strength of my breathing, the sight of my hands swinging in and out of my peripheral vision, etc. all at the same time. All these were not "front and center," but they were all there.

For a while my strongest focus was on the thoughts. At the same time, my body effortlessly adjusted to turns in the path, my feet accommodated stones and small depressions along the way, and I felt the pleasantness of the air and the wind in the trees. When a coyote stepped out from behind a tree, my thoughts slipped into the background and the animal came into the foreground.

It's easy to see that we can walk, chew gum, listen to an iPod, and watch people all at once. After all, these involve different systems — leg muscles, jaw muscles, listening, and seeing. However, multiprocessing happens within the mind itself. Multiple thoughts can go through the mind all at once.

Several years ago this became clear to me during my first meditations each day. I usually get up between 3:00 and 6:00 in the morning to meditate for a few hours. As I begin to settle in, I silently recite three refuges, seven precepts, and three aspirations (as detailed on pp. 297–315). A voice in the mind recites the words in sequence. Often another part of the mind checks "ahead" to remember which precept is coming next ("Is the next about refraining from stealing or is it about refraining from lies and gossip?"). At the same time, stray thoughts about yesterday or today might drift around. As all that is going on, the mind monitors those thoughts to decide if they are intrusive enough to Six-R or if it's wiser to not pay attention to them.

Mostly, the reciting voice is "front and center." The other voices are rarely full sentences. Sometimes they try to elbow their way in; more often they are faintly in the background. And sometimes they fade away and I'm left with a string of recited words that glow and fade like a string of fireflies.

But before the mind settles, there are clearly multiple thoughts in the mind at once.

Perhaps some people believe the mind does only one thing at a time because it has a wonderful ability to put some things on the front burner and let others simmer in the back. If the mind couldn't do this, we'd be flooded with collages of sights, cacophonies of sounds, and deluges of thoughts all at once.

I knew a schizophrenic woman who was deluged with thoughts and perceptions. She was very bright and wanted to know how "normal" minds worked. She asked me how I knew what to pay attention to and what to ignore. "If I'm sitting in a restaurant talking to a friend and a dog slips in the door, how much attention do I give to my friend? To the dog? To the approaching waitress? To the conversations drifting over from the next table? To the sounds of dishes in the kitchen? How do I decide?"

After reflecting on her question, I said, "Most of the time *I* don't decide. My mind just moves the attention. I can tell it to focus on one thing or another. But mostly, it just does it by itself."

We began to appreciate that her brain had little ability to move some things to the foreground and put others in the background. Everything came in equal strength. I can get a sense of this by recording a conversation in a restaurant. The tape recorder picks up everything indiscriminately: my voice, my friend's voice, voices from other tables, sounds from the street, and more. The playback is an unintelligible deluge. But in the live conversation in the restaurant, my mind easily sorts out the foreground from the background.

This natural capacity of the mind can be misunderstood as thinking that the mind can only do one thing at a time or that it's unnatural to multiprocess.

I intentionally use the word "multiprocess" rather than "multitask." Multitasking is trying to keep several tasks front and center at once: writing a report while making phone calls to friends while listening to the news. The research is very clear that multitasking degrades performance. The stress of doing too much tightens the mind and distorts perception, feeling, and thinking.

But even when we are single-tasking, the mind is multiprocessing. Driving home the other evening, I noticed that I had not been conscious of the pressure of my foot on the gas pedal or the motions of my hand on the steering wheel. Front and center was watching the road. As I scanned for cars, traffic signals, road conditions, and people on the sidewalks, the mind was deciding whether to shift lanes, speed up, slow down, and more. Fortunately, my feet and hands did not have to be front and center in order for the mind to tell them what to do.

Multiprocessing has many implications for meditation training.

Samadhi

A quiet, clear, stable awareness is crucial for meditation and living well in the world. The Pāli word for this quality is *"samādhi."*

If we think the mind naturally does only one thing at a time, we may try to cultivate samādhi by concentrating on a single object to align us with the mind's deeper nature. Indeed, many people translate "samādhi" as "concentration."

However, if the mind naturally multiprocesses, then concentrating on one object works against the mind's nature.

A better translation of "samādhi" is "calm abiding" or "collectedness." We quietly observe what arises in the mind and relax any tension. If the mind is multiprocessing, that isn't a problem. If there is tension, that is a problem. So we relax the tension.

Since we aren't fighting the nature of the mind, this softening allows a natural, quiet, clear, and stable awareness to come forward. This open, stable awareness is samādhi.

To say this differently, we meditate with a wide-open awareness, rather than a focused awareness. Focused awareness may inadvertently push other things aside, which results in tension. Wide-open awareness relaxes even with several things going on at once. The result is ease.

Distinguish Multitasking and Multiprocessing

One of the differences between multitasking and multiprocessing is intention. If we intend to do several things at once, we are multitasking. If we intend to do one thing, we are single-tasking. If we relax while single-tasking, we may notice multiple processes: hearing, feeling, thinking, etc. If, upon seeing these, we try to reduce them to one, then we are multitasking: we are trying to pay attention to the original task and at the same time trying to control our attention.

The mind gets tense if we try to push some things out of awareness to create the illusion of single-processing.

In meditation, it is better to be simple. We adopt one task, such as being aware. If, in doing that task, we notice several processes, we just notice, let them be as they are, and relax.

Self-identity

We often try to create a self-identity around what is "front and center" in the mind. "This is me. This is mine. This is who I am." If we try to focus in on one thing, it enhances a sense of self. We think "I am happy" rather than "I feel happy" or "There is happiness in the mind."

At the same time we create a sense of "other" out of the things that are in the background of the mind. "That is not me, it's a distraction. That's not mine, it's an intruder. This is not myself, it's my unconscious making a mess."

But if we see all of these phenomena as just the mind's natural multiprocessing, then we do not categorize them into "me" and "not me." Instead there is an array of impersonal phenomena that arise, float around, and drift away. None of it is me. None of it is other. None of it is myself. None of it is them. None of it is mine. None of it is not mine.

If we aren't trying to control or attenuate experience, it is easier to see the impersonal nature of thoughts and other mental experiences.

Wisdom

The mind doesn't know the difference between conscious (foreground) thoughts and background ones. They all affect perception, feeling, and consciousness.

If we're angry and push the anger into the background (or try to ignore it), the mind doesn't know it's not supposed to know it. The anger still has a dramatic effect. It colors our perceptions, feelings, and thinking. If we have fear, desire, confusion, or other unwholesome qualities, they distort the mind whether we recognize the distortion or not.

In fact, one of the paradoxes of the mind is how strongly we can identify (at least unconsciously) with things we don't see clearly: they hang around in the background. When we see foreground and background as foreground and background, we see both more clearly. This simple clarity is the essence of wisdom. The mind-heart becomes suffused with a relaxed and fascinating flow of impersonal phenomena. Many things are arising and passing at the same time.

Related Chapters

46. Awareness Is Magic

Explore the nature of pure awareness.

– Atiśa

One of the natural laws governing the mind-heart is that pure awareness has an almost magical calming effect. "Pure" means awareness with no agenda: it sees without judgment. I don't know why this is so. But if we pay attention, we can see how it works.

For example, if the mind-heart is restless, depressed, irritated, or worried and we observe these qualities without preference, the mind-heart calms down. But if we have the slightest aversion to our experience or desire for it to be different, the mind gets edgy and agitated. Similarly, if we're calm or joyful and aren't aware of our mood, our mood tends to tighten. But if we are serene and know it, the serenity deepens.

Pure awareness has this uplifting effect if we can remember to observe awareness itself. But it is hard to remember to do.

Walking through Paris one day, P. D. Ouspensky vowed to be continuously aware. A few moments later he saw his favorite tobacco shop and turned in. Three days later he remembered his vow to be aware.

The mind likes to wander. It is curious about people, sights, sounds, thoughts, irritations, longings, memories, reruns of conversations, and just about everything but itself.

Remembering to be aware of awareness is difficult in the beginning — but not impossible. The Six Rs help. We can sense it for a short time. You can do it now:

What is the quality of your awareness right now? Is it light or heavy? Focused or scattered? Easygoing or tense? ...

If we observe the mind without judgment, it becomes a tad quieter. As it quiets it becomes clear. The more we see how the mind works, the calmer we become. The calmer we become, the more clearly we can see.

The process snowballs. With time and practice, peaceful lucidity becomes self-sustaining.

The Buddha discovered that awareness of awareness can be a foundation for enduring happiness. It brings forth the mind's natural peace and calming luminosity. He called it "waking up."

Related Chapters

47. Clarity and Acceptance

At all times simply rely on a joyful mind.

— Atiśa

To love someone requires that we see them clearly as they are. If we don't, we may love an image we have of them or a hope we have for them. But we don't love who they are right now.

To love someone requires that we accept them as they are, warts as well as beauty. If we don't, we may accept who they could be or might have been, but not the real person today.

Likewise, to love ourselves requires that we see ourselves clearly and accept ourselves as we are. We may have improvements we'd like to make or qualities we want to cultivate. But to start from a base of kindness and love, we first must fully accept that we are what we are in this moment.

When we look inside, we may not always see ourselves so clearly or feel so accepting. The concept of original sin is deeply embedded in Western culture. It says that our core nature is corrupt, that we are not acceptable without intervening divine grace.

Many in the West do not accept the doctrine of original sin but have its residue in the psyche, called "the inner critic." When we look inside, there may be a voice that is a little too enthusiastic in its objections. It is neither loving nor accepting.

Buddhism starts from a premise of original goodness or the potential to awaken in all of us. This side of enlightenment, we have flaws. These flaws may cloud or cover that potential, but they don't destroy it. It remains to be realized.

So in meditation we are not seeking to fundamentally change what we are. We are seeking to discover it, to reveal it, to see it clearly.

This makes the practice simpler and more pragmatic. We try to see exactly what we experience and accept it without judgment. This is not the same as saying that everything is always just fine as it is. But it is saying that everything is what it is.

Clarity and acceptance are the on-the-ground practice of love and kindness. They are a tangible expression of Wise Attitude and Wise Effort.

Related Chapters

48. It's Only Pain

If we stir a teaspoon of salt into a glass of water, it makes the water undrinkable. If we put the same salt into a five-gallon cistern, we hardly notice it.

— Ancient adage[21]

I hit a big pillow as I yelled, and cried. Gradually the hurt of old emotional wounds subsided. I felt spent, vulnerable, and alive. The old pain lingered a little. My therapist looked at me gently for several long minutes. She smiled and said, "Doug, it's only pain."

"Oh yeah," I thought. "It is only pain. What's the fuss?" I relaxed and seemed to expand. The hurt receded to a whisper. It was as if I'd been looking at a spider: up close she's terrible. If I step back and see her spinning her web in the garden, she's not so bad. If I step back further and see her in the cycles of nature — part of the texture of everything, she's not a problem at all.

Physical and emotional pain triggers a contraction. It's a protective instinct. But if there is no real danger, the tension just makes things worse. The trick in meditation and in daily life is to step back, relax, and let our natural wisdom expand.

The adage says that life has its teaspoon of salt: its pain, its discomfort, and its soreness. Sometimes it's just a pinch of salt, sometimes a whole tablespoon. We have no control over the quantity. But we can make ourselves bigger. When we are expansive enough, the salt is no longer a problem — it's just a faint flavoring.

---

[21] Perhaps the adage comes from the "Lonaphala Sutta: The Lump of Salt," found in the *Anguttara Nikāya* 3.99: "Suppose a man would drop a lump of salt into a small bowl of water ... Because the water in the bowl is limited, thus that lump of salt would make it salty and undrinkable. But suppose a man would drop a lump of salt into the river Ganges ... Because the river Ganges contains a large volume of water, thus that lump of salt would not make it salty and undrinkable."

Related Chapters

IV.
Cleaning Up
Our Act

Your actions speak so loudly I cannot hear what you are saying.
— Ralph Waldo Emerson

49. Engaging Precepts Mindfully

Open heart and good boundaries.

In the relative world in which we live, there are no absolutes. The Buddha's precepts are not a behavioral code to be followed at all costs. Neither are they frivolous suggestions to be tossed aside casually. Rather they are guidelines to be engaged mindfully and heartfully. After all, the Buddha's path is a middle way.

The middle way is not necessarily an easy way. At times we face choices that are neither clear nor simple. Strictly following precepts does not keep us safe or let us off the hook. However, in the long run, engaging precepts mindfully can help us navigate rough waters and learn how to live well.

To unpack how this works, let's start with stories about Suzie and Bandit and situations I found heart wrenching.

Suzie

Suzie was a tabby cat given into my care when I was seven. We became close friends. She slept on my pillow. She even allowed me to be in the closet with her when she delivered kittens. I watched her purr and meow and push the little blobs from her body and lick them to life.

One afternoon when I was ten, my father backed the car out of the garage. I walked around the corner just in time to see Suzie go under the rear wheel.

My father noticed the unnatural bump and jumped out of the car. Suzie lay on her side unable to get her feet under her. Yet she thrashed so violently she threw her body several inches into the air. My father murmured something about a knife and her throat and rushed into the house.

I didn't think I could watch. I saw the yellow plastic kitchen wastebasket standing empty by the back door. I filled it with water and gently lowered Suzie into it head first.

She struggled with surprising strength and coordination. I held her head firmly underwater until she stopped moving. I released her and slowly removed my arms from the pail. A bubble escaped her mouth.

I looked up to see my father watching from the back steps. He held a long carving knife in his right hand. He didn't say a word. I turned away and walked into the backyard to be alone.

A half hour later I noticed long scratches on my forearms. I'd been too emotionally numb to notice.

My father never spoke to me about it.

Bandit

I've owned cats all my life. They've been fond friends and companions.

When Bandit was nineteen (which is very old for a cat), he became lame and had spells of confusion. Sometimes he stood beside my bed and meowed for a half hour. But most of the day he seemed comfortable, sleeping on the foot of the bed or resting in his favorite garden in the backyard. Despite spells of disorientation and pain, on the balance he still seemed to enjoy being alive.

Then one afternoon my wife called to me. She had found Bandit lying on his side in the garden. Ants crawled over him, including across his eyes. He was breathing but couldn't blink.

"He doesn't want to be alive like this," I said. My wife agreed. I considered drowning him in the nearby hot tub. But I remembered how Suzie had struggled. Once I had brushed the ants off him, Bandit's situation was not acute. So my wife and I drove him to the vet who gave him an injection as we stroked him gently. I asked the vet how long until he dies. She said, "He already has."

Precepts

The Buddha's first precept is to "refrain from killing or harming living beings on purpose." He said that breaking this precept requires four things: (1) knowing of a living being who (2) we want dead and (3) doing something that (4) directly results in its death.

Killing Suzie and Bandit were literal violations of this precept. Though I grieved their deaths and missed them both, I am at peace with what I did. Kindness and alleviating my friends' suffering felt more important than non-killing. Even if I thought my deeds created bad karma, I'd do them again.

We're Never Off the Hook

After hearing my stories about Suzie, a serious, long-time meditator said to me, "I'd never do what you did. I would sit with her. I'd send her loving kindness. I'd comfort her. But I wouldn't do anything to hasten her death."

When I asked him why, he said, "Because that violates the first precept about killing."

I responded, "But Suzie preferred to be dead rather than spend her last few moments of life in excruciating pain. Why wouldn't you break a precept to relieve her agony?"

He said, "Breaking precepts can disturb my meditation and create negative karma."

I said, "That sounds selfish. Selfishness can disturb inner peace and have negative karmic consequences as well. The precepts are guidelines, not magic shields to be used by rote in all situations."

We agreed to disagree.

Other yogis have raised a different objection. "Doug, what makes you so sure you knew what Suzie and Bandit really wanted?"

This is a valid concern. We don't want to be too casual about "putting a pet to sleep." It's difficult to know what another human really wants, much less a non-speaking pet. Many feelings can disrupt our ability to intuit another's wishes. Perhaps we're uncomfortable witnessing another's discomfort. Perhaps we're annoyed cleaning up after an incontinent pet (or person). Personal tensions can distort our ability to "read" another. Selfishness comes in subtle guises.

Despite the valid concern about knowing another's wishes, behind the yogi's question may be a dubious assumption: when in doubt it's safer to do nothing; if we aren't certain what a pet or person really wants, it's best to be passive.

However, ethically there is little distinction between doing something that causes suffering and refraining from doing something that would relieve suffering. Inaction doesn't necessarily get us off the hook.

On the other hand, action doesn't necessarily get us off the hook either. I suspect there are consequences of harming others no matter how kind our motives. Occasionally I have killed a squirrel running across the road in front of my car. Despite doing everything I could to swerve, I hit it anyway. My intentions were save it, but my actions still killed it. I could feel the effect of this for days. Intentionally killing it would have had deeper and longer lasting effects. But harming unintentionally or harming with the kindest of intentions can still have an effect.

It's the nature of life in the world that sometimes the best we can do is to choose the least-worst alternative. To put this in old-fashioned terms, being an adult means making decisions based on our best understanding and living with the consequences.

The Buddha said that the motives behind our action or inaction are very important. They can even shape our perceptions. If our best understanding is ambiguous, it helps to look deeply and clearly at all our various motivations, make a decision as wisely and kindly as we can, and learn from the results.

We will make mistakes: errors of commission and errors of omission. Nothing lets us off the hook. But the more open we are with ourselves about our heart's intentions, the easier it is to learn. Sometimes this is the best we can do.

Hamburger Dilemma

Despite my willingness to kill a beloved pet to ease its suffering, there are times when I think the Buddha's injunction against killing doesn't go far enough.

Buying a hamburger doesn't meet the Buddha's criteria for breaking the precept against killing because (1) we didn't know the cow before it was killed, (2) we never intended harm to that particular cow, and (3) we did nothing directly to cause its death. The cow (4) died, but that is not linked directly to our intention or action. So eating a hamburger does not break the precept, according to the Buddha.

But living in the world of supply and demand economics, buying hamburger contributes a tiny amount of demand for cow meat, which encourages someone else to kill a cow. Knowing these subtle cause-and-effect relationships is enough to give me qualms about consuming meat in today's society.

I was a pure vegetarian for many years. I ate eggs and milk products but explained to my wincing friends that I would not eat any "flesh."

Then an acupuncturist convinced me that my blood protein was low. I'd be healthier if I ate a little fish from time to time. She reminded me that our bodies evolved on a diet that included meat.

As I reflected on this, her reassurance was not comforting. I knew I could get all the protein I needed from vegetables, but it took more work than I wanted to expend.

I reflected further that I couldn't survive without eating something that had once been alive. I had a friend who ate only the parts of plants — like fruits and leaves — that could be harvested without killing the whole plant. But this felt like philosophical hair-splitting.

Many Native Americans say that what's important is being humble, mindful, and grateful to the life forms that died so that we might live.

Today I don't eat any "flesh" except occasional fish.

This may sound like convenient rationalizing or a self-centered, "If it feels good it's okay." But I'm not suggesting you should model your diet on mine. I am suggesting that in the relative world there are no absolutes. We have to wrestle with our actions and their effects. The conclusions you reach may be different than mine. How we engage the precepts is more important than the conclusions we reach.

Spirituality and Action

So let's look more deeply at how the Buddha intended the precepts to be used.

The goal of spirituality training is not rigid adherence to a code of conduct. The goal is a mind-heart free of distortion. Such a mind-heart can see clearly and dispassionately how the mind-heart works. It can see how the mind's attention moves. A mind-heart like this is free.

If we were fully enlightened, "if it feels good it's okay" would be a good criterion. We wouldn't need formal precepts. As Thich Nhat Hanh said, "When we are mindful, we know what to do and what not to do." But this side of enlightenment, our minds are not always clear enough. Our perceptions, feelings, and thoughts get distorted in many directions. Some things feel good in the moment and later cause regret. And some things feel bad or guilt-producing in the moment, so we back away and later wish we hadn't. Because of our propensities for confusion, it helps to have tools to navigate the world. It is in this context that the Buddha offered the precepts.

He saw a relationship between certain qualities of consciousness and certain behaviors.

He considered some qualities to be defilements or unwholesome states. They have tension and tightness that distort the mind-heart and obscure its natural clarity. High on the Buddha's list of unwholesome qualities were desire, grasping, aversion, hatred, confusion, and willful ignorance. Collectively they are called taṇhā, which is often translated as "craving" and literally means "thirst."

Some behaviors are generally unskillful and likely to cause harm. High on the Buddha's list of unskillful actions were killing, harming, stealing, sexual misconduct, lying, gossiping, spreading rumors, harsh speech, idle chatter, and taking intoxicants.

Tensions and distortions can easily give rise to unskillful actions. Unskillful actions easily give rise to unwholesome qualities. They feed each other.

The opposite is also true. A wholesome mind-heart is filled with kindness, compassion, joy, equanimity, or peacefulness. Such a mind gives rise to skillful actions like generosity, caring for others, and treating yourself and others well. These skillful actions, in turn, generate a peaceful, kind, clear, compassionate mind-heart with little distortion.

When we are confused, it is easier to see our outward actions than it is to notice our inward qualities. By flagging behaviors that give rise to unwholesome qualities, the Buddha was saying, "When you break a precept, it is a good time to reflect mindfully on what's going on inside." And "If you are tempted to break a precept, it is a good to time refrain from saying or doing something you may later regret. Instead, reflect on the quality of your mind-heart."

Killing

From the perspective of wholesome motivation, killing Suzie and Bandit was not a problem. I saw clearly what the situations were and was motivated by kindness and compassion — wholesome qualities. The problem with killing is that this is very rarely the case. Most often, killing and harming are motivated by aversion, hatred, anger, or fear. Even swatting a fly usually begins with annoyance — which is a form of aversion.

Killing is most likely to arise in everyday life when we're interacting with creatures we think are less important than us — mosquitoes, flies, ants, termites, rats, and other so-called "pests." We might imagine the inconvenience they bring us is more important than their lives: killing them is not a big deal.

But in those situations, if we look inside, there are contracted states. The contractions may be small enough to ignore as we swat a bug and go back to matters of greater consequence to us. But in subtle moments of meditation, those acts of mindless violence can be disturbing and leave us restless without knowing why. Ignorance, whether intentional or unintentional is not conducive to well-being for us or for the creatures around us.

Devaluing life is the root of war and ecological crisis. So coming into a more harmonious relationship with all the creatures — large and small — increases our own peace and contributes to peace on the planet.

Ants

It is not always easy.

When I walked into my apartment a few months after moving to Sacramento in 2000, there were several streams of ants winding across the kitchen and down the drain in the sink. My first thought was, "I hope nobody sees them. They'll think I'm a sloppy housekeeper." I quickly turned on the garbage disposal. Ant carcasses spewed out of the disposal and splattered all over the kitchen. I was horrified at what I had done and vowed to find some way to live more harmoniously with these little beings.

I began to clean up the kitchen more thoroughly. Using trial and error, I learned what they liked and didn't like. Now, during the times of the year when the ants are more active, I'm careful to not leave food out that they find enticing.

Today, if I look carefully, I can often see a tiny ant here or there in the kitchen — scouts looking for something to harvest. But since they find nothing, they don't send for their buddies.

It feels good to know that I can share the space with them in ways that both of us are comfortable. I like living harmoniously around them.

Rats

My relationship with local rats was more difficult to work out. We bought a house near the American River in Sacramento.

This means we live along a greenway with lots of fields, woods, and a variety of creatures: birds, deer, coyotes, and rats, to name a few.

Rats are resourceful. They can squeeze through the tiniest cracks and survive for long periods on very few calories. They mostly keep to themselves, so I didn't mind having them in the backyard at night — I wanted to accommodate them. But I didn't want them in the house itself. I used hardware cloth and steel wool to seal tiny openings in the walls and roof. I used Havahart® traps to catch them and release them into the fields. I sealed food in containers.

Yet after several years, we could still hear squeaking in the walls at night, see holes chewed through food boxes, and find droppings in pans in the cupboards. One evening rats ran across our feet as we sat in the living room.

The next day I called an exterminator.

He carefully placed lethal traps around the foundation of the house and in the attic. Over the next several months, on my behalf, he killed about a half dozen rats. And that was it: no more rats. After six months we terminated our contract with him.

Several years later, we still don't have rats inside. Perhaps I had sealed the house sufficiently — we just had to get rid of the rat families that were already inside. Perhaps the new roof that we had to put on the house sealed up holes in our defenses. Whatever the case, we now have boundaries that allow us to live around the rats while keeping them out of the house itself without having to kill them.

Termites

The creatures with which I've been completely unsuccessful are termites. I cannot afford the damage they can cause to our living quarters when they chew through joists and beams unimpeded. We have an exterminator who drives chemically treated stakes into the ground to set up a chemical barrier. Every four or five years, they manage to breach the ramparts and start to burrow through the house. The exterminator uses poison before they get very far.

I have an uneasy truce.

I've had more success with spiders, wasps, and other crawling or flying bugs. For years our practice has been capture and release.

Seriously

I take the precept to refrain from killing or harming beings quite seriously even if I haven't been able to figure out how to follow it literally in all circumstances. It has taught me a lot nonetheless.

I've recognized that we humans are the most predatory species on the planet. We quake in movies when we see velociraptors, wolves, or lions tearing animals apart. But we humans continue to do much more damage than they. We are taking out creatures and entire species at an alarming rate.

Despite our collective impact, few of us view ourselves as violent aggressors. We just do what feels comfortable. If that means swatting mosquitoes, shooting deer, or poisoning termites, we may shrug and say, "That's just how life is."

Seriously taking the precept of non-killing means I can't shrug any more. I've had successes and failures in trying to live by it. But it is harder and harder for me to do harm without recognizing what's going on inside as well as around me. Often that's enough to stop me.

Today I'm more aware than ever that our world is full of intelligent creatures and sentient beings. We live in a sea of relationships with many, many species. The birds and squirrels outside my window have the intelligence of small children. We can have quite complex relationships with small children.

My relationship with my nonhuman brothers and sisters feels more harmonious than before I began working with these precepts. And I'm learning more all the time.

The precepts are meant to be trainers in just this way: to help us learn to live with more wisdom and harmony in the world as it is.

Stealing

The second precept is to "refrain from taking what is not freely given." I inserted the word "freely" into the translation to make it clear that non-stealing includes being aware of how we use our influence on others. Browbeating somebody into giving up something they would otherwise keep is a form of stealing. We live in a world where the exploitation and the misuse of power are all too common.

The opposite of non-stealing is generosity. By taking this precept and using it wisely, we can move from the contraction of greed to the expansion of generosity.

Most of us can see the problems with robbing a bank, ripping someone off, or shoplifting. We can imagine rare exceptions where kindness or compassion may lead us to take something that is not freely offered. For example, Lawrence Kohlberg, in his study of moral development, proposed a scenario: your child is dying of a rare illness. The pharmacist has a medicine that will cure the disease, but he's charging an unreasonably high price. You don't have the money to buy it. Is it morally better to steal the medicine or let your child die?

As with Suzie's and Bandit's scenarios, this scenario is very rare. But it's enough to make the point that non-stealing is not an absolute. The Buddha included it as the second precept because stealing is generally precipitated by greed, desire, or intentional disregard — all are contracted states. In most situations, taking what is not freely given is harmful to the person gaining an object as well as to the person losing it. Adopting this precept encourages us to explore our motives when we are tempted to take what is not freely given.

For example: How do we feel when we take a pen home from work? Do we rationalize it? Do we think it is okay as long as nobody notices? How would our boss feel if she knew?

How do we feel about taking a pen from the office with the intent to use it for work we bring home? Is this a situation in which the pen is "freely given"? If it is, how do we feel if, when our work is done, we use the pen to create a family grocery-shopping list? Is that okay? Do we even think about it?

When is it okay to download music, movies, or documents from the Internet? Can we always tell if they are truly freely given?

I knew a monk who would not accept gifts that were left on the doorstep of his *kuti* (meditation hut) because he could not be absolutely sure they were freely given to him. When is it okay to take something even if we aren't sure if it's unencumbered?

When somebody tries to patent a human gene, they did not actually create the gene. They just claimed it. Is working with that gene a violation of this precept?

What does it mean to own something? What is our true relationship to objects?

Balance

The number of questions that can be asked about the relative world is infinite. One of the insights of situational ethics is that if we have one rule, we can live by it. But if we have two rules, there will be times when those rules conflict. So we need a third rule to sort it out. Now we have three rules. Each will conflict with the other two at times, so we need more rules to sort those out.

We cannot answer all the questions that can be asked about our actions. Trying to do so may lead to endless thought proliferation.

Finding the middle way between ignoring rules and overindulging is an art. Walking the spiritual path is an art.

To help us in daily life, the Buddha offered lay people five precepts. For retreats, he offered eight. I use seven. These are listed in the appendix (see p. 299).

Theravada Buddhist monks have 227 precepts and nuns 311. They have taken a path that is less involved in the affairs of the lay world and have more time to engage fruitfully in a larger set of guidelines.

How many precepts are useful for us? That's something we each have to work out. The Buddha did say that doing anything we feel is wrong damages us even if it doesn't break a formal precept. We have to work this out for ourselves.

Summary

If our mind and heart are serene and luminous, we sense easily what kinds of actions deepen our equanimity and strengthen our awareness. But if we are upset, angry, or disturbed, we may get caught up in events and take actions that leave us unsettled.

In the earliest saṅghas around the Buddha, there were no formal precepts. But as the saṅghas grew and a greater variety of people became monks, more and more of them would get caught in old habitual patterns — they'd do things that they later regretted or that scattered their minds.

So the Buddha and the saṅghas created precepts. They point to actions that arise from a mind-heart caught in tensions or distortions. The tensions and distortions might be subtle and difficult to see in an emotional moment. But actions are concrete and easy to spot even when we are overwrought.

Precepts are flags that say, "Hold on a minute. You are about to break a precept. This is a time for you to take a few breaths and pay attention to the quality of your mind and heart. Are there disturbances or defilements present? If so, reflect deeply before taking this action. Don't proceed until you are at peace."

For a precept to work, we must take it seriously. If we're willing to dismiss it when it is emotionally inconvenient, it will not be helpful. We're likely to get caught by unbalanced feelings.

On the other hand, mechanical adherence to precepts creates a mind-heart that is rigid and righteous when it stays within the rules, and rigid and guilty when it doesn't. Rigidity, righteousness, and guilt are not conducive to awakening. On the other hand, kindness and clarity are. They are the overarching qualities to be used when engaging precepts mindfully.

I undertake the precept to be
kind and generous to myself and all beings.

Related Chapters

50. Wise Acceptance and the Six Rs

Don't be swayed by outer circumstances.

– Atiśa

Many years ago I worked with an educational psychologist and school consultant named Mark. A high school had requested his help. During the initial interview, Mark asked about absenteeism. The principal said, "Our students have to come to school. They have no other choice."

Mark smiled slightly, scratched his head, and replied, "Your records show an 8.7% truancy rate. Apparently, one youth in twelve exercises a choice you say doesn't exist. You may not like the number of students who skip school, but unless you accept the fact that they do, it'll be hard to figure out why and what to do about it. On the other hand, if you accept the truth and relax, you'll be able to respond more effectively."

This was my first encounter with an attitude I later called "wise acceptance." Up to that point in my life, I had thought acceptance meant believing something was okay as it was. Or, if it wasn't okay, acceptance meant acquiescing. But for Mark acceptance didn't necessarily mean okaying or acquiescing. It meant seeing a situation clearly as the first step in engaging and doing something about it.

Crazy and Crazy-Making

Lack of acceptance is a little crazy. The principal's non-acceptance of unexcused absences clashed with reality. Being out of touch with reality is one definition of insanity.

If I break an arm and don't accept it, my understanding of my condition is at odds with reality. If I have a drug problem, marriage difficulty, or health issue and deny it, this is crazy. Seeing and accepting things as they are is essential for living sanely in the world.

On the other hand, casual acceptance can feel crazy-making. Sometimes casual acceptance is helpful. If traffic makes me late for a meeting and someone says, "C'est la vie. That's life," that light touch is helpful. If I spill food on my shirt and think "no big deal," that may put it into a better perspective. But if I'm diagnosed with cancer or a friend dies, "C'est la vie," may feel dismissive. It denies the depth of fear or heartache. It feels crazy-making and lonely.

Wise acceptance is different from lack of acceptance on the one hand and casual acceptance on the other. It's a middle way. It sees things as they are but doesn't dictate how we are supposed to feel. It accepts our inner responses without conflating them with outer reality. It's not a pat, one-size-fits-all answer. But it can loosen the grip a problem has on us and it can change our relationship to it by helping us see it more clearly.

Seeing Clearly

Seeing clearly is the first step in solving a problem or in deepening our meditation. It sounds simple — just look and see what's there. But it is easy to confuse our inner thoughts with the outer reality. Let me share a story that illustrates how tricky it can be.

A long time ago my wife left me. I had been deeply depressed. She mistook the depression for a sign that I didn't care for her. She thought it best to move on. I didn't blame her. But when she moved out I was devastated and mute.

I remember three or four weeks later sitting in the parsonage living room that was my home at the time. It was a big parsonage. And now I was alone in it. It was snowing that afternoon, muffling the sounds from outside. I sat next to a window, looking at a living room wall. The wall was blank except for a clock. I was miserable. I thought I'd always be alone. I felt my life was over and I had failed.

As I gazed blankly into space, a bit of my attention noticed the second hand moving around the face of that clock.

As the hand came back to the "12," I had an epiphany: "This last sixty seconds wasn't so bad." I thought, "The snow is beautiful. I am depressed and sad. The fire in the wood stove radiates lovely warmth. My wife isn't here, but she's never been here in the afternoons — she has a job. I have a job as a minister. Maybe we'll never get back together, but I doubt I'll always be alone. And right now, the room is peaceful — almost serene. The cat is purring in my lap. This moment isn't so bad."

I had compressed my life into a sound bite called "miserably alone." Suddenly it opened up, revealing disparate elements. I recognized events, thoughts, feelings, mental elaborations, moods, possibilities, and many other aspects of my life. Some things were difficult; others were nice. My mental projections into the future were glum, but the present moment wasn't so bad.

The next forty-five years unfolded differently from my fears. My wife and I got back together. We raised two kids. My depression dispelled with dedicated inner work. We've had a long and satisfying marriage.

So what issues do you face today? Recognizing reality is tricky, particularly when we feel stuck. Too often we reduce the issues in our lives to sound bites.

The eleventh century Buddhist Atiśa wrote, "Don't be swayed by outer circumstances." Seeing clearly means looking deeper than sound bites. It means seeing events as just events, feelings as just feelings, fears as just fears, hopes as just hopes, mental projections as just mental projections. *And it means seeing possibilities as possibilities and not as inevitabilities.*

It takes a little time to sort all this out. It takes a little time to see the larger context of our lives. Seeing clearly takes time, practice, and patience.

So whether our issue is a relationship difficulty, disease, worrisome kids, fears for the world, or whatever else, mindful awareness is not glancing over the situation lightly. It's stopping what we are doing and giving it clear, dispassionate attention.

Clear Awareness and the Six Rs

One of the best tools I know to cultivate clear, dispassionate awareness is the process called "the Six Rs." Bhante Vimalaraṁsi and his students developed it as a paint-by-the-numbers implementation of what the Buddha called "wise effort." It is mentioned throughout this field guide, described briefly in Appendix A (p. 287) and discussed in more detail my book *Buddha's Map*[22] and elsewhere.

The Six Rs in Meditation

Recognize

Release

Relax

Re-Smile

Return

Repeat

Clear awareness cannot be created directly by cogitation, strain, or effort. But clear awareness can be revealed indirectly using the Six Rs to relax strain and tension. Strain and tension distort the mind-heart. They block its natural clarity. By releasing and relaxing tightness skillfully, the six Rs allow the mind-heart's clear wisdom to come forth.

Most often the Six Rs are described as part of a formal meditation practice. But they can be useful in our day-to-day lives. The first five Rs are virtually the same whether in meditation or in the world. But they manifest slightly differently. So let's look at them in each context.

In formal meditation, wise acceptance is passive. If the school principal is meditating and his mind is disturbed by the truancy rate, the standard guidance is to Six-R the distraction.

To do this, the principal would **Recognize** that his attention had been drawn away; **Release** the distraction by letting it be what it is without getting involved in its content; **Relax** any tension in his mind, body, or emotions; **Re-Smile** and allow peace, kindness, or other uplifted qualities to come into the mind-heart[23]; and **Return** to his practice of radiating uplifted qualities to himself, to a spiritual friend, or to all beings.

---

22 Doug Kraft, *Buddha's Map: His Original Teachings on Awakening, Ease, and Insight in the Heart of Meditation*, (Carmichael, California, Easing Awake Books, 2017), Chapter 11, pp. 145-157.

Whenever his mind would become completely distracted again, he would **Repeat** the Rs as needed.

With time and practice, the first five Rs begin to roll together into one process that includes all five: recognize-release-relax-re-smile-return as a smooth flow.

Notice that the school principal does nothing about the truancy in formal meditation practice. Meditation is about learning how the mind operates. Accepting the mind as it manifests is very important. It helps to be passive in the sense of not doing anything with the content of the issue. Sitting still without moving helps develop more inner clarity.

However, when the school principal is at work, part of his job is diagnosing and reducing truancy. He is supposed to responsibly engage the school community, not just sit around peacefully doing nothing. He's paid to act. The Six Rs may still be helpful in this context. But they manifest differently.

The principal wants to **Respond** skillfully to the problem, not just react to it. So before he responds, he can **Reflect** on a wise course of engagement. This Reflection might involve mentally reviewing what he knows about the situation. It might involve collecting more information by talking with students, parents, and teachers, reviewing records, studying research, and so forth.

If he's upset while he's talking with people or thinking about the problem, the tension can distort his reflections, perceptions, feelings, and decisions. A relaxed, kind, and spacious awareness is more sensitive and intelligent than a mind–heart that is tied up in knots. So before Reflecting, he wants to gently cultivate a relaxed, wholesome state.

This is where the first five Rs are so helpful. They bring forth acceptance, peacefulness, mindfulness, and wisdom.

---

[23] Brain research confirms that even mechanically smiling tends to encourage the mind to lighten up. Physically smiling evokes an uplifted mood.

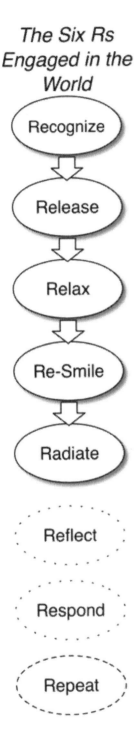

The Six Rs
Engaged in the
World

Recognize

Release

Relax

Re-Smile

Radiate

Reflect

Respond

Repeat

Just as in formal sitting meditation, the principal will want to **Recognize** his worry, upset, or other feelings; **Release** them by letting them be what they are without ignoring or changing them; **Relax** tension; smile or **Re-Smile** or bring up wholesome qualities; and **Radiate** those qualities. This helps him settle and open his awareness. After radiating, he'll be in a clearer place to **Reflect** on the situation and **Respond**.

He'll **Repeat** this whole process any time he tightens. And after he's responded, he may **Repeat** the process as a way of evaluating the evolving situation to see if there is more to be done.

Meditation versus Engaged Six Rs

Notice that the Six Rs are almost the same in both contexts. The single biggest difference is what we do with the contents of the mind. In formal meditation, the contents – the stories, concepts, ideas, beliefs, and so forth – are not relevant. We just observe how attention moves. We're concerned with the activity of the mind and the natural laws that govern how it operates. We ignore the content so that we might better see the processes themselves.

It's as if we are curious about the inner workings of a factory. Only this factory doesn't produce cars or washing machines. It produces thoughts and images. If we stand on the street and watch the neatly packaged thoughts flow out of the factory onto the shipping platform, we won't really see how those thoughts were formed. However, if we release and relax our fascination with the packages and go inside, then we can directly observe the pre-thought — the raw elements — and what the mind-factory does with them.

In other words, *it is best not to use Reflecting and Responding in formal meditation.* They will defeat its purpose and slow down meditation progress. Sometimes it is helpful to reflect on our meditation experience before or after a sitting, *but not during the meditation itself.*

Formal meditation is about observing without thinking, pondering or doing anything that engages the content of the mind. When thinking, pondering, and reflecting arise, we drop the content using the meditation version of the Six Rs.

However, if we want to live responsibly in the world, if we want to do our best to raise our kids, work out relationships, perform well at work, plan a vacation, and so forth, then thoughts and ideas can be helpful. Sometimes, the contents of the mind-heart are very relevant.

So the Six Rs engaged in the world make room for a little space to Reflect and Respond after the mind has quieted. That is the only substantive difference between the Six Rs in meditation and the Six Rs in the everyday world: we make some space to examine the contents of the mind or explore the world.

For example, what would we do if our child brought home a report card showing a D in math? We may find it upsetting, particularly if he loves math and generally does very well. What's going on?

While meditating, if this issue distracts us, we recognize the distraction as a distraction without getting involved in the content. We notice the upset, worry, or concern without getting caught up in the details of our child's life. We release the content by relaxing into it without thinking about the thoughts. In this way, we observe and learn how the mind responds to worry and concern. We don't try to solve the D-in-math problem.

However, when we aren't meditating, as compassionate parents we want to help our child. Our reflections are relevant. Does our child have a personality clash with the teacher? Do family issues distract him? Is his social life upsetting him? Have his interests genuinely shifted away from math? Is he tired in the morning? Does he need new glasses? Is there anything else going on?

We'd like to help him sort it out. To the extent that our mind-heart is peaceful and receptive, we'll manage these questions much better. So even as we actively engage the contents, we'll first spend a little time Six-R'ing tensions within us.

Return versus Radiate

You may have noticed that the label for the fifth R is "Return" in meditation and "Radiate" when we're engaged in the world. Substantively they mean the same thing. "Return" means to return to our home base. Depending on our stage of practice this can mean "return to radiating uplifted states to ourselves" or "return to radiating to our spiritual friend" or "return to radiating to all beings." "Return" covers these evolving practices.

When we use the Six Rs in the world, we still *Radiate* uplifted qualities but we don't necessarily *Return* to a base meditation practice. Rather, we *Reflect* about the issue at hand and possibly *Respond* actively. So the label "Radiate" is less confusing than "Return."[24]

---

[24] A technical point: Advanced meditators sometimes do not Radiate at all. In the eighth jhāna and beyond, the practice Returns from a distraction to Rest awareness in clear, luminous mind. There is no more Radiating at this stage. But it is not possible to be in the eighth jhāna while navigating the world. So a meditator who is used to the eighth jhāna in meditation would still Radiate uplifted qualities when engaged in the world.

The Larger World

There are many difficulties in the world that none of us can fix by ourselves: climate change, species extinction rate, income inequality, corporate aggression, war, human rights abuses, prejudice, racism, political gridlock, and more. The sea of suffering is great. Fear, worry, anger, guilt, despair, bewilderment, and more can overwhelm us. We may want to withdraw from the world. Nevertheless, the human heart naturally wants to help. How do we manage this dilemma?

Human society is large and complex. It needs lots of different roles: political leaders, conscious parents, bus drivers, poets, teachers, plumbers, computer programmers, healers, activists, meditators, and so much more. While none of us can do it all, I believe each of us has a role we can play which deepens us spiritually and moves the world toward greater kindness and generosity. How do we find a role that works for us and is truly helpful? We need insight not only into ourselves but also into the world and how we can relate to it.

The meditation practices that the Buddha taught create the conditions in which insight is most likely to arise. The Six Rs are a key to his practice. They relax tension in all its manifestations and help awareness and wisdom to emerge. When we use the Six Rs when engaged in the world, it helps us sort out even this most complicated issue.

Sorting out the specifics of our roles in the world is a huge topic beyond the scope of this field guide. But I did want to make the case for using the Six Rs even for these very complex questions. They are the essence of wise effort and wise acceptance. Rather than leaving us feeling pushed around by the world, they help us notice how and where we feel drawn. I'll leave this topic with the words of Ralph Waldo Emerson:

> *To laugh often and love much,*
> *To win the respect of intelligent people and affection of children,*
> *To earn the appreciation of honest critics and endure the betrayal of false friends,*
> *To appreciate beauty,*

To find the best in others,
To leave the world a little better whether by a healthy child, a
garden patch, or a redeemed social condition,
To know even one life has breathed easier because you have lived,
This is to have succeeded.

Wise Acceptance and the Six Rs

Whether used in formal meditation or informal engagement in the world, the Six Rs help cultivate wise acceptance. Wise acceptance encompasses all these qualities – recognize, release, relax, re-smile, radiate, reflect, respond, and repeat – as a unified flow. It is passive and active, dispassionate and engaged, caring for ourselves and caring for the world, forgiving and responsive. And it takes the issues in our lives seriously while encouraging us to take ourselves lightly.

If we engage this way, it becomes easier to see the soft spot — the luminous center — of other people, and to recognize it in ourselves. And it is easier to let the past be the past and move wisely into the present and beyond.

What we want or don't want is irrelevant.
Life is what it is.

Related Chapters

V.
Expanding Infinitely

*The way is perfect like vast space where nothing
is lacking and nothing is in excess.*

– Sengstan

© David Dawson

51. Self as Process

Be gentle with yourself. You are the truth unfolding.
— Joseph Goldstein

In this final section of this field guide, our focus shifts from awareness to how we interpret awareness, from raw phenomena to what we think about them, from phenomenology to philosophy.

Meditation is generally about awareness, the strengthening of awareness, and insights that arise from direct experience. Most of the Buddha's teachings are about awareness: suffering, release of suffering, impermanence, dependent origination, hindrances, jhānas, and so forth. These are phenomena we can know directly.

However, there is one important exception: his teachings about self and non-self — attā and anattā — are not about *what* we perceive. They are about how we *interpret* what we perceive. Self is not something we experience but something we infer from sensations and thoughts. Our inferences can quietly and stubbornly bring our practice to a standstill as we personalize our self rather than see it clearly.

Understanding the sense of self requires understanding how human intelligence constructs a self-concept out of sensory and mental phenomena. Understanding human intelligence — how it matures in children and evolves in the human species — gives us access to advanced meditative techniques and insights that would otherwise remain obscure.

Knowing Begins with Contact

In the middle of the twentieth century, the Swiss psychologist Jean Piaget did groundbreaking research on the development of intelligence in children. He said that *knowing* begins at the point of contact between an organism and its environment. It's here that we experience touch, tastes, sights, sounds, and smells. From these raw sensations, we extrapolate outwardly into the world to try to surmise what caused those sensations. And we extrapolate inwardly to try to surmise who or what experienced them. The only thing we know for certain is the direct experience. The further we extrapolate, the more abstract our conclusions become. Therefore, the further we go in forming an understanding of the self, the further we move from direct awareness into concepts we create. It's the nature of the territory.

Part of Piaget's genius was identifying and describing the schema (cognitive structures) that we use to construct maps of the world and ourselves.

Our minds are not passive. They don't just take snapshots of what's "out there" or "in here." They dynamically build images out of raw sensations and cognitive structures. Piaget documented these schemas and how they emerge and change as the child's neurology matures and engages the world.

When I was an undergraduate student, I became fascinated with Piaget's work and conducted modest research validating some of the changes in these schema. Years later when I became fascinated with Buddhist psychology, I noticed parallels between what the Buddha taught and the work of Piaget.

Piaget's primary interest was the maturation of intelligence. The Buddha's primary interest was how suffering arises and subsides. Their explorations led them in different directions. But they agreed that ordinary experience begins with, and dynamically builds from, raw sensation. They even used similar language. Piaget spoke of contact between the organism and the world. The Buddha spoke of *phassa*, which is translated as "contact" or "contact between a sensory energy (like light), a sensory organ (like an eye), and sensory awareness (like seeing)."

Perhaps the parallel between the Buddha's and Piaget's work should not be surprising — they were both looking at human minds.

No Word for "Process"

Reading between the lines, it's clear that the Buddha saw *self* as a dynamic process — as verb in motion rather than a noun in stasis. He implied that everything is in process.

But in describing this to his contemporaries, he had a few handicaps. First, the dialect the Buddha spoke and the Pāli language used to record his talks had no word for "process." It simply was not in the Pāli lexicon.[25] Without a word to name it directly, he had to rely on similes and metaphors like "impermanence," "rising and passing," "aggregates affected by clinging," "dependent origination," and so forth.

Evolutions of Consciousness

The Buddha's other handicap was the level of complexity of the cognitive structures in the people around him. Piaget demonstrated how these structures mature as a child grows. In the last half-century, many other researchers have demonstrated how the highest levels of cognitive sophistication in the general adult population have evolved dramatically in the 2,600 years since the Buddha's time. The structures in the Buddha's mind may have been more evolved than those in most people around him. But his contemporaries and their descendants shaped his teachings as they transmitted them down to us. The evidence for the evolution of the stages of consciousness is quite persuasive. [26]

Because of this evolution, there are techniques and practices we can utilize that may not have been helpful to the Buddha's contemporaries. The Buddha was a genius at identifying techniques appropriate to the varying abilities and temperaments of his students. He would not have suggested practices that would not have been suitable for them.

---

[25] Richard Gombrich, *What the Buddha Thought* (Sheffield, United Kingdom and Bristol, Connecticut: Equinox, 2013), 10–11.

[26] Ken Wilber has written extensively about the development of consciousness. *Integral Spirituality* (Integral Books, London, 2007) provides a good overview.

Were he alive today, he most likely would offer techniques suitable to us, even if they would have been less effective two and a half millennia ago.

So this section of the book talks less about states of awareness and more about stages of consciousness — less about *what* we experience and more about *how* we shape our experience into an ever-shifting sense of self.

In the coming chapters, we'll first clarify the difference between states of awareness and stages of consciousness. Then we'll briefly survey how the stages of consciousness have evolved and what states of awareness are emerging now. Finally, we'll look at how we can take advantage of our own consciousness structures to help get us out of our own way.

Though this material may feel theoretical at first, as we engage in it, it can lead to tangible, practical techniques. Many yogis find it helpful and inspiring. Others, not so much. As our practice deepens, each of us decides which teachings are skillful means for our temperaments and which are not. However, a book with a section entitled "Getting Our Selves Out of the Way" would be incomplete without investigating the dynamic process through which we create a notion of self.

Related Chapters

52. The Evolving Self

Don't take yourself so personally.

What would the Buddha say to us if he were alive today?

I suspect that his core teachings would be much the same. He had that together. But as mentioned in the last chapter, the way the average person thought about life in the Indian, agrarian culture of the fifth century BCE was different from that of the average person in the Western information culture of the twenty-first CE. Human consciousness has evolved dramatically in the past 2,500 years. If he were alive today, might he offer new approaches and practices?

As audacious as it is to answer this question for him, surely he would respond "Yes." He had a genius for creating styles of meditation suited to the proclivities of his students. Undoubtedly he would offer new techniques to our 21st century mindset.

I suspect that one of the most dramatic differences would be his teaching about selflessness or the impersonal nature of phenomena (*anatta*). The Buddha never said we don't have a self — only that there is no enduring self-essence or soul independent of everything else. We could call this "selflessness." Or we could call it an "infinite self" that expands to include everything. Selflessness implies getting rid of the self. The infinite self implies allowing it to encompass all that is. These methods move in opposite directions to arrive at the same place.

The path to selflessness or non-self may have been more accessible to people in the Buddha's time. The path to the infinite self may be more accessible to us today. But both release the tension in self-identity and arrive at the same place.

In this section we'll pick up themes introduced earlier in the book and look at them through a 21st century lens. The themes were:

- Finding a compass that heads us in the direction of seeing the impersonal, selfless nature of everything;
- Getting ourselves out of the way;
- Cultivating a pure awareness that reveals the mind-heart's natural glow; and
- Cleaning up our act so we relate to the world in ways that are more aligned with the welfare of all.

In the next chapter we'll look at the actual stages of consciousness that have emerged or are emerging in humanity. We'll be particularly interested in the highest stage generally available in the Buddha's time (Traditional Literal Consciousness) and how much further we've come today. In the following chapters we'll look at the implications these stages have for our practices and our lives.

But first it would help to clarify the difference between states of awareness and stages of consciousness, and how each relate to self-identity. We'll start with self-identity itself and how it might have first arisen.

Evolving Self

Imagine two prehumans walking through the primeval forest. The first is at one with the birds, trees, mountains, bears, wolves, and everything else. He ambles along peacefully. His life is content. And short. His mellowness makes him an easy target for large carnivores looking for lunch.

The second person is spooked by every shadow and rustle. He has a thick sense of self he wants to preserve. He scurries through exposed fields like a paranoid squirrel. His life is anxious. And long.

Guess whose DNA we inherited?

When we were a marginal species in a world of powerful predators, there was no evolutionary advantage to feeling at one with all life, and every advantage to feeling a dense sense of self to be protected from all those beasts.

It worked. We have contained or wiped out creatures that posed significant existential threats to us. We are at the top of the food chain. Now our desire to protect ourselves is the most significant threat to our existence. We are our most significant enemy. [27]

Yet that sense of self is still wired into us. The Buddha called it *bhava taṇhā*, the desire to exist as a separate individual. It's known as an *anusaya* or underlying tendency. An anusaya is a hidden hindrance because it is hard to see directly. It colors our experience and shapes our behavior without drawing attention to itself. When it is triggered by a threat, we see the threat, not the instinct itself.

Evolving Consciousness

Over a million years ago, the human brain became large, complex, and malleable. Its ability to learn from fellow creatures and the environment skyrocketed.

Since then human evolution has had less to do with DNA and genes and more to do with how we train the flexible minds of our children. Human evolution today has little to do with changes in body structures — teeth, claws, and bones — and a lot to do with changes in consciousness.

---

[27] This theory is, of course, speculative. It's difficult to get hard empirical evidence for forces that played out millions of years ago. However, we do know that humans descended from scavengers who found food and safety through their knowledge of the world more than through claws, teeth, or unconscious instincts. They developed large, complex brains that allowed them to map the world. When a strong survival instinct interacted with a complex neural network, they probably developed a map of themselves as well — a self concept. This highly developed — some would say "hyper-developed" — sense of self that helped our ancestors to survive is now a threat to our survival. Most of the major problems we face from income polarization to political gridlock to environmental change to war can be traced to a hyper-developed sense of self.

In English, the word "consciousness" has two different meanings. One is "awareness." When we say, "I lost consciousness," we mean awareness ceased. When the suttas say, "eye consciousness is different from ear consciousness," they mean seeing awareness is different from hearing awareness, which it obviously is!

The other meaning of the word "consciousness" is *how we process information and assign meaning to it.* When a five-year-old, fifteen-year-old, and fifty-year-old walk down the street together, they see and hear the same things. But they are in different worlds because they process those sights and sounds differently. When a conservative and a progressive look at the political scene, they process similar information differently and draw different conclusions.

Consciousness is like a mental lens that focuses, filters, defines, and distorts raw awareness. When looking through a pair of glasses, we don't notice the lenses, only the objects we see. Similarly, we are rarely aware of our consciousness, but it has a dramatic effect on how we see.

So when we talk about the evolution of consciousness, we are talking about changes in how the mind processes information and assigns meaning to it — changes in the lenses through which we see the world.

States versus Stages

There are various states of awareness and stages of consciousness. States of awareness and stages of consciousness are very different from each other.

All states of awareness are theoretically available to us all the time. They are right under our noses, if you will. Some ways to describe the spectrum of awareness states include:

- Gross awareness of the physical world — sights, sounds, smells, tastes, tactile sensations
- Subtle awareness of thoughts, feelings, images, and aspirations

- Very subtle awareness of how the mind works
- Non-dual awareness of the gross and subtle coexisting with and interpenetrating one another

Stages of consciousness are very different from states of awareness. All stages are not available at once: they develop in sequence over time because each stage builds upon earlier ones. If we know our stage of consciousness and work hard to cultivate the next, it takes about five years to move up to the next. Meditation can be a catalyst for moving up through stages more quickly because meditation takes the structures of consciousness apart and puts them back together again. They feel more fluid and shift more easily.

Stages of consciousness can dramatically affect our sense of self. Some ways to describe the spectrum of stages include:

- Tribal Consciousness — self-identity is merged with the tribe, similar to the way an infant's identity is merged with the mother.
- Magical Heroic Consciousness — a sense of "me" emerges with very little sense of "you," similar to two-year-old parallel play.
- Traditional Literal Consciousness — a strong sense of me and my family/clan/tribe. Everyone else is "other" or "outsider."
- Modern Rational Consciousness — seeing the self and others objectively and scientifically.
- Postmodern Pluralism — ability to sympathize with others who may be different.
- Integral Consciousness — ability to think and feel the way others think and feel.
- Transcendence — self-identity merges with a larger and larger breadth of people and creatures.

These brief descriptions of stages are very different from states. They hint at how dissimilar states of awareness are from stages of consciousness.

We'll explore the stages of consciousness in more detail in the next chapter. For now, it's enough to appreciate how different the states of awareness are from the stages of consciousness. Awareness allows us to enjoy beautiful music. Consciousness allows us to compute the physical laws that govern how the strings vibrate. They are very different realms indeed.

Anattā Is Not about Awareness

One of the Buddha's most difficult ideas is non-self or selflessness (anattā). It is tough because this teaching is fundamentally different from most of his other teachings.

Most of the Buddha's teachings are about awareness. The jhānas are about cleansing the mirror of awareness until we come to pure awareness. His teachings about suffering and impermanence are about awareness of things we can experience directly.

However, his teaching about anattā is not about awareness — it's about how we interpret awareness. It's about how our consciousness creates a sense of self. Anattā is about consciousness.

One reason anattā can be tough to follow is because his teachings were directed toward a fifth-century-BCE culture whose consciousness was very different than ours today.

So the next chapter looks further into anattā and stages of consciousness.

*I found that the chief difficulty for most people was to
realize that they rarely heard new things,
that is, things that they had never heard before.
They kept translating what they heard into their habitual
language. They had ceased to hope and believe there might be
anything new.*
— P. D. Ouspensky

Related Chapters

53. Stages of Consciousness

How we see changes what we see.

Jean Houston was one of the pioneers of the Human Potential Movement. In her younger years she lived on the Upper East Side of New York City. One morning she was late for her school bus, as usual. She whipped around a corner and ran smack into an elderly gentleman, knocking them both off their feet.

"I'm sorry, sir. I'm so sorry." She tried to help him up.

As he dusted himself off, he looked her in the eyes: "Young lady, are you going to be in such a hurry all your life?"

"Well, sir. I don't know, sir," she said. "I guess so, sir."

He smiled with sparkly eyes and said, "Well then, Bon voyage!"

In the following days, their first abrupt encounter grew into longer conversations. She couldn't get his name because of his heavy French accent. It sounded like "Tear" or "Tier." She took to calling him "Mr. Thayer." Soon they were strolling in Central Park together.

He had a bright and playful spirit. "Jeanne, Jeanne, come see this caterpillar! How does he move all those feet together?" And "Jeanne, Jeanne, look at this spider. How does she spin this beautiful web?" He was enchanted by the natural world.

Then she didn't see him for many days. She couldn't check on him, because she didn't know where he lived.

One day she saw his portrait on the bottom of a page in the New York Times. "It's Mr. Thayer," she called to her mom. The adjoining article said, "On the evening of Easter Sunday, Teilhard de Chardin died of a heart attack."

Teilhard de Chardin was a scientist and Jesuit priest. He'd been censured for ideas in his manuscript *The Phenomenon of Man.* The Church didn't know what to do with him. So they sent him to live out his remaining years at the Church of St. Ignatius Loyola on Park Avenue.

Jean Houston had been rambling in the park with one of the twentieth century's greatest mystics and theologians.

I love the image of the old man with sparkly eyes wishing the young lady a buoyant "Bon Voyage!" I love the image of strolling in the park with an elderly priest, delighting in the trees, spiders, caterpillars, and sun. His sense of self didn't cling to a body, emotions, or thoughts. He was "out there," merged with the natural world.

What would it feel like to relax so completely that our awareness loses its borders and blends with the world? To have an awareness as crisp and clear as a cool spring day and not weighted down by concerns over "my body," "my thoughts," "my feelings," "my person?" What would it be like to be Teilhard de Chardin merged with the wonder of life itself?

Teilhard de Chardin was Catholic — at least nominally. I am Buddhist — at least nominally. Yet Buddhism leads to the same consciousness and spirit embodied by Teilhard de Chardin.

Jean Houston's description of Teilhard de Chardin offers an example of a stage of consciousness which researchers call "Transcendent." The sense of self merges with the natural world. It gives us an experiential peek into what the Buddha may have meant by anattā, selflessness or the impersonal.

However, before we discuss Transcendent Consciousness, it would help to trace how consciousness evolved to reach this level. In the last chapter we looked briefly at these stages: Tribal, Magic Heroic, Traditional Literal, Modern Rational, Postmodern Pluralistic, Integral, and Transcendent Consciousnesses.

Now we'll look inside each to understand how it ticks. All children grow through at least the earlier stages. And the highest stages generally available have been evolving through the centuries.

It is through these stages that people's sense of self ("who I am") has changed. A four-year-old's sense of self is formed quite differently from a forty-year-old. The typical adult in the Buddha's time thought about the meaning of life quite differently than the typical adult in advanced society today. (See

"G. Awareness, Consciousness, and Enlightenment," p. 321, for a discussion of what this means for enlightenment.)

Without understanding these stages, we tend to think other people look at their lives the way we look at ours. However, the research indicates otherwise. People like Clare Graves[28] and Ken Wilber[29] have mapped how human consciousness has evolved over the last several thousand years.

So let's go back in time to see where our species began and how our "selfing" has shifted so profoundly. Hopefully this will give us some insight and inspiration to keep expanding our consciousness and our understanding of the dynamic process we call "self."

Tribal Consciousness

Hundreds of thousands of years ago, when our ancestors were furtive creatures living in primordial forests, some had instincts that bound them together to look out for one another.

This gave rise to what could be called "Tribal Consciousness." It had no sense of individuality as we understand it today. Self-identity was fused with the tribe, customs, and traditions passed down from the ancestors. Members of the tribe operated as a unit, similar to a hive of bees.

Their instinctual cooperation allowed them to live longer and reproduce more. But Tribal Consciousness was inflexible. During unstable times (such as an enemy invasion or drought), it couldn't adapt quickly.

Magic Heroic Consciousness

So thousands of years ago, Magic Heroic Consciousness emerged and with it the beginnings of a sense of self. Rare individuals had thoughts, feelings, or impulses that didn't fit

---

[28] Don Edward Beck and Christopher C. Cowans, *Spiral Dynamics* (Malden, Massachusetts: Blackwell Publishing, 2006).
[29] *Integral Spirituality* (Boston and London: Integral Books, 2007) is a good introduction to Ken Wilber's many books on this topic.

the tribal mentality. Rather than filter them out, they acted them out. This felt magical and powerful.

The rest of the tribe refocused its loyalty and obedience from tradition to this flamboyant leader.

Menelaus was a king of Sparta. His wife, Helen, ran off with Paris, the wayward prince of Troy. Menelaus was angry and went after her. The armies followed him into the Trojan Wars. Whether this was in the personal best interest of the average Spartan was not considered by Menelaus or the soldiers. "Ours is not to question why, ours is but to do or die. Oorah!"

I was talking to an ex–Special Forces guy in the gym. After a while he paused and said, "You're a thinker." He prided himself in being a "Doer." He was intelligent yet perfectly comfortable letting the chain of command do the thinking.

Magic Heroic leaders don't think about the needs of others. Magic Heroic followers define their interests as whatever the leader wants. Besides Menelaus, other examples include the Egyptian Pharaohs, Genghis Khan, Attila the Hun, feudal systems, and Jesus the magician who raised Lazarus from the dead and changed water into wine. In modern times we have street gangs, villains in James Bond movies, wild rock stars, and frontier mentality. In children we have the terrible twos and parallel play where there is no cooperation — each child follows his or her own interests.

Traditional Literal Consciousness

A few thousand years ago, a new consciousness emerged that expanded the circle of caring from "me" to "us." Today we call this Traditional Literal Consciousness. People care about the people in their family, clan, or tribe: "We take care of our own."

An example was the twelve tribes of Israel. Rather than each tribe having its own local gods, Yahweh emerged as a trans-tribal God. One set of rules applied to everyone. When different tribes encountered one another in the desert, they had a common leader — Yahweh — under whom they could cooperate. This allowed larger groups of people to live together in cities and nations.

The rules were understood to be passed down from ancient, divine authority. They tended to be rigid, literal, authoritarian, and group-centric rather than self-centric.

Examples today include ethnocentrism, love-it-or-leave-it patriotism, fundamentalism, Jesus as Law Giver, Lake Woebegone, "traditional values," and ISIS.

Modern Rational Consciousness

In the mid-17th century, a new Modern Rational Consciousness emerged that included "me," "us," and "them." God's laws could be discerned not just by studying the sacred texts but by studying the world He made. Rather than look through the Bible to understand the universe, Galileo looked through a telescope to see for himself.

This gave rise to the scientific method. Modern Rational Consciousness was more interested in bottom-line results and was willing to set traditional authority aside.

Examples of Modern Rational Consciousness include the Western Enlightenment, the emerging middle class, Jesus as Tradition Breaker, the Scientific Revolution, the Industrial Revolution, Wall Street, the Monroe Doctrine, the advertising industry, chambers of commerce, and transnational corporations.

Modern Rational Consciousness has been wildly successful. Slavery was outlawed in Modern societies. Science extended life expectancy by more than a decade.

And there are limitations. For example, transnational corporations want to understand people in order to exploit them. Many overlook the well-being of others or ravage the environment in deference to their spreadsheets.

Postmodern Pluralist Consciousness

In the middle of the 20th century, a new Postmodern Pluralistic consciousness emerged that truly valued everyone. It valued feelings, inclusiveness, consensus, collaboration, and helping the oppressed. It sang, "Everything is beautiful in its own way."

Postmodern Pluralism gave rise to the Civil Rights Movement, feminism, gay rights, and other liberation movements. Other examples include Jesus as Humanitarian, Greenpeace, the American Civil Liberties Union, Doctors without Borders, animal rights, deep ecology, sensitivity training, and the Occupy Wall Street movement.

Limitations

As we go from Tribal to Heroic to Traditional Literal to Modern to Pluralistic Consciousnesses, the circle of caring expands. Each stage includes more and more people and creatures. Each increases inclusivity and complexity, which are measures of maturity.

However, one limitation of all these stages is that each believes its own way of thinking is reasonable while earlier stages are Neanderthal, and higher stages are New Agers lost in a psychedelic haze. Even Postmodern Pluralists, despite valuing others, don't really understand how others think.

Looking around the world, we see the last three stages — Traditional Literal, Modern Rational, and Postmodern Pluralism — trying to destroy each other. Regardless of our motives to invade Iraq, our attempts to impose Modern Rational democratic values on them were a disaster. Similarly, most conflicts around the world are between groups that are centered in different stages of consciousness. And they're literally at war with each other.

Integral Consciousness

By the end of the 20th century, another stage of consciousness emerged called "Integral." It understands all the earlier stages empathetically and knows how to engage each on its own terms *without being patronizing.*

It recognizes earlier stages of consciousness as developmental — each stage develops out of the ones that came before. In fact, children grow through them as well. And it recognizes that different ways of thinking are appropriate in different situations.

If the building is on fire, we probably don't want to hold a Pluralistic meeting, sing "We Shall Overcome," check in on everyone's feelings, search for a consensus about what to do and in what order, and see if anyone wants to volunteer to help. We'd rather have a Hero taking charge: "You get the kids. You call the fire department. You check to see if the rooms are clear. Now move!"

Integral consciousness holds in mind and integrates earlier stages, and works with all of them. Without more Integral consciousness, the human species may tear itself apart.

Transcendence

The next stage of consciousness is just starting to emerge. It's too soon to have much research data on it, but it seems to look like this:

In Integral Consciousness, we have the ability to objectively see our own ways of thinking, as well as the ways of others. We can step back from our consciousness and appreciate other's perspectives.

In Transcendence, self-identity comes unmoored from any specific stage consciousness. Self-identity extends beyond one body, one personality, one set of habits, one set of memories, or one style of thinking. It expands to include more people and creatures.

Teilhard de Chardin's mystical merge with the natural world is an example. He wasn't just observing and appreciating nature; he felt at one with it. If the story resonates with you, you may have had a glimpse of this consciousness.

Transcendent Consciousness is a more or less permanent shift of self-identity from a single organism to the larger collectives: one awareness looking through many perspectives.

It has been called "Transcendence" because the sense of self transcends its innocent beginnings in one organism and envelops more of the world than just one person.

Meditation

To get a taste of transcendent consciousness, try this:

Close your eyes and relax. Meditate in a way that is comfortable. Settle in.

As thoughts and images arise, Six-R them and come back to sending out peacefulness and well-being ...

Now, as you send out uplifted qualities, flow out with them. Rather than just send peace and ease, flow out with them ...

Expand to include more and more ...

The awareness looking through your eyes and thoughts could be the same awareness that looks through the eyes of those around you. It is just looking through different eyes, listening through different ears, thinking through different brains.

It's the same awareness but a different perspective ...

Be with the awareness itself. Release the perspective ...

Related Chapters

54. Consciousness and Selfing

To study the self is to lose the self.

– Dogen

I wonder if the Buddha was stymied when he began to teach anattā. The urge to project a sense of self — *bhava taṇhā* — onto our experience is deeply wired into us.

So he said, "Stop interpreting. There is no me. There is no mine. There is no myself. Stop the workings of consciousness. See things directly as they are." That is not easy to do.

In the "Chachakka Sutta" (*Majjhima Nikāya* 148), he says:

The eye is impermanent. It comes and goes in time. There is no permanent self in the eye. To think the eye is self is just wrong.

Light is impermanent. It comes and goes. There is no permanent self there. To think light is self is just wrong.

Seeing is impermanent. It comes and goes. There is no permanent self there. To think seeing is self is just wrong.

He drones on to name every possible combination of sensation, feeling tone, and liking and disliking. There is no permanent self in any of these. "To think there is, is just wrong."

It takes over an hour to read the whole sutta. It's as if he was trying to pound it into the heads of his monks: "Stop interpreting. Stop creating a sense of self. Stop constructing sand castles in the air."

One of the reasons the Buddha used this strategy was that in his time the highest stage of consciousness generally available was Traditional Literal: the same as present-day Fundamentalism. It has a very strong sense of self: you and me, us and them, good guys and bad guys.

The Buddha was at least Modern Rational. He said, "Explore your own experience. Work it out for yourself." Those are Modern Rational values. They are at odds with the Traditional Literal values of obedience to ancient scriptural authority.

Perhaps he had an even higher consciousness. We'll never know because the words he spoke were remembered, interpreted, and codified by followers who were mostly Traditional Literal.

This is like me listening to Stephen Hawking and telling you what I remember. What I pass along is seriously constrained by my understanding of theoretical physics.

The Buddha's followers' understanding of what the Buddha taught was seriously constrained by their Traditional Literal Consciousness. Modern Rationalism would not emerge into any human culture for another two thousand years. (See "G. Awareness, Consciousness, and Enlightenment," p. 321, for a discussion of what this means for enlightenment.)

Despite these obstacles, the Buddha did okay. Thousands of people woke up during his ministry. His path worked.

Our situation today is very different from the time of the Buddha. In the sanghas I've been part of, most of the people are Postmodern Pluralistic. For example, they value feelings, caring for the oppressed, decision by consensus, and ecology; and they believe everything is relative and beautiful in its own way. These are Pluralistic values.

In the general populations of the developed world, about 5 percent are Integral, about 20 percent are Pluralistic, and the rest are earlier stages of consciousness. In sanghas those percentages are probably higher.[30] (See "53. Stages of Consciousness," pp. 263.)

We are not that far from Transcendent Consciousness. Many of us have had glimpses. In our meditation, awareness became pure, clear, and luminous. This awareness felt closer to who we

---

[30] Ken Wilber has written extensively about these stages and the prevelance. For example, *A Theory of Eveything*, (Shambala Publications, Boston, 2000) and *Integal Spirituality*, (Integral Books, Boston and London, 2006. Don Edward Beck and Christopher C. Cowan, (*Spirial Dynamics*, (Blackwell Publishing, Malden Massachusetts, 2006) talk about the same topics using a slightly different model.

are than any thought, feeling, or memory we've ever had — because this awareness attended to every thought, feeling, or memory we've ever had. The awareness felt kind and clear and intimate.

And yet, it was also impersonal. It went way beyond the bounds of our sense of self as a body, personality, or collection of thoughts and preferences.

© William Poulos, unsplash.com

Then it faded.

In Transcendent Consciousness this shift becomes more or less permanent. If we've had a taste of this at some time, then it's not that far away now. We can nudge ourselves in that direction.

Today, rather than fight against the sense of self, we can surrender into it and those evolutionary forces pushing us toward Transcendence. Rather than trying to shrink the self, we can expand out and out, including more and more people and creatures. As we spread out, self gets thinner and thinner.

The more inclusive that sense of self, the less it separates us from other creatures and life itself. And the less substantial it feels.

This is one way to describe what the Buddha taught: release a contracted self that suffers, and expand into an infinite self that is light, joyful, and merged with everything.

One of the easiest places for most of us to do this is in nature. We'll look at an example of this in the next chapters.

Related Chapters

55. We're Not So Different

Suffering is complex. Happiness is simple.
— Nietzsche

I was walking through the woodland along the American River when two snakes reared up out of the grass about eight feet from me. They were at least four feet long. Their exposed creamy underbellies gave little hint as to species, but their triangular heads suggested venom.

They were not within striking distance, so I watched, fascinated. After a few moments, I saw the back of one with a diamond pattern. And a tail with a rattle. Rattlesnakes are usually shy of humans, so this puzzled me. I wondered if they were fighting each other.

But as I watched, their motions seemed more affectionate than combative. They wound around each other, fell back into the grass, rose up again, wound around each other ... I smiled softly. "They're making love," I thought. "They're too distracted to notice I'm here."

I'm not particularly scared of snakes. But I had never felt so warmly toward two rattlesnakes in the wild so close to me.

Snakes and humans and all sentient beings feel urges that lead to generating life. I don't know what snakes feel, but I felt a commonality with them. It made me smile.

After a while I moved on. There were lots of butterflies out that day — black ones with white spots. I didn't know their name. But that's fine because they didn't either.

I passed one on the ground on the edge of the path. He fluttered his wings without rising in the air — just moved through the dust a few inches.

I turned back to take a closer look. His wings were dusty and ragged.

"Near the end of your life cycle," I whispered to him. I wanted to reach down and touch him to see if he could take flight. But I couldn't imagine that a big fleshy finger descending from the sky would be a pleasant experience for a butterfly. So I just observed.

His wings moved slowly with his breathing. Butterflies don't live very long. But from their perspective, they live full lives. From their perspective humans are ancient creatures who live near eternity.

One day, I, like the butterfly, will be near the end of my cycle. I'm past the middle of mine (probably) and not too near the end (hopefully).

I wasn't trying to empathize with the butterfly. How could I know what it feels? But I knew that eventually, life will ebb from both of us. In this, we are the same.

I walked down the path, leaving the butterfly to die in peace.

The urge that starts new life. The ebbing of life. As I gazed at the green woods and meadows around me, I felt touched to be part of it all. My eyes were moist.

I think Nietzsche, in a rare soft mood, said that suffering is complex but happiness is simple. Walking through the fields, I felt simple. I felt ordinary. I felt blessed.

One of the lovely things about nature is it really doesn't care. As I sit beside the river, the water, trees, and boulders don't care if I'm happy or sad, quiet or turbulent, joyful or melancholic. The river just flows on by, the trees sway gently in the breeze, and the rock I'm sitting on doesn't budge in one direction or another. Even the snakes and the butterflies don't care. Whoever I am — whatever I am — seems to be just fine. I have no inclination to hide or pretend or posture. It's easy to just be, without even thinking about it.

When we are just being without thinking about it, we naturally flow out to be with all that's around. For many people, feeling the expanding self is easiest in nature. We feel touched by the ordinary because we are part of it all. We don't even project ourselves onto the other creatures. Nature lets us be what we are. We can let it be what it is. And separation fades.

To study the way is to study the self.
To study the self is to lose the self.
To lose the self is to be enlightened by all things.
To be enlightened by all things is to remove the barrier
between self and other.

– Dogen

Related Chapters

56. We're Not in the Driver's Seat

Water gives life to the ten thousand things
and does not strive.

– Lao Tzu

I like the vignette of "Josie and the Turkey" (p. 163) in which a wild turkey attacks a dog four times its weight. I mistook the turkey for a mean, stupid bird because I didn't see the whole story — she was distracting the dog from her hidden baby chicks. The original draft was a journal entry in which I reflected on seeing below the surface of our lives to understand the whole story.

When I tried to insert the entry into this book, it didn't work. "Seeing the whole story" clashed with the metaphor "getting ourselves out of the way." Weaving the two images together felt clumsy. I made peace with dropping it from the draft.

The next morning, I woke up with a different understanding of "Josie and the Turkey" and added it back to the draft with a different commentary.

This process is familiar to most of us. We have a problem — an artistic difficulty, a relationship snafu, a job conundrum. We ponder and reflect, but a resolution seems impossible. We give up. The next morning, the solution is clear. Or while out walking, an entire new perspective pops into our head.

We call this phenomena "sleeping on it," meaning "not thinking about it and seeing if something new comes into our mind." We explain this process as relaxing the conscious mind so the unconscious can go to work. But the actual experience feels more like God, muses, or a guiding spirit inserted a new insight into our head. "Something told me."

Small Mind and Big Mind

We can think of this as "small mind" and "Big Mind." Small mind is the "self" that we normally identify with: a collection of aspirations, fears, memories, emotional tendencies, beliefs, and inclinations. It is the stuff of ordinary psychology.

Big Mind is vaster than ordinary psychology. As meditation and the spiritual journey go deeper, it becomes clear that life is more complex than our limited brains can compute. There are sources of wisdom and guidance we can draw upon. We do not have to adopt any metaphysical beliefs to access them. In the suttas they are called "wisdom's eye." In modern parlance we call it "intuition." Awareness knows much more than we know it knows.

To draw upon this intuitive wisdom, we have to get small mind out of the driver's seat and let Big Mind take the wheel. Most of us don't know Big Mind so well. When we surrender control, rather than Big Mind taking over, old wounds and neuroses can slip into the driver's seat. That is not so pretty. It can do harm. In the relative world, we are responsible for our actions. To think otherwise is ethically untenable.

Rather than retire small mind, we let it ride shotgun. We can let it sit up in the front seat and stay in dialog with Big Mind. We are wired for relationships, so imagining our ordinary self in dialog with a broader wisdom can bring some of our relational intelligence into service too.

In the end, not being in the driver's seat simply means listening more deeply and communing more comfortably with intuition. Expanding infinitely is not doing away with anything as much as it is relaxing into something much larger. It is allowing small mind to expand out into Big Mind.

To do this, here are a few suggestions we've explored in this section of the book:

- Try the guided meditation on p. 270.
- Study the stages of consciousness we just talked about. Many of the misunderstandings in the world and in our lives have less to do with information and more to do with how we process information. Understanding the lens of

consciousness through which others look at the world can deepen our empathy, kindness, and effectiveness.

- Understand transcendence. In grosser states of awareness and earlier stages of consciousness, we can develop a meditation practice that deals only with awareness because states and stages are so different. However, at the high end of the spectrum, states and stages begin to come together. Subtle and non-dual awareness is more accessible with Integral or Transcendent consciousness. Transcendent consciousness is more available through subtle and non-dual awareness.

- Gently Six-R tension and distortions whether they arise inside or outside of meditation. This patiently moves us up through the jhānas toward higher, clearer states of awareness and more nuanced and inclusive stages of consciousness.

- Send out mettā to counter the tendency to contract into a dense self. As awareness gets more spacious, rather than just radiating uplifted qualities, we can let ourselves flow out to become part of it all and let attention rest in the glow of pure awareness.

- Let the self expand infinitely. Don't fight the urge of "selfing." It is deeply wired into us. Rather, let it expand in all directions. Let the self relax, spread out, and expand to include more and more until there is no separateness. Only space. Only awareness.

Related Chapters

57. I Rest in Emptiness

Appendices

He who binds to himself a joy
Does the winged life destroy;
But he who kisses the joy as it flies
Lives in eternity's sunrise.

− William Blake

A. The Six Rs and Five Ss Overview

Resistance is futile.

– The Borg[31]

While meditating, sooner or later, a distraction completely hijacks our attention. In meditation, these distractions are often called "hindrances" (*nīvaraṇa* in *Pāli*). We may not even see them coming: one moment we're sending compassion, the next we're rehearsing a conversation, planning our day, reminiscing about yesterday, or attending to something other than the object of meditation.

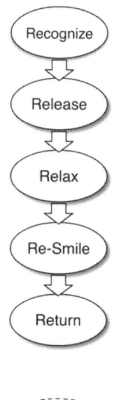

This drifting mind is a symptom of tension that is disturbing our underlying peace. This side of awakening, we all have many tensions. So the distraction points out tightness — it shows exactly where it is so that we can release it skillfully.

The trick is to do it wisely. An unwise way is to condemn ourselves, "Oh, I can't do this!" That criticism and aversion create more tension and destabilizes the mind further. Another unskillful strategy is to buckle down and try harder — a kind of greed for something different. This too creates more tension and restlessness. Another unhelpful way is to give up and stop meditating.

---

[31] The Borg are a fictional collection of species in the *Star Trek* series. Before assimilating another species they typical told them "resistance is futile." In meditation the phrase is a reminder that hindrances are strengthened by our opposition to them. The Six Rs allow them to relax and quietly disappear.

A better approach is employing a six-phased process called "the Six Rs" that was developed by Bhante Vimalaraṁsi and his students.

Recognize

The first step is Recognizing that our attention has moved away from the primary object of meditation. Seeing how the mind's awareness shifts from one thing to another is crucial. In time it will be clear that something specific drew us to that particular distraction. The reason may not be clear now. That's fine. If a thought drew us away, there's no need to get involved in its content. It's not important. If the content of a thought could awaken us, we would have become enlightened a long time ago. Instead, we notice the feeling in the mind-heart. There will be some tension: worry, curiosity, aversion, fear, desire, doubt, or some other attitude.

Recognizing this tightness on its own terms is very helpful. We want to recognize sensations as sensations, feelings as feelings, and thoughts as thoughts rather than confusing a thought or label with a sensation or feeling. See "Chapter 50. Wise Acceptance and the Six Rs," pp. 240-241 for a more detailed discussion of how this can sometimes be tricky.

Release

The second phase is to Release the hindrance. Our culture has a bias toward fixing things or getting them under control. The Six R practice is the opposite. We just let the distraction be without trying to change it. If we're upset, we don't indulge the turmoil or try to squelch it. We just notice, "Ah, there is a lot of hurt and anger in my system." If we notice daydreaming about an imagined vacation, we don't go off into the fantasy or try to shut it down. We just notice daydreaming is happening.

As Suzuki Roche put it, "The best way to control a cow is to put it in a large pasture." Release means giving the distraction some space. It may wander across the pasture and out of our lives. Or it may come back and stare us in the face with big brown eyes. Either is just fine.

Releasing isn't pushing the distraction away. It's just letting go of our grip on it. To truly let something be means it can do what it wants. We no longer hold it close or hold it off. The best way to control a cow is to Release it into a large pasture and let the cow be a cow.

Relax

The third phase is to Relax. The first two phases are passive: we Recognize the distraction and Release it or let it be. In this third phase, we start to act. This action is directed inward — soothing our stress by softening the tension in it. We aren't trying to change the hindrance or our thoughts or feelings. We aren't trying to Relax the distraction; we've just Released it to do what it wants. We look inside, notice any physical, mental, or emotional tensions, and Relax them. That's all. The term the Buddha used was dramatic: he said "abandon" the tension. Walk away from it. We don't have to search for tension like an enthusiastic detective. Just relax. That's enough.

There's no need to force Relaxation. It is just a gentle invitation — like a sigh. Yet this opportunity to Relax physically, emotionally, and mentally is very helpful!

Re-Smile

The next phase is to invite a lighter state of mind. One way to do this is to smile — not a forced smile, but a gentle, sincere one. A frown takes more energy and tension. So as we Relax, smiling comes easily.

It's called "Re-smile" because we do it over and over (and because we needed an "R" word). But in truth, Re-smiling refers to any uplifted state — lightness, kindness, joy, ease, gratitude, spaciousness, or any state with little tension in it.

Sometimes this lightness comes by acknowledging, "Boy, that situation sure has me by the throat. Cool." It helps to take ourselves lightly.

The smile may be on our lips, in the mind, in our eyes, or in the heart. If no uplifted state comes on its own, we raise the corners of the mouth slightly. Brain research affirms that even if we do it mechanically, it effectively encourages the mind to lighten up. Having a good sense of humor about how the mind drifts is helpful.

Return

Now we take the Relaxed mind-heart and this brighter, lighter state back to radiating happiness and well-being. We Return our attention to our base meditation practice.

Repeat

The final phase is to Repeat the process when it's needed and as often as needed. This step does not flow automatically from the preceding Rs. But it is included as a reminder that we may need to use the Six Rs a lot. During meditation, if distractions keep grabbing our awareness, it is not a problem if we Six R each time. Meditation is not about sustaining any particular state. States come and go. Meditation is about seeing how the mind moves around. By six-R'ing, we see the mind-heart's movements more and more clearly.

If one or several uses of the Six Rs didn't release all the tension, it will let us know by arising again. We Recognize, Release, Relax, Re-smile, and Return again, perhaps going a little further each time.

That is the beauty of this process. We don't have to do it perfectly. Doing it just a little is good enough. As we Repeat, it gradually works itself out.

Rolling the Rs

The first five Rs are not entirely separate from each other. As we learn this process, the Rs begin to blend together. They become less a set of isolated steps and more a dynamic flow of energy.

To Recognize a hindrance clearly, we naturally step back from it a little. "Let's have a look at this," implies getting a little distance from the hindrance so we can turn toward it and see it clearly. Stepping back is part of the Release. As we Release, we tend to Relax. As we Relax, our mood brightens. From this brighter place, we naturally Return to radiating well-being.

Think of this as "rolling the Rs." Don't push for this flow, but don't be surprised if the stages start to flow together naturally into a single process with multiple aspects: recognize-release-relax-resmile-return.

Wise Effort

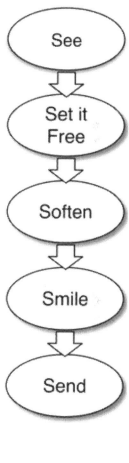

The purpose of the Six Rs is not to get rid of anything. It is to see clearly what's going on, accept it as it is, soften any tension, and then go back to radiating kindness, happiness, or equanimity. If we use the Six Rs to try to make a distraction go away, we are practicing aversion. That doesn't help!

The Six-R process is a practical implementation of Wise Effort (or "Right Effort"), the fourth step of the Buddha's Eightfold Path. The Eightfold Path is the fourth of the Buddha's Four Ennobling Truths. So in practicing this way, we are engaging the Buddha's core teachings.

Five Ss and a P

The Six Rs are effective enough to be used over and over. However, after a while, repetition can become rote and dry.

Words don't have absolute meanings. Different words have different connotations for different people. So my sangha and I thought about another set of letters that might serve as alternate reminders. Because "soften" is sometimes

a good synonym for "Relax," and "Smile" is an obvious substitute for "Re-smile," we looked at Ss.

Because a majority of people (but not all) are visual thinkers, "See" became a good stand-in for "Recognize."

"Send" was a good stand-in for "Return." It means go back to the practice of sending out mettā or other uplifted states.

It was a little harder to find a stand-in for Release. But since my favorite quote about it is Suzuki Roshi's, "The best way to control a cow is to put it into a large pasture," we settled on "Set the cow free" or simply, "Set it free."

That left the final R, "Repeat." We could not come up with a good S verb. However, the Six Rs are really a sweep of Five Rs with the Repeat coming later when the mind gets hijacked again. The point of including "Repeat" is not that the step is done right away, but a reminder that we'll be doing the Rs a lot. And doing a lot of Six Rs is good practice.

"Patience" captures this attitude and looks at "Repeat" from a different vantage. Good enough.

"Patience" is the Buddhist equivalent to "grace."
    – Chöyam Trungpa Rinpoche

B. Forgiveness Meditation

Give up all hope of ever having a better past.
— Lily Tomlin

Sometimes the meditation practice comes to a stop. We may be overwhelmed with grief, remorse, regret, or discouragement. We Six-R as best we can, but remain flooded with emotions. Or there may be no obvious emotion but the practice comes to a standstill nevertheless. Something is in the way, but we can't see what.

During these times, forgiveness meditation may help. Forgiveness heals by helping us lovingly accept whatever is going on without trying to control it. It's not a tool to drive off sadness, anger, frustration, or any other emotion. It gently and kindly accepts whatever arises, softening tension that we may not even see.

This meditation uses phrases similar to the beginning mettā practice, but the phrases center on forgiving:

I forgive myself for not understanding.
I forgive myself for making mistakes.
I forgive myself for harming myself or someone else.
I forgive myself for not following my own sense of what's right.

We can make up our own phrases, but these four can be very helpful.

We say a phrase or two over and over slowly until we feel it. We radiate that feeling of soft acceptance to ourselves. If the mind resists, insists on blaming, or wanders off track, it helps to be patient. We gently Six-R those feelings and thoughts and come back to forgiving ourselves. It doesn't help to fight the distractions. We use the Six Rs to softly come back to forgiving.

The mind may naturally go to a person who left us, died, or hurt us in some way. If this happens, we use any appropriate phrase to direct forgiveness to the person:

I forgive you for not understanding.
I forgive you for making mistakes.
I forgive you for harming yourself or someone else.
I forgive you for not following my sense of what's right.

We see the person in our mind's eye and sincerely forgive them. We don't get involved in the storyline; that doesn't help. Instead we just repeat whatever phrases seem best until we feel them. We stay with the feeling while it lasts. When the mind becomes distracted, we gently Six-R and start again.

The mind may naturally go to someone we hurt or abandoned. If we feel remorse, guilt, or regret, we shift the practice again. We imagine them looking at us and hear them saying, "I forgive you for _____. I truly do forgive you." We allow that feeling to soak in.

We have come full circle from forgiving ourselves, to forgiving the person, to the person forgiving us.

If we get stuck and are unable to forgive or feel forgiving, then we have a subtle attachment or aversion to anger, guilt, or allowing ourselves to be forgiven. This holding on or pushing away can be forgiven and released as well.

When we aren't engaged in formal meditation, we can take this practice into the rest of our life by forgiving everything. We forgive ourselves for dropping something, knocking something over, spilling something, bumping into someone, burning ourselves while cooking, forgetting to do an errand. We can forgive ourselves for distracting thoughts and forgive the thoughts for distracting us. Anytime our inner critic starts to speak, we forgive ourselves and forgive the critic for being too enthusiastic. We forgive ourselves for everything from how we squeeze the toothpaste tube to how our voice quivered in that meeting. We forgive everything.

Most of us have an inner critic that is so familiar we don't even recognize it. Continuous forgiveness helps bring that overlooked tension to the surface and allows it to relax in a kind embrace.

After a few days or a few months, those subtle overlooked tight places inside relax. The forgiveness may feel more and more like simple kindness and compassion. The details of the forgiveness process may not feel as needed or helpful. We are ready to return to our regular practice.

C. Refuges

The mind is in no way amenable to force; the least bit of force closes the heart.

– Steven Levine

Every morning I say the three Buddhist refuges along with seven precepts (see p. 300) and three aspirations (see p. 315) before I enter my first meditation of the day. These remind me of my deepest intention and the spirit of this practice.

A refuge is a place to which we turn for restoration, comfort, and inspiration. People take refuge in lots of things: working hard, meditating, eating, watching TV, pretending to be happy, trying to be kind, and more. Some of these refuges are helpful and wholesome. Some are not. Traditionally there are three things we can take refuge in that are considered particularly beneficial: the Buddha, the Dhamma, and the Saṅgha.

The most obvious understanding of these is: taking refuge in the historic Buddha Gautama as a guide and teacher; in his teachings (the "Dhamma") as a practice; and in the community of seekers (the "Saṅgha") who are following the Buddha and the Dhamma as a source of inspiration and support.

But I think the refuges go deeper than that.

The Buddha was fierce in insisting that we "be a lamp unto ourselves" and take our own deepest experience as our ultimate guide. We have the potential to fully awaken just as he did. We may not know it or be confident in it. But taking refuge in it means the willingness to deeply explore this possibility in our own experience. It's a commitment to learn to listen deeply enough to get past distortions. We don't have to turn ourselves into something we aren't already. We just have to realize the potential that is already here.

The word "Dhamma" literally means "law." But these are not man-made laws. These are natural laws: the truth of how the mind and awareness actually work. Of particular importance is how the mind-heart can naturally unfold from confusion into wisdom.

The saṅgha is not just a community of contemporary seekers. I draw great inspiration from the fact that women and men have been following these practices for several millennia and that many have fully awakened. And we live in the reality that all beings are interconnected and interdependent.

When I say the refuges to myself, I do them first using the Pāli terms (Pāli being the language in which the earliest suttas were recorded), then once in English, and the third time in Pāli again, like this:

I take refuge in the Buddha.
I take refuge in the Dhamma.
I take refuge in the Saṅgha.

For the second time I take refuge in
the process of awakening.
For the second time I take refuge in
the natural laws of how the mind-heart unfolds.
For the second time I take refuge in
the community of fellow seekers,
those who have walked this path before me,
and the interdependence of all beings.

For the third time I take refuge in the Buddha.
For the third time I take refuge in the Dhamma.
For the third time I take refuge in the Saṅgha.

D. Precepts

We are the heirs of our actions.
– The Buddha

Since ancient times, spiritual traditions have offered precepts to help mitigate attitudes and activities that can disrupt meditation and spiritual maturation.

In the *Book of Discipline (Vinaya)*, Buddhist monks are enjoined to not "whistle and snap their fingers ... and having spread their upper robes as a stage, say to a *nautch* (dancing girl) 'Dance here, sister,' while they applaud." (*Saṅghādisesa* 13). I have never been tempted to invite somebody to dance on my clothes as I whistled and snapped my fingers. However 2,600 years ago, apparently monks who professed to be followers of the Buddha were allured this way. So rules were created to guide them.

The rules were gradually codified into 311 precepts for nuns, 227 precepts for monks, 8 precepts for lay folks on retreat, and 5 precepts for laity in daily life.

The Buddha did not sit in deep contemplation and come up with these policies. Rather they were created and modified in response to situations that arose among fifth century BCE monastics. Most of the rules were created by the saṅgha, not by the Buddha. Some rules are so quaint as to not be useful to us today. Contemplating the metaphorical equivalent of dancing girl temptation might be helpful. But unless we spend time with *nautches*, the specific injunction is archaic.

Other precepts, like non-killing and non-stealing, are painted in broad strokes. They transcend a particular time and culture and remain as germane today as they were for the ancients. If we're tempted to break one of these precepts, it is best to refrain and reflect on the inner states urging the action. However, since they were drawn so broadly, we must engage them deeply and wisely to figure out specifically how they apply to 21st century life. In Chapter 49. Engaging Precepts Mindfully," pp. 225–237, we began exploring issues around engaging precepts.

In this appendix I want to expand this exploration by first offering precepts for daily life followed by stricter precepts for retreat. They are followed by a detailed discussion of interpreting these precepts and applying them to our lives.

I have found this to be a highly charged topic for many people. So I want to proceed carefully making a clear distinction between, on the one hand, what the ancient precepts actually say and don't say, and on the other hand, our interpretations of what they mean and don't mean to each of us.

My intention is not to tell you what you should do. I only want to share my own struggles in sorting them out in the hope it will help you sort them out for yourself.

First, the precepts themselves.

Daily Precepts

I recite seven daily precepts before my first sitting each day. The first five are traditional. The sixth is in many of the Buddha's talks. It is an overall reminder of what the precepts are about. The last precept summarizes them all in positive terms of kindness and generosity.

> **I undertake the precept to refrain from killing or harming on purpose.**
>
> **I undertake the precept to refrain from taking what is not freely given.**
>
> **I undertake the precept to refrain from sexual misconduct.**
>
> **I undertake the precept to refrain from lies, gossip, harsh speech, and idle chatter.**
>
> **I undertake the precept to refrain from drugs and alcohol to the point of heedlessness.**
>
> **I undertake the precept to refrain from speaking or acting with ill will.**

I undertake the precept
to be kind and generous to myself and all beings.

Retreat Training Precepts

I use the following nine precepts in retreats and offer them to my students when I am leading a retreat. They are more rigorous than the daily precepts in order to take advantage of the quiet of a retreat to reflect more deeply.

I undertake the precept to refrain from
killing or harming on purpose.

I undertake the precept to refrain from
taking what is not freely given.

I undertake the precept to refrain from
all sexual activity.

I undertake the precept to refrain from
lies, gossip, harsh speech, and idle chatter.

I undertake the precept to refrain from
drugs and alcohol.

I undertake the precept to refrain from
eating solid food after the noonday meal.

I undertake the precept to refrain from entertainment
and distractions, and to groom and dress modestly.

I undertake the precept to refrain from
speaking or acting with ill will.

I undertake the precept
to be kind and generous to myself and all beings.

Bringing Ancestors Back from the Dead

The Buddhist precepts were recorded in the Pāli language. Before looking at specific precepts in English, let's look at translation in general.

When Pepsi Cola went into China, it translated its slogan, "Come alive with the Pepsi generation" into Chinese. It came out, "Pepsi brings your ancestors back from the dead." In English, "come alive" is usually metaphorical. In Chinese, it is usually literal. These and other differences in nuance implied a message far different from what Pepsi intended.

Most words don't translate readily from one language to another because words don't have a single meaning. Rather they have clusters of definitions and connotations that differ from one language and culture to another. And within a given language, words' meanings are fluid, shifting from generation to generation and even from year to year. To confidently understand what the Buddha meant requires a nuanced understanding of the time, culture, and language around him. Many of those details have been lost to us.

When we translate the Buddha's teachings, we have an additional difficulty: during his time, writing was considered too crude for spiritual matters. Important teachings were conveyed orally. The Buddha spoke a language called *Magadhi Prakrit*. His teachings were passed verbally for generations before finally being recorded in the Pāli language. English did not exist at that time. The translations we have today are the product of a 2,600-year game of Telephone.

Scholarly detective work can uncover clues about original intent. But if we take these clues too literally, we risk thinking Pepsi brings our ancestors back from the dead.

Intoxicants and Intoxication

The fifth precept about alcohol and drugs illustrates some of the complexities of translations. It is also a relatively charged precept, perhaps because of the widespread use and misuse of intoxicants of all varieties in our 21st century lives. Let's begin with a little historical background so that we might understand what this precept meant in the Buddha's time when it was created.

In the early years of his ministry, the Buddha and the sangha used only four precepts. Alcohol was not mentioned. The Buddha's Middle Way implied moderation in drinking, but his followers weren't teetotalers.

During the ninth year of his ministry, a dispute arose amongst the monks near the city of Kosambi. A monk had broken a rule about washing: after using the latrine and washing their hands, monks should throw out any unused water so bugs couldn't grow in it. A monk forgot to throw out the water and confessed his transgression. Then an argument arose over whether his infraction was a minor or a major offense. The dispute became so acrimonious that the citizens of the city were losing faith in the saṅgha.

The Buddha went to Kosambi to try to settle the bickering. Upon approaching the city, he saw a monk passed out dead drunk beside the road. Within a few months, the saṅgha put forth the fifth precept. In *Pāli* it reads:

Surāmerayamajja pamādaṭṭhānā veramaṇī sikkhāpadam samādiyāmi.

The first two words are the substance of the precept. The last three words are a standard formula for all precepts: *veramani* ("to refrain from"), *sikkhāpadam* ("the training precept"), and *samadiyami* ("I undertake"). Rearranging these to conform to English syntax, we get: "I undertake the training precept to refrain from …"

The first two words tell what this particular precept recommends we refrain from. Both words are compound. The first compound is made up of three words. "*Sura*" and "*meraya*" were different kinds of alcohol. One probably refers to simple fermented drinks like wine and beer. The other probably refers to fermented and distilled drinks like liquors. The third word, "*majja*" is controversial. Like most words in most languages, it has multiple meanings. It can be read as "intoxicant" or "intoxication."

In Pāli compound words, the final word in the series is usually the root word while the preceding ones are modifiers. So "*suramerayamajja*" can mean "an intoxicant made from alcohol" or "intoxication from alcohol" depending on how we read "*majja*."

The second compound word, *"pamādaṭṭhāna"* is made up of *pamāda* ("heedlessness," "carelessness," or "negligence that leads to moral lapse") and *thāna* ("place"). So *pamādaṭṭhāna* literally means "place of heedlessness" and metaphorically "condition of heedlessness." However, it is unclear whether "place" or "condition" refers to the condition of the mind of a person drinking alcohol or the "condition" of the drink to potentially intoxicate.

If we go with the first meaning, the precept is about refraining from intoxicants that can give rise to heedlessness. In other words, abstaining from all alcohol. If I'm invited to join a champagne toast at a wedding and no other beverage is available, I should not participate. If we go with the second meaning, the precept is about refraining from the mind condition of intoxication. In other words, modest use of alcohol is okay as long as we don't get drunk. I can take a sip of champagne so long as it's not enough to fuzz the mind.

So which is it? Do we refrain from intoxicants or from intoxication? Sincere scholars and teachers earnestly advocate each interpretation. If we could take a time machine back 2,600 years and talk with the saṅgha in their native *Prakrit*, we could find out if they intended one interpretation over the other. But in the *Pāli* language as we understand it, both meanings are equally valid.

The controversy around this precept is ironic. Behind the dispute in Kosambi were monks holding differing views of precepts and rules. Some said rules should be followed to the letter. Others said rules were guidelines to help us better examine our intentions. They should be applied sensitively and flexibly to the natural ambiguities of life.

The Buddha did not take sides in this fight. Instead he said, "I wish you would quit arguing. The wise do not dispute with one another." He left it at that.

Tightly or Gently

How do we apply this ambiguous fifth precept to our lives?

Since the text is unclear, we can look for clues in the larger arc of the Buddha's teaching and in our own intuition. These are not likely to lead to a definitive answer that will please everyone. Indeed, even among serious scholars and practitioners, I find little disagreement about what the text *says* even as there is marked disagreement as to what it *means*. The text is ambiguous. The differing views are usually justified by differing personal experiences, insights, and beliefs about human nature. Some hold the precept tightly while others hold it gently. My views fall into the "gentle" camp. Here are some of my thoughts:

- The Buddha's path is a Middle Way that avoids extremes. In this case, the middle is somewhere between abstinence and indulgence.

- One argument for abstinence is that the only reason someone would take alcohol is craving to dull the mind. Such intentional ignorance is seriously unwholesome.

  This argument implies that we should never act with craving. But until we are near full awakening, we will have craving that can give rise to suffering. The Buddha recommended we understand suffering rather than suppress it.

  In truth, there are lots of other reasons someone might drink alcohol, such as not wanting to offend someone by rejecting an offered drink.

  And if someone does want to dull the mind, the solution is not necessarily abstinence. That may suppress the behavior without working wisely with the craving itself. It can become a kind of craving for non-craving and lead to rigidity rather than freedom.

- The data is clear that people with a history of alcohol abuse or addiction do much better with abstinence and support from others for abstinence.

- On retreats, I recommend abstinence. Keeping the saṅgha healthy and sober is valuable to everyone. And retreat time is so precious that I don't want to risk muddying the mind-heart even a little.

  Some argue that for them personally, a little alcohol or recreational drug helps them relax or see more clearly. In some cases this might be true. But I still recommend against it because there may be others on retreat who have a history of alcohol or drug abuse. It may be wisest for them to abstain completely. Having everyone abstinent is a support to them. Keeping the saṅgha healthy and sober is more valuable to everyone than a few indulgences might be to anyone.

- Both *sura* and *meraya* refer to alcoholic drinks. The precept doesn't mention other drugs. Yet most contemporary Buddhist teachers include recreational drugs as part of this precept. It is reasonable to assume that, were the Buddha alive today and looking at the wide variety of mind-altering substances available to us, he might include other substances under the precept.

- Most teachers make an exception for prescriptions. They say prescriptions are "medicine" not "drugs." However, an opioid, for example, has the same effect on the body and mind with or without a note from a doctor. This exemption says in effect, "If a wise and knowledgeable expert agrees that the benefits of a drug outweigh the problems, it's okay to use in an appropriate dosage."

  I think this is a wise standard. If we want to use a modest amount of a substance, it is helpful to consult a wise and knowledgeable expert — a doctor, teacher, or friend – who has our highest best interest at heart and see if they agree.[32]

---

[32] I never recommend using a substance that requires a medical prescription without having a doctor's prescription. And I never recommend not using a substance a doctor has prescribed. If a necessary medication has an adverse effect on the mind, there are

- Some mind and mood altering substances don't fall into the conventional understanding of alcohol, drugs, or medicine. For example, small amounts of caffeine make my mind restless and groggy at the same time — a useless condition. So I avoid all caffeine unless there is a compelling reason to take it. Other people are not affected the way I am. So I don't consider caffeine to be part of the precept. The precepts do not cover every contingency.

Refined sugar can be harmful for some people. Partial or complete abstinence may be wisest for some people, even if it's not part of the precept. It's important to understand your own system and get qualified advice where appropriate.

In truth, anything we ingest has some effect on our bodies and minds. If we refuse to put anything into the body, we die. Precepts can only point out some general principles about how to manage. It's up to us to be kind and wise in how we treat the body-mind.

Bottom Line

Rules and thoughtful reflection can only take us so far. At some point we have to look at our own experience and discover what is most helpful.

I have found that even small amounts of alcohol can disrupt subtle awareness for hours, a day, or longer. As such it is incompatible with advanced meditation. So is caffeine, too much sugar, poor diet, lack of exercise, lack of sleep, too much time on computer or TV screens, too little time in meditation, working too hard, and difficult people, to name a few. As best as I can figure, I probably consume an average of about six ounces of alcohol per year. Each time it prevents my meditation from going to its greatest depth for a time. But in the larger scheme of things, it hasn't slowed my progress more than other bad habits.

---

ways to work with it in meditation.

I think it is vitally important for us to understand how our own body-mind-heart system responds to various substances and activities and then be kind, clear, and fiercely honest with ourselves about our motivations to engage in anything that doesn't support our highest best interest. That is how wisdom grows.

Wisdom does not grow through indulgence or rigid abstinence. We can treat the desire for alcohol like any other desire by being aware of our intentions and relaxing any tension in them using the Six Rs. If we have any concern about them, we can have a conversation with a wise and knowledgeable friend.

Ajahn Sumedho was talking about the suttas in the following passage. But he could have been talking about the precepts when he wrote:

Suttas [or precepts] are not meant to be 'sacred scriptures' that tell us what to believe. One should read them, listen to them, think about them, contemplate them, and investigate the present reality, the present experience with them. Then, and only then, can one insightfully know the truth beyond words.

Killing and Harming

The first four predate the Buddha. Other groups, like that Jains, used the same language as Buddhists. The Buddha merely adopted these four from long-standing traditions. As with other things he adopted, he tweaked them to match his understanding.

The original language of the first precept refers to abstaining from "striking":

Pāṇātipātā veramaṇī sikkhāpadaṃ samādiyāmi

Most later translations refer to abstaining from "killing" or from "killing and harming." The early meaning emphasized the action. The later emphasized the effect. The shift in emphasis may reflect changes in the meaning of *pāṇātipātā*. But the intentions are similar and clear.

Taking What is Not Freely Given

The second precept is to abstain from taking what is not freely given:

Adinnādānā veramaṇī sikkhāpadaṃ samādiyāmi.

Some people translate it as refrain from "stealing." But "taking what is not given" has a wider connotation. I prefer "not *freely* given" to make it clear that coaxing or manipulating somebody into giving us something can be in the same category as stealing.

Sexual Misconduct

The third precept is about sexual misconduct:

Kāmesumicchācāra veramaṇī sikkhāpadaṃ samādiyāmi.

The earlier meaning was sensual misconduct. That is a much higher standard than just sexual misbehavior. But it has been so consistently translated and elaborated on in the text as sexual misbehavior, that I use that.

Sexual misconduct is considered any sexual behavior that is directly or indirectly hurtful to anyone. On retreats, people are encouraged to refrain from all sexual behavior so the time can be used fully for meditation training and observing the mind-heart itself.

Lies, Gossip, Harsh Speech, Idle Chatter

The Buddha had more to say about speech than any other precept. When we open our mouths, mindfulness tends to fly away. The precept itself is usually translated as incorrect speech or lying:

Musāvādā veramaṇī sikkhāpadaṃ samādiyāmi.

But given the importance of speech in our everyday lives, I like to include a few of the other qualities the Buddha spoke about: lies, gossip, harsh speech, and idle chatter.

On retreats, correct speech is usually silence.

Solid Food After Mid-Day

These first five precepts are the ones for the laity to use in everyday life. On retreats they are modified to include abstaining from all sexual activity, all non-essential speech, and all use of alcohol and non-prescription drugs.

Traditionally there are three additional precepts used on retreats. The first is to not eat at "incorrect times":

Vikālabhojanā veramaṇī sikkhāpadaṃ samādiyāmi.

The only "correct time" is between the time you can see the lines of your hand when outdoors — that is around dawn – and before the sun reaches its zenith.

Daylight Savings means that the zenith is not always high noon. And many rented retreat centers offer the mid-day meal at noon rather than before noon. So I follow Bhante Vimalaraṁsi's looser interpretation of not eating after the noon meal. This also means that advanced meditators who want to sit for many hours in the morning and through the middle of the day can still get a meal even if the "noon-day meal" is not until the afternoon.

"Solid food" is considered anything that does not naturally melt and turn to liquid before we swallow. So ice cream, chocolate, and hard candy are traditionally not considered solid. It seems to me that such exceptions are skirting the intention of the precept. So some people interpret it more strictly.

If somebody must have a later meal for medical reasons, I tell them not to take the precept at all.

Entertainment, Distractions, and Immodesty

The seventh precept is long:

Nacca-gīta-vādita-visūkadassana
mālā-gandha-vilepana-dhāraṇa-maṇḍana-vibhūsanaṭṭhānā
veramaṇī sikkhapādam samādiyāmi.

It translates roughly as refraining from dancing, singing, and music because they were considered frivolous distractions and restraining from beautifying the body with garlands, perfumes and cosmetics because they were considered vain.

Today there are problems with these. First, not all music and dance are frivolous. Second, "beautify," "garlands," "perfumes," and "cosmetics" sound like they target women. This list could include the scents of deodorants, soaps, and colognes or grooming practices such as shaving so that the list addresses both genders. The culture during the Buddha's time was misogynistic. I'd rather not continue wording that reinforces that aspect of the tradition. Furthermore, today movies-on-demand, cellphones, computers, and other electronic devices offer distractions not on the ancient list. So I update and simplify the precept *"to refrain from entertainment and distractions, and to groom and dress modestly."* The concerns are the same as in the Buddha's time but these specifics align more closely with the 21st century distractions and vanity and with gender equality.

High Beds

The eighth traditional precept is to refrain from using high beds. This is a cultural artifact from a time when high beds were a sign of privilege or haughtiness. In the context of modern society, this is no longer meaningful. I don't use it.

Ill Will

When talking about ethical behavior in his discourses, the Buddha rarely mentions just five precepts. He often mentions ten behaviors. For example in *The Sammādiṭṭhi Sutta: Right View* (*Majjhima Nikāya 9.6*) he advises abstaining from:

killing
taking what is not given
sensual pleasure

false speech
malicious speech
harsh speech
gossip
covetousness
ill will
wrong view

Notice that he doesn't mention drugs or alcohol, perhaps because that precept came from the saṅgha later or perhaps because he didn't think alcohol was as important as the other ten.

Also notice that he says a lot about speech. Perhaps because wise speech is so difficult he mentions four specifics.

The second to last item is abstaining from ill will. Without ill will, the previous items would not arise. This is a good summary of them all. So I include it as an additional precept. However, precepts are about specific physical or verbal actions. Ill will is an attitude or feeling. We have very little control over the attitudes and feelings that arise in us at any given moment. We can't wish them away. However, if we refrain from speaking or acting with ill will, we don't reinforce it. Over time it will fade. So the precept is about refraining from speaking or acting with ill will. (See pp. 134–135.)

Kind and Generous

The precepts are framed as refraining from harmful actions or speech. This way we are more likely to catch ourselves when we are tempted to speak or act unwisely.

However, it can be helpful to frame them positively. So the last precept I use summarizes them affirmatively. The opposite of ill will and covetousness is kindness and generosity.

Wisdom

The last item on the list is wise view — or refraining from wrong view. When we take the precepts to heart, we don't take life so personally. When we don't take life personally, we have wise view.

Related Chapters

E. Aspirations

Trying to transform yourself is an act of self-aggression.
— Pema Chödrön

I use these three aspirations each morning as a reminder of the overall direction of this path.

I seek to observe the mind-heart without preference.

The Buddha's meditation is based on insight into how the mind really functions. "Citta" is one of the Buddhist words for mind. It includes the qualities that, in the West, we think of as belonging to the mind and the heart. So I prefer the term "mind-heart."

We can't see the mind-heart clearly if it is clouded with judgments or preferences. As the Third Chinese Zen Patriarch put it, "The Great Way is not difficult for those who have no preferences" (see p. 41).

I seek to get myself out of the way.

We can't see the mind-heart clearly if we personalize it and add to it a sense of "me, myself, and mine." Rather, we want to see the processes by which they operate as impersonal phenomena (see p. 33). It helps to relax our sense of self so it doesn't get in the way.

I seek clarity and acceptance.

We can observe the mind-heart not for purposes of control but for the purpose of learning (see p. 199). In learning, all we need is clarity and acceptance — that is, wisdom and love.

Related Chapters

F. The 3-4-6-8-11-12-16-Fold Path

Journey away from the soundless desert
of mapped out reality.

– Herman Hesse

The Buddha's descriptions of the spiritual path included many different numbering schemes. Buddhism is known for its numerals: Four Ennobling Truths, Seven Awakening Factors, Eightfold Path, Twelve Links of Dependent Origination, and so forth. The numbers were probably not created by the Buddha. Monks added them later to make them easier to memorize. The numbering is not so important though the sequence can be helpful.

For example, the Buddha first referred to the path in his talk to his old meditation buddies in the deer park in Sarnath shortly after his awakening (see pp. *xxx*). He described Four Ennobling Truths:

1. Dukkha: Suffering (bummers) is to be understood.
2. Taṇhā: Tension (which may be experienced as desire, aversion, or confusion) is to be abandoned (or relaxed).
3. Nirodha: The cessation of taṇhā is to be realized (recognized for what it is and savored).
4. The path to the cessation of suffering is to be cultivated.

At other times and places, the Buddha spoke about eight dimensions of the spiritual journey: the Eightfold Path. These eight dimensions are grouped into three categories: "wisdom," "ethical conduct," and "practice." I prefer more evocative titles: "Finding a Compass," "Cleaning Up Our Act," and "Getting Our Selves Out of the Way." Putting these together we get:

Group / Fold / Aspect	*Pāli Term*
Finding a Compass (Wisdom)	*paññā*
1 Wise View	*sammā diṭṭhi*
2 Wise Intention	*sammā saṅkappa*
Cleaning Up Our Act (Ethical Conduct)	*sīla*
3 Skillful Speech	*sammā vācā*
4 Skillful Action	*sammā kammanta*
5 Harmonious Lifestyle	*sammā ājīva*
Getting Our Selves Out of the Way (Practice)	*samādhi*
6 Wise Effort	*sammā vāyāma*
7 Awareness (Mindfulness)	*sammā sati*
8 Stability of Mind	*sammā samādhi*

In the "Mahācattārisaka Sutta: The Great Forty" (*Majjhima Nikāya* 117) the Buddha said that three of these eight folds are primary. The other five tend to flow out from these three. The three primary ones are 1 Wise View (sammā diṭṭhi), 6 Wise Effort (sammā vāyāma), and 7 Wise Awareness (sammā sati).

Notice below that the fourth ennobling truth is the Eightfold Path. So by replacing the fourth truth with the eightfold, we have eleven stages, or eleven aspects, to cultivate:

1   First Ennobling Truth: Suffering or dissatisfaction (dukkha) is to be understood.

2   Second Ennobling Truth: The source of suffering (taṇhā) is to be abandoned.

3   Third Ennobling Truth: The cessation of suffering (nirodha) is to be realized.
    Fourth Ennobling Truth: The path (magga) is to be cultivated including:

4   1. Wise View (sammā diṭṭhi)

5   2. Wise Intention (sammā saṅkappa)

6   3. Skillful Speech (sammā vācā)

7   4. Skillful Action (sammā kammanta)

8   5. Harmonious Lifestyle (sammā ājīva)

9   6. Wise Effort (sammā vāyāma)

10 7. Awareness or Mindfulness (sammā sati)

11   8. Stability of Mind (sammā samādhi)

Or we could remove the secondary folds and turn them all into verbs to create a streamlined action plan of six:

1. Understanding Bummers
2. Relaxing Tension underlying these bummers
3. Realizing the Cessation of Suffering/Bummers
4. Wise Viewing
5. Wise Efforting
6. Cultivating Awareness

While we're making numbered lists, we could add the path of eight jhānas (which sometimes are called four jhānas with the fourth having four bases), the four stages of enlightenment (each of which has two sub-stages: attainment and fruition) — though some think the first (stream entry) and the last (liberation) are all that matter. Or we could put all the jhānas and stages of enlightenment into a Sixteen-Stage Path.

We might ask, "What's going on here? Why didn't the Buddha organize these lists more consistently?"

The answer is simple: people aren't consistent. They aren't the same as one another but have varying strengths and vulnerabilities. The Buddha was a gifted teacher who custom fit the path to the person. And as I said, it is likely that the Buddha's followers added these organizing schemes long after he died.

There are consistent themes that run through all these organizing schemes. In pursuing our own path, it helps to recognize both the consistent themes and the variations to find something that works best for us.

In practice this means trying on a version of the path that makes sense. If it works, we can continue. If it plateaus, we may want to reflect on various descriptions of the path to find out what we might need to tweak or experiment with. It is a middle way. So finding a "middle" means being wise about our own strengths and vulnerabilities and adjusting our practice to take them into account.

G. Awareness, Consciousness, and Enlightenment

When the mind exists undisturbed in the Way, nothing
in the world can offend, and when a thing can no longer
offend, it ceases to exist in the old way.

– Sengstan

Awareness and Consciousness

States of awareness and stages of consciousness are quite different from on another, as we saw in chapter 52. The Evolving Self, (p. 255–260). A few examples of states of awareness include sobriety, inebriation, dream sleep, deep sleep, infinite space, no-thing-ness, neither-perception-nor-non-perception, and other jhānas.

All states of awareness are available to us all the time, at least in theory. It may take training to learn to access some of the more refined ones. But all the states we know today have been known and accessed by seekers for thousands of years.

Stages of consciousness are different. They are not about awareness. They are about how we *interpret* awareness. A few examples of stages of consciousness include Tribal Consciousness, Traditional Literal Consciousness, Postmodern Pluralism, and Transcendent Consciousness. These and others are described in chapter 53. Stages of Consciousness (pp. 263–270).

Not all stages are available to us all the time, theoretically or otherwise. They develop and evolve over time. Each stage builds slowly on the ones that came before it. Children grow through the earlier ones as they mature. However, one way to help *stages* mature more quickly is to cultivate higher *states* through meditation. In higher states such as the higher jhānas and beyond, the stages of consciousness are broken down temporarily. Experiencing consciousness structures dissolve and come back loosens our grip on any particular stages. This allows higher stages to emerge more easily.

The highest stages generally available in a culture have evolved significantly over the millennia.

The highest stage available in the Buddha's time was Traditional Literal Consciousness. The highest generally available to us today is Integral Consciousness. Throughout history, there have been extraordinary individuals who went beyond the stages of their culture. The Buddha was probably an example. But such individuals have been rare and far between.

Enlightenment

This raises an interesting question: what does it mean to be enlightened? There were a lot of fully enlightened monks around the Buddha. They would have had full access to all states of awareness. And their stage of consciousness would likely have been Traditional Literal. That was the highest stage generally available at that time.

If we imagined taking one of these enlightened monks and transporting him 2,600 years into the future and dropping him into twenty-first-century America, he would see women as second-class citizens and have other values typical of Traditional Literal Consciousness (see p. 266–267).

Even without conjuring fantasies of time travel, we have examples today of shamans who are capable of accessing very refined states of awareness and yet have a value system typical of Magical Heroic Consciousness. (see pp. 265–266).

Would an enlightened monk in the Buddha's time be considered enlightened today? Should we consider the shaman enlightened?

The philosopher Ken Wilber says "No." He makes the case that the description of enlightenment today should include all states of awareness and all generally available stages of consciousness.

The conventional descriptions of enlightenment have been about awareness only. The jhānas, cessation, and nibbāna are all described in reference to awareness. In the highest states, normal awareness flickers out. But the descriptions make no reference to stages of consciousness or how we interpret awareness.

Cultivating states of awareness and cultivating stages of consciousness seem like separate development lines. However, in Transcendent Consciousness, we become deeply aware of oneness and the dissolution of a separate self. In this experience, the states of awareness and the stage of consciousness begin to merge. We can't have one without the other.

Ken Wilber suggests that today we should define enlightenment as the ability to access all states of awareness and the highest stages of consciousness generally available.[33]

This means that the definition of enlightenment today is more demanding than in the Buddha's time because consciousness has evolved to higher stages. It also implies that the specific criteria for enlightenment will continue to move. Today, having access to all states of awareness and to Integral Consciousness may be sufficient. But soon, we'd also need full access to Transcendent Consciousness (see p. 269–270) as it emerges more fully in the culture. And in the future, there may be higher stages that we don't yet even know about.

---

[33] Ken Wilber, *Integral Spirituality: A Startling New Role for Religion in the Modern and Postmodern World* (Boston: Integral Books, 2006).

H. Glossary

You're rich when you know you have enough.

– Lao Tzu

Different kinds of glossary entries are denoted by their formatting:

- *Pāli terms* are in *lower case italics.*
- *Sutta Titles* are in *Title Case Italics.*
- Names of people and places are in Title Case Roman. People who were not a contemporary of the Buddha have an asterisk (*) after their name.
- English words that have a special meaning in Buddhism are displayed in lower case roman.
- <u>Underlined</u> words have their own glossary entry that can be looked up for more information.

Achaan Chaa*

A Thai Forest monk who was instrumental in establishing <u>Theravada</u> Buddhism in the West. He died in January of 1992 at the age of 73.

acceptance

Seeing something clearly as it is. In Buddhism, "acceptance" does not necessarily imply approval, support, or preference. I can clearly accept that my mind is restless without preferring it. I can clearly accept that I feel discouraged without wanting it.

acinteyya

<u>Imponderable</u>; incomprehensible; questions or topics that cannot be answered.

Ahimsaka

A ruthless serial killer who became a follower of the Buddha and became fully enlightened. He is an exemplar of the redemptive power of the Buddha's teaching and the universal human potential for awakening. (See <u>Angulimāla</u>.)

Ajaan Tong*

The lineage holder of the Mahasi tradition in Thailand and one of the countries most venerated Theravada meditation teachers. He resides at Wat Phradhatu Sri Chom Tong Voravihara temple in north Thailand.

ājīva

Lifestyle; livelihood; how we take care of our basic needs while living in the world. *Ājīva* is the fifth aspect of the Eightfold Path. (See *ariyo aṭṭhaṅgiko maggo*.)

ājīvaka

A class of naked ascetics who believed in fate and predeterminism. An ājīvaka named Upaka was the first person the Buddha spoke to after his full awakening. Upaka recognized something special about the Buddha. But when the Buddha tried to teach him, Upaka didn't get it. In the suttas, ājīvaka are rarely referred to favorably and are often derided for their ideas.

Alara Kalama

A highly respected yogic meditation teacher in the Buddha's time. He became Siddhārtha Gautama's first teacher. When Gautama mastered the realm of nothingness, Alara Kalama said, "You are the same as I. Stay here and teach my students with me." Gautama left and found another teacher, Uddaka Rāmaputta.

Ānāpānasati Sutta

"The Discourse on Mindfulness of Breathing" (see *Majjhima Nikāya* 118). The Buddha gives an exposition of sixteen steps of mindfulness (*sati*) of breathing (*ānāpāna*) and its relationship to the four foundations of mindfulness and the seven awakening factors.

Angulimāla

When Ahimsaka finished his training at the university at Takkaskila, his teacher asked for a payment of 1,000 fingers. With unwavering devotion to his teacher, Ahimsaka tried to comply. As he killed people, he collected their fingers on a string around his neck. Not knowing his identity, the people in the surrounding countryside called him Angulimāla, which means "finger garland." The Buddha persuaded him to give up his violent ways.

anattā (Sanskrit: atman)
No unchanging self. Not taking things personally. Selflessness. <u>Attā</u> means "self" and "an-" is a negation. So anattā is often translated as "no self." But since the Buddha's contemporaries often believed in a higher, eternal, unchanging, true self, those listening to the Buddha would have understood the word to mean no eternal, unchanging, self essence. (See <u>attā.</u>)

anicca
Impermanent. It is one of the <u>three characteristics</u> of all things in the conditional world: nothing lasts; nothing stays as it is forever.

Anupada Sutta
The discourse "One by One As They Occurred" (see *Majjhima Nikāya* 111). The Buddha describes <u>Sāriputta</u>'s development in meditation, including a succinct description of the <u>jhānas</u> and how they unfold.

anusaya
<u>Underlying tendency</u> or latent tendency. It is a deep hindrance that is hard to see until it is expressed.

applied and sustained thought
"Applied and sustained thought" is a common though ambiguous translation of two different kinds of thought. They might be better translated as "noticing and examining." For more, see *vitakka* and *vicāra*.

arahant (Sanskrit: arhat)
Someone who has reached the final stage of awakening but has not become a Buddha. It literally means "one who is worthy" or "perfected person."

ariyo aṭṭhaṅgiko maggo (Sanskrit: āryāstāṅgamārga)
The Noble Eightfold Path. This is one of the major teachings of the Buddha where he laid out important aspects of the

path to awakening. It is a checklist to help fine-tune one's practice.

The Noble Eightfold Path (Ariyo Aṭṭhaṅgiko Maggo)		
Pāli	English	Other Translations
Sammā Diṭṭhi	Harmonious Perspective	Wise View, Right View
Sammā Saṅkappa	Harmonious Intention	Right Thought, Wise Aspiration, Wise Intention
Sammā Vācā	Harmonious Communication	Right Speech, Skillful Speech
Sammā Kammanta	Harmonious Conduct	Right Action, Skillful Conduct
Sammā Ājīva	Harmonious Lifestyle	Right Livelihood, Wise Livelihood
Sammā Vāyāma	Harmonious Practice	Right Effort, Wise Effort, Skillful Use of Energy
Sammā Sati	Harmonious Mindfulness	Right Awareness, Wise Observation
Sammā Samādhi	Harmonious Collectedness	Right Concentration, Steadiness of Mind

Ariyapariyesanā Sutta
The discourse "The Noble Search" (*Majjhima Nikāya* 26). In describing the difference between the noble and the ignoble truth, the Buddha gives one of the fuller descriptions of his own path to awakening.

arūpa
Without body; "a-" means "without" and "rūpa" means "body." The first three of the eight jhānas are considered "rūpa" because of the prominence of sensory sensations. The fourth and higher jhānas are considered arūpa because of the fading of sensory perceptions.

Atiśa*
An 11th-century Bengali prince and spiritual master. He studied with all the most respected teachers of his time and became a religious teacher and leader. He was a major figure in the spread of both Mahayana and Vajrayana Buddhism.

attā (Sanskrit: atman)
Self or soul. The Buddha used the negation, anattā, to say that we have no unchanging eternal self.

avijjā (Sanskrit: avidyā)
Unawareness, ignorance, delusion about the nature of the mind. *Avijjā* is commonly translated as "ignorance," though it has fewer pejorative connotations than in English. As in English, the root is "ignore" and indicates a tendency to overlook the true nature of things. Avijjā is the beginning of the downstream flow of *paṭiccasamuppāda* (Dependent Origination). Without it there would be no suffering.

awakening factors (*bojjhaṅga*)
Seven factors of the mind-heart that are conducive to awakening, particularly when they are brought into balance together. There are three energizing factors: investigation (*dhamma vicaya*), energy (*viriya*), and joy (*pīti*). There are three calming factors: calm / tranquility (*passaddhi*), collectedness (*samādhi*) and equanimity (*upekkhā*). There is one so-called neutral factor, mindfulness (*sati*) that can both energize or calm depending on what's needed.

awareness jhāna
The specific type of jhāna described by the Buddha. Some schools of meditation describe a jhāna as deep states of mental absorption where awareness of the surrounding environment is completely lost. But in the earliest recordings of the Buddha's talks, some awareness of the environment remains through all but the last jhāna. The term "awareness jhāna" is used to refer to non-absorption jhānas as the Buddha intended.

Basho*
Matsuo Bashō was a 17th-century Japanese poet and master of haiku.

Batchelor*
See Stephen Batchelor

Bhante
  Title used to address a monk or nun. It literally means
  "Venerable Sir" and may be used for a monk or a nun.

Bhante Vimalaraṁsi*
  An American Buddhist monk who is currently Abbot of the
  Dhamma Sukha Meditation Center in Annapolis, Missouri.
  He ordained in Northern Thailand in 1986. From 1991 to
  2000 he studied and practiced the suttas intensely. He
  trained with many Asian teachers and may be best known
  for the Six R practice and for teaching the <u>awareness jhānas</u>.

bhava
  Habitual tendency or emotional habitual tendency. It is the
  tenth movement in the flow of <u>*paṭiccasamuppāda*</u> (Dependent
  Origination). It is often translated as "becoming" or
  "existence." But these meanings are confusing. In meditation,
  bhava is experienced as the arising of familiar or habitual
  patterns of thought and emotion.

bhikkhu
  An ordained male monastic in Buddhism.

bodhi tree
  "Bodhi" is usually translated as "awakened" or
  "enlightenment." The Bodhi tree is the particular fig tree
  under which <u>Siddhārtha Gautama</u> meditated and became
  the fully awakened Buddha. The tree was in a grove along
  side the <u>Nerañjarā River</u> near present day Bodh Gaya India.
  Today, the large fig tree that grows in that location is
  thought to be a direct descendent of the original bodhi tree.

bojjhanga
  See <u>awakening factors</u>.

brahmavihāra
  The four "sublime states" or "divine abodes." They are <u>*mettā*</u>
  (friendliness, kindness or goodwill), <u>*karuṇā*</u> (compassion),
  <u>*muditā*</u> (joy or appreciative joy), and <u>*upekkhā*</u> (equanimity).

Buddhaghoṣa*
A fifth-century Indian Theravādan Buddhist scholar and commentator. He is best known for writing the *Visuddhi* or *Path of Purification*. This summary and analysis constitutes the orthodox understanding of Theravada texts since at least the 12th CE. There are significant differences between some of Buddhaghosa's understandings of meditation and those found in the earlier recordings of the Buddha's talks. Where differences exist, the earlier texts are a better guide to effective practice. (See "Visuddhimagga.")

cattāri ariya saccani
The Four Noble Truths. These are the core of the Buddha's teaching. "Noble" refers not to the truths but to the mind that can perceive them correctly. The Four Truths are *dukkha* (dissatisfaction or suffering), *taṇhā* (tightness or craving), *nirodha* (cessation or the release of *taṇhā*), and the Eightfold Path (*ariyo aṭṭhaṅgiko maggo*).

cetanā
Intention; directionality. It is a mental factor that organizes the mind in a particular direction. Cetanā includes both conscious will power and unconscious inclinations that we may not notice but nevertheless incline the mind-heart in a particular direction.

chanda
Wholesome desire. Not all desires are all bad. Wanting to be more loving, compassionate, or generous are examples of wholesome desires. However, as the mind becomes more serene and receptive, all tightness that accompanies any kind of desire must be relaxed and released. Even wholesome desires can block the mind-heart's natural clarity from emerging.

Channa
A royal servant and head charioteer of Śuddhodana. Śuddhodana entrusted Channa to attend to the needs of his son Siddhārtha who would later become the Buddha. Tradition credits Channa with teaching the young Siddhārtha about old age, sickness, death, and the life of a

monk. When <u>Siddhārtha</u> decided to leave home and become a monk, Channa protested but eventually helped him set out on his quest.

Chöyam Trungpa Rinpoche*

A preeminent teacher, scholar, poet, and meditation master who helped bring Tibetan Buddhism to the west. Trungpa coined the term "crazy wisdom" and may be best known for his book, "Cutting Through Spiritual Materialism." Some of his teaching methods and actions were topics of controversy.

citta

Mind. There are three overlapping terms for mind. The other two are *māna* (prideful mind) and <u>*viññāṇa*</u>. Citta often refers to the quality of the mental process as a whole.

concentration

Collectedness; calm abiding; stability of mind. The <u>*Pāli*</u> term <u>*samādhi*</u> is often translated as "concentration" because the attention stays easily on an object. However, <u>samādhi</u> does not have the tension or strain that "concentration" may imply. It is collected and stable because there is little tension to pull it away. Forcing the mind to stay on one object creates tension, not <u>samādhi</u>.

contemplate

Observe. In English the word "contemplate" often implies actively thinking about a topic. In the suttas, the <u>*Pāli*</u> word "contemplate" is usually a translation of a word like <u>*sati*</u> which means merely to observe with an open awareness without cogitating upon it.

delusion

Personalizing; taking as self something that is not self; lack of objectivity.

Dependent Origination

See <u>*paṭiccasamuppāda*</u>.

Devadatta
> Cousin and brother-in-law of Siddhārtha Gautama the Buddha. He is probably best known for several failed attempts to kill the Buddha.

dhamma (Sanskrit: dharma)
> The law, the way things are, the natural order. The term can also mean a phenomenon in and of itself, a mental quality or a teaching. When capitalized, Dhamma refers to the teachings of the Buddha. To take refuge in the dhamma (lower case) means to take refuge in how things really are. To take refuge in the Dhamma (upper case) is to rely on the Buddha's teachings.

Dhammacakkappavattana Sutta
> "The Discourse on Setting the Wheel of Dhamma in Motion," *Saṃyutta Nikāya* 56.11. In this text the Buddha gives his first successful teaching to his old meditation partners, the five ascetics. He explains the Middle Path and the Four Noble Truths.

Dhammapada
> A collection of short sayings of the Buddha in verse form. It is one of the most widely known Buddhist texts.

dhammavicaya
> Investigation, or investigation of the dhamma. It is one of the seven awakening factors.

dhammachanda
> Love of or desire for the dhamma, to live in harmony with all that is.

dharma
> The Sanskrit spelling of dhamma.

Dīgha Nikāya
> The collection of the long discourses of the Buddha.

diṭṭhi (Sanskrit: dṛṣṭi)
> View, perspective, or position. In Buddhism, a view or position is not a simple abstract proposition but a charged interpretation that can shape experience and thought. Right

view or harmonious perspective (*sammā diṭṭhi*) is the first
fold or aspect of the Eightfold Path. It refers not so much to
holding a correct view as to having a way of seeing which is
clear and holds to no position. (See *ariyo aṭṭhaṅgiko maggo*.)

dukkha
Dissatisfaction, suffering, stress, discontent. *Dukkha* is the
first Ennobling Truth, indicating that life has dissatisfaction.
The Buddha never said that life *is* suffering, only that
nothing in the relative world of constant change can be a
reliable base for happiness. A more colloquial translation of
dukkha that conveys its wider range of meaning is
"bummer."

Eightfold Path
Harmonious path. (See *ariyo aṭṭhaṅgiko maggo).*

gatha
Technically a gatha is a song or verse. The Zen Master Thich
Nhat Hanh popularized the term as a verse or short saying
to be recited mentally as part of a meditation practice or
means of bringing wise awareness into daily life.

Gautama
The Buddha's family name or surname. By tradition, his first
name was "Siddhārtha." However, this might be a spiritual
name given to him after his awakening.

imponderables *(acinteyya)*
Four topics the Buddha considered imponderable or
incomprehensible. They can be vexing or drive us crazy to
try to solve. They are: What are the powers of an
enlightened being? What can meditation ultimately achieve?
What karma caused a specific event to occur? Where did the
universe come from?

intention
See *saṅkappa*.

Jain
An ancient Indian religion known for its main premises of
non-violence, many-sidedness, non-attachment, and

asceticism. Followers of Jainism take five main vows: non-violence, truth, not-stealing, chastity, and non-attachment.

jarāmaraṇa
The final "down river" event in the flow of Dependent Origination or *paṭiccasamuppāda*. "Jarā" literally means "old age." "Marana" literally means "death." "Jarāmaraṇa" refers to the "whole mass of suffering": "sorrow, lamentation, pain, grief, and despair."

jāti
Birth or birth of action. The term traditionally refers to the arising of a new entity. In Dependent Origination it can also refer to the beginning of a mental, verbal, or physical action.

jhāna
A stage of meditative knowledge gained through direct experience. The nature of the jhānas and how to work with them is discussed in detail in *Buddha's Map*[34] and elsewhere.

Kabir*
A 15th-century Indian mystic poet whose writings were mostly concerned with devotion, mysticism, and discipline.

kammanta
Action, movement, or conduct. In the Eightfold Path, "sammā kammanta" refers to behaving in ways that are harmonious with life and that encourage awakening. (Also see "*ariyo aṭṭhaṅgiko maggo,*" the Noble Eightfold Path.)

Kandaraka Sutta
The talk the Buddha gave to the mendicant Kandaraka (see *Majjhima Nikāya* number 51). He describes some of the practices used by accomplished meditators and makes the distinction between people who live in ways that harm or disturb themselves or others, and those who live according to the Dhamma.

---

[34] Doug Kraft, *Buddha's Map: His Original Teachings on Awakening, Ease, and Insight in the Heart of Meditation,* (Carmichael, California, Easing Awake Books, 2017), Chapter 11, pp. 145-157.

kamma *(Sanskrit: karma)*
The effects of our physical, verbal, or mental actions. Everything we do creates the potential for other things to happen. If we are wise, we will act in ways that tend not to create difficulty or unhappiness in the future.

karuṇā
Compassion. It is the second of the four brahmavihāra or sublime states.

kasiṇa *(Sanskrit: kṛtsna)*
One of ten meditation objects, each of which is an element (earth, water, air, fire) or a color. The meditator focuses his attention on the object. The suttas mention kasiṇa meditation; it is likely that these were borrowed from the Brahmin traditions and inserted into the text at a later time.

kāya
Body. "Kāya" refers to the material body alone—what is present in a corpse. "Rūpa" refers to a living body.

khandha (Sanskrit: skandha)
Aggregate, heaps. The five khandha (body, feeling tone, perception, concepts and storylines, and consciousness or awareness) refer to the various phenomena people often identify as self. In this context they are often called "aggregates affected by clinging." Bhante Vimalaraṁsi calls them "aggregates affected by craving and clinging."

kier
A rice pudding typically made by boiling rice, broken wheat, milk, sugar and spices. It may be served as a meal or a dessert. The young Sujata brought kier as an offering to the tree spirit of her village and found the Buddha-to-be sitting beneath it close to death. She offered him the kier and helped restore his health.

kilesas
Mental states that cloud the mind and may manifest in unwholesome actions. Kilesas include anxiety, fear, anger, jealousy, desire, depression, and other states that distort the mind.

kōan
> A paradoxical story or riddle used in Zen Buddhism to move the mind beyond logical reasoning and to provoke awakening.

Kosala
> A town in India that may have been subjugated by the Shakya Clan, to which the Buddha belonged.

Kosambi
> A great city in the time of the Buddha. Several Buddhist monasteries were in the vicinity of Kosambi. A great schism among the monks of Kosambi is described in the early texts.

kuti
> A small hut used for meditation.

Lao Tzu*
> An ancient Chinese philosopher, writer, reputed author of the Tao Te Ching, and founder of Taoism. He may have been a contemporary of the Buddha, but there is no direct evidence that the two knew each other.

latent tendency
> See *anusaya*.

maggo
> Path. "Ariyo aṭṭhaṅgiko maggo" is the Eightfold Path taught by the Buddha.

Majjhima Nikāya
> The Middle Length Discourses. The Pāli Canon is a collection of over 10,000 suttas or discourses attributed to the Buddha or his chief disciples. It is divided into three *pitakas* ("baskets"). The second basket, the *Sutta Pitaka*, is divided into five *nikāyas* (collections). The *Majjhima Nikāya* is the second of the five. It contains 152 suttas. They provide a comprehensive body of teaching concerning all aspects of the Buddha's teachings.

Mara
He is depicted as a demon who tried to seduce the Buddha in various ways, always failing. Mara is described as "the personification of forces antagonistic to awakening."

mettā
Loving kindness, goodwill, and gentle friendship. Mettā is the first of the four sublime states (brahmavihāra) the Buddha recommended be cultivated. These can be very effective objects of meditation. Mettā is usually translated as "loving kindness" but a more accurate rendering is "friendliness."

mindfulness
See *sati*.

mind-heart
Buddhism does not make the distinction between mind and heart often made in the West. I use the term mind-heart to refer to all those qualities together.

mind-stream
That which may pass from one body to the next. Various religious traditions use the term in different ways. Some say the mind-stream contains some of the memories and impressions from one lifetime to the next. It should not be confused with soul or self, because our sense of self is made up of many more transient phenomena.

mudita
Joy, especially but not exclusively the joy that arises from seeing someone's good fortune. Mudita is the third of the four sublime states (brahmavihāra) used as a very effective meditation object.

nāmarūpa
Mind-body. As a phase of Dependent Origination, it refers to a condition before mind or body has arisen as separate phenomena. Mind (nāma) and body (rūpa) are said to co-arise.

Nerañjarā River
The Buddha became fully enlightened sitting under a tree near the banks of the Nerañjarā River in northern Indian near the present day town of Bodh Gaya.

nibbāna (Sanskrit: nirvāṇa)
Extinguished. The word literally means "blow out" as in a candle that is extinguished. In the scientific thinking of the Buddha's time, when a fire goes out, the heat element in the flame does not go away. It simply ceases to cling to the burning object. It disperses. So to those who heard the Buddha use the term, it meant the complete cessation of craving and clinging. Through meditation training, we can relax so deeply that all perception and consciousness cease for a period of time. Coming out of this state, we can see Dependent Origination so clearly that we no longer identify with psychophysical processes. When this is deep and full enough, we wake up.

nibbidā
Disenchantment. Seeing the truth of how the things actually operate, the enchantment or attachment to the world fades. At first it can be quite disturbing. But as it deepens, it moves toward dispassion.

nikāya
Volume; collection; assemblage; class. Nikāya most commonly refers to one of the five collections of the suttas that make up the Pāli Canon. These five are: the *Dīgha Nikāya* (long discourses), the *Majjhima Nikāya* (middle-length discourses), the *Saṃyutta Nikāya*, (thematically linked discourses), *Anguttara Nikāya*, (the discourses grouped by content enumeration), and the *Khuddaka Nikāya* (minor or shorter discourses).

nimitta
A mental sign or vision that can arise during meditation, particularly during the fourth jhāna and beyond. Often it is seen as a white light or a white disk. Some traditions use it as an object of meditation to go into a state of absorption. However, it is wiser to simply know that it is there and

Six-R it like anything else. That allows the <u>mind-heart</u> to go even deeper.

nirodha
Cessation, absence, or extinction. Nirodha is the third of the Four Noble Truths, which points to the cessation of perception, feeling, and consciousness. With this is the cessation of suffering.

nirvāna
See <u>nibbāna.</u>

Nisargadatta*
An Indian guru who owned a tobacco shop in Mumbai from which he taught and gave talks. His guru was Siddharameshwar Maharaj. He retired from his shop in 1966, but continued to teach in his home until he died in 1981.

nīvaraṇa
Hindrance; veil; something that gets in the way of meditation progress. The term literally means a covering – it covers something valuable. So the problem is not what we perceive but how we relate to it. If we are skillful, we can use nīvaraṇa to point out something that needs wise attention. The Six Rs are the best way to work with hindrances and turn them to our advantage.

Pāli
The language used in recording the suttas and many early texts. It was close to the language the Buddha spoke (*Prakrit*), but not actually the same.

pamada
Heedlessness; carelessness; negligence that leads to moral lapse.

paññā
Wisdom; insight; seeing into the true nature or reality. In Buddhism it has the more specific meaning of understanding Dependent Origination (see <u>*paṭiccasamuppāda*</u>).

papañca
Mental proliferation. The kind of thinking that wanders around sometimes aimlessly.

Pasenadi
King Pasenadi was the ruler of the principality of Kosala in ancient India. He was a devoted lay follower of the Buddha and built many monasteries for the Buddhist saṅgha.

pas'sambaya
Relax, tranquilize as in "bring tranquility to ——." This term can be used as a noun, verb, or modifier. However, in the suttas it is most often used as a verb as in "bring tranquility to the mind-heart."

passaddhi
Calmness, tranquility, serenity. It is the seventh awakening factor and part of the "higher path" in Dependent Origination.

paṭiccasamuppāda (Sanskrit: pratītyasamutpāda)
Dependent Origination. This is the central teaching of the Buddha about how everything arises because of causes and conditions. Seeing this clearly is central to his path to awakening.

Pema Chödrön*
An American Tibetan Buddhist and student of Chögyam Trungpa Rinpoche. She is the director of the Gampo Abbey in Nova Scotia. She has written many books emphasizing bringing wisdom and heart to difficult times.

phassa (Sanskrit: sparśa)
Contact, raw sense impression. It is defined as the coming together of three factors: sensory data (e.g., light), sensory organ (e.g., eye), and consciousness (e.g., eye consciousness). It is the first movement in Dependent Origination that is noticeable by the average person who has no advanced meditation training.

pīti (Sanskrit: prīti)
> Joy. It is sometimes translated as "rapture," but "pīti" need not be overwhelming. It can range from a huge, overwhelming joy to a peaceful, all-pervasive joy. It is one of the signs of the first jhāna.

Prakrit
> An ancient Indian language that has many dialects. Prakrit means "natural," "normal," "artless," or "vernacular" as contrasted to the more literary and religious orthodoxy of Sanskrit. The Buddha probably spoke the Ardhamagadhi ("half-Magadhi") dialect.

pure awareness
> Awareness without an agenda or tension; awareness of awareness itself.

Rāhula
> The son of the Buddha (before the Buddha awakened) and his wife Yasodharā. Rāhula become the first novice monk in the Buddha's saṅgha.

Rājagaha
> Ancient name for the modern city of Rajgir. In the Buddha's time it was the capital of Magadha. It was probably built by Bimbisāra, a lay follower of the Buddha.

right
> See *sammā.*

rūpa
> Body, physical phenomenon, sense information. It has different meanings in different contexts. As a sensory object, rūpa is the object of the sense of sight. As the first khandha, it is physical phenomena or sensations picked by sensory organs. In "nāmarūpa" it means physical as opposed to mental phenomena ("nāma").

saddhā (Sanskrit: śraddhā)
> Confidence, faith. In some contexts it means faith in the Buddha's path. It is part of the "higher path" of Dependent Origination. With stream entry, it becomes unshakable.

samādhi
Collectedness, calm abiding. Often it is translated as concentration or one-pointedness. But it has neither the strain implied by "concentration" nor the blocking out of other phenomena as implied by "one-pointedness." It is a unified and quiet quality of consciousness. Samādhi is one of the awakening factors as well as part of the Eightfold Path. (Also see *"ariyo aṭṭhaṅgiko maggo,"* the Noble Eightfold Path.)

sammā
Harmonious, skillful, wise. In the context of the Eightfold Path, it is often translated as "right." But the *Pāli* term does not carry the sense of right and wrong or good and bad implied in English. The name of the eight aspects of the Eightfold Path starts with "sammā." (Also see *"ariyo aṭṭhaṅgiko maggo,"* the Noble Eightfold Path.)

sammā diṭṭhi
Wise view. The first fold of the Eightfold Path. (Also see *ariyo aṭṭhaṅgiko maggo.)*

sampajañña
Commonly translated as "clear comprehension" or "clear knowing" means knowing what's going on in the moment and knowing the larger context at the same time. It's like a wide-angle lens that sees both depth and breadth.

saṃsāra
The world and the suffering found in it. The word literally means "continuous flow" and refers to the continuous flow from birth to life to death to rebirth.

samudaya
Origin, source. It is the second Noble Truth that refers to the origin of dissatisfaction (dukkha).

Saṃyutta Nikāya
The Connected Discourses. This nikāya is part of the *Pāli* Cannon. This collection of over 10,000 suttas (discourses) is attributed to the Buddha or his chief disciples. It is divided into three *pitakas* ("baskets"). The second basket, the *Sutta Pitaka,* is divided into five nikāyas (collections). The

Saṃyutta Nikāya is the third of the five. The suttas are grouped into five avgas (sections), each of which is further divided into *saṃyuttas* (chapters) on related topics.

saṅgha

Originally it referred to the community of Buddhist monks and nuns. Today it is often used to refer to any community of people dedicated to the Buddha's teachings.

Saṅghādisesa

A division of the *Pāṭimokkha* or the code of conduct for Buddhist monks. The Saṅghādisesa division contained rules that, if broken, were serious enough to require a meeting of the entire saṅgha.

Sanskrit

A primary language of Hinduism, Sikhism, Jainism, and Buddhism. It is a "high" language used in liturgy and scholarship. The relationship between Sanskrit and Pāli is similar to the relationship between Latin and Italian.

saṅkappa

Intention. It has also been translated as "thought" or "aspiration," but "intention" is closer to the original meaning. It is the second aspect of the Eightfold Path as it grows naturally out of wise or harmonious view of life. (Also see "*ariyo aṭṭhaṅgiko maggo,*" the Noble Eightfold Path.)

saṅkhāra

Thoughts, concepts, storyline, or anything else that has been mentally formed or put together. Saṅkhāra is a complex term that is used in lots of different ways. *Khāra* means "action." "*Saṅ-*" puts added emphasis on it. So the word is often translated as "volitional formations." But this can be confusing in English. "Volitional" in English implies conscious intention or even willpower. But the Pāli term can imply unconscious inclinations and tendencies. And "formation" in English implies something solid and lasting. But in Buddhism the sense is fragility — anything that has been put together or formed easily falls apart. (See volition.)

sañña (Sanskrit: Saṃjñā)
Perception, label. It is seen as a subtle but active process whereby we compare an experience to our past experiences and figure out what it is (i.e., what to label it).

Sāriputta *(Sanskrit: Śāriputra)*
One of the Buddha's main disciples who was "renowned in wisdom," meaning he had an exceptionally clear understanding of the Dhamma.

Sarnath
A small town not far from Varanasi. It was here in the Deer Park that the Buddha first taught the Dhamma to five ascetics who had been companions of his before his enlightenment.

sati (Sanskrit: smṛti)
Mindfulness, heartfulness, the state of being fully present without habitual reactions. It is a very important quality in Buddhist practice. The Pāli language does not make a distinction between mind and heart, so sati includes both these qualities. It is the balancing factor of the seven awakening factors. It is also the seventh aspect of the Eightfold Path. (See *"ariyo aṭṭhaṅgiko maggo,"* the Noble Eightfold Path.)

Satipaṭṭhāna Sutta
The Discourse on the Foundation of Mindfulness, *Majjhima Nikāya 10.* This sutta is considered by many Theravada Buddhists to be the core of the Buddha's teachings.

Sayadaw
A Burmese Buddhist title for a senior monk or abbot of a monastery or a highly respected teacher.

Sayadaw U Tejaniya*
A Theravādan Buddhist monk of Burmese Chinese lineage whose teachings have attracted a global audience for their clarity and sense of humor.

Sengstan*

Jainzhi Sengstan is the Third Chinese Zen Patriarch. He is best known as the putative author of the famous Zen poem, "Hsin-Hsin Ming" or "Inscription on Faith in Mind."

Shakya

A warrior clan of the late Vedic period (1000 to 500 BCE) in the upper Ganges valley in present-day northern India and southern Nepal. The Buddha was born into this clan where his father, Śuddhodana, was the chosen leader.

Siddhārtha

"Siddha" means "accomplished" and "aretha" means "goal." "Siddhārtha" means "one who accomplished his goal." By tradition, this was the Buddha's first name. However, it is more likely that it was a spiritual name given to him after his awakening.

Six Rs

A six-phase technique used in meditation and all of life to deal wisely with distractions and disturbances in the mind-heart. Its effectiveness comes from its simplicity and its foundation in what the Buddha called Wise Effort or *sammā vāyāma*. (See Appendix A. The Six Rs and Five Ss Overview, p. 287.)

sīla

Moral conduct.

Stephen Batchelor*

A British author, teacher, and scholar of Buddhism. He trained and ordained as a novice Tibetan monk and went on to study intensively with Theravada and Zen teachers. Years later he disrobed and married. He is probably best known for his writings about secular Buddhism.

Śuddhodana

Leader of the Shakya clan in ancient India and father of Siddhārtha who later became the Buddha.

Sujata
A young woman who brought food to the Buddha-to-be and helped restore his strength after he had been depleted by severe aesthetic practices. Shortly after his recovery he became fully awakened.

sukha
Happiness. An important factor in the first two jhānas.

sutta (Sanskrit: sūtra)
A talk given by the Buddha. The suttas are part of the canonical text. The term literally means "thread." The implication is that to understand the "whole cloth" of the Dhamma, it's important to know how the suttas are woven together.

Sutta Nipata
A collection of suttas that is part of the Khuddaka Nikāya (collection of shorter suttas). Many scholars believe these may be some of the earliest suttas.

Suzuki Roshi*
A Sōtō Zen monk who is renowned for founding the first Buddhist monastery outside Asia. His book, *Zen Mind, Beginner's Mind,* is one of the most popular books on Zen and Buddhism in the West.

Takkaskila
A city in ancient India famous for its university.

taṇhā (Sanskrit: tṛṣṇā)
Craving, tightness, holding. Though "taṇhā" is most often translated as craving, it can be very subtle. It is a preverbal tightening as we try to avoid something uncomfortable, hang on to something pleasurable, or space out with something neutral. The Buddha identified it as the "weak link" in Dependent Origination—the easiest place to stop the "down stream" of events by relaxing the tightness. Besides being the eighth phase of Dependent Origination, it is subtly present in all phases as well as being the second of the Four Noble Truths.

Tejaniya*
(See Sayadaw U Tejaniya.)

Theravada
Theravada literally means "school of the elder monks." It uses the Buddha's Teachings in the Pāli Canon as its primary source. It is probably best know for Vipassanā or Insight meditation.

Thich Nhat Hanh*
A Vietnamese Buddhist monk who first came to the attention of the West during the Paris peace negotiations for the end of the Vietnam war. He coined the term "engaged Buddhism." He has published over 100 books about the peace movement, nonviolence, and meditation.

three characteristics
Three qualities that the Buddha taught are part of everything in the relative word, namely impermanence (*anicca*), unsatisfactoriness or suffering (*dukkha*), and no unchanging self (*anattā*).

tilakkhaṇa (Sanskrit: trilakṣaṇa)
The three characteristics of all things in the conditioned world: unsatisfying (dukkha), impermanent (anicca), and selfless or impersonal (anattā).

upādāna
Clinging. It is always experienced as thinking or the beginning of thinking. It is the seventh phase of Dependent Origination. It arises when taṇhā is not relaxed and released.

Uddaka Rāmaputta
A famous teacher and contemporary of the Buddha. "Putta" means son of, so his name literally means son of Rama, who also was a famous teacher. Uddaka became Siddhārtha Gautama's second teacher. Siddhārtha mastered all Uddaka could teach and then left to train on his own.

underlying tendency
See *anusaya*.

Upaka
See ājīvaka.

upekkhā
Equanimity. It is the fourth of the sublime states (brahmavihāra) and one of the awakening factors. It is very important, particularly in the higher jhānas.

vācā
Communication, speech. In the Eightfold Path, it is usually translated as "speech" but refers to more than spoken words. It includes written, typed, and any other kind of communication. (Also see "*ariyo aṭṭhaṅgiko maggo,*" the Noble Eightfold Path.)

vāyāma
Practice; skillful or wise effort; effort without strain. It is the sixth aspect of the Eightfold Path and is commonly translated as "effort" or "right effort." But the term should not be confused with pushing or straining. Skillful effort is to remember to relax and release, not to strive. (Also see "*ariyo aṭṭhaṅgiko maggo,*" the Noble Eightfold Path.)

Veda
Veda literally means "knowledge." The Vedas are a large body of texts originating in ancient India.

vedanā
Feeling tone. Vedanā can be pleasant, painful, or neither. It arises out of raw perception.

venerable
Title of a monk.

vicāra
The kind of thinking that wisely discerns. For example, in meditation if a small distraction arises, you may decide whether it is minor enough to ignore or if you should Six-R it. Vicāra is the type of thinking that skillfully decides what to do. It is not the wondering or free associational kind of thinking. (Compare to *papañca.*)

Vimalaraṁsi*
(See Bhante Vimalaraṁsi)

vimutti
Release, liberation, freedom from the constraints of the conditioned mind.

Vinaya
One of the three main parts of the Buddhist text. It is primarily concerned with the rules for monks and nuns.

viññāṇa (Sanskrit: viññāṇa)
Awareness, consciousness. It is the third phase of Dependent Origination and the last of the five aggregates (khandhas).

vipassanā
Insight into the true nature of reality. Vipassanā is not just perceiving what's around us but also being aware of the mind's response to the perception. The term is often used to refer to the Buddha's meditation practice based on mindfulness.

virāga
Dispassion. It is similar to being unconcerned. However, in virāga, the mind is attentive without being invested in outcomes. It is important for entering the eighth jhāna and for the "higher path" of Dependent Origination.

vitakka
The kind of minimal thought that recognizes an experience and often puts a label on it. (Compare to *papañca*.)

Visuddhimagga
The Path of Purification. A text composed by Buddhaghosa in about 430 CE. It is probably the most influential text in the Theravādan tradition. Buddhaghosa was attempting to find common ground between the various Buddhist schools at that time. He was not as motivated to decide which aspects coincided best with the Buddha's earliest teachings but gave equal credit to each school's interpretation. Thus the texts

differ from some of the Buddha's original teaching in important areas. (See "Buddhaghoṣa.")

viriya (Sanskrit: vīrya)

Energy, enthusiasm. This is one of the seven awakening factors. It is naturally arising balanced energy. It is both relaxed and at the same time energized without tension.

volition

A common translation of the Pāli term *cetanā*. It applies to things that arise in the mind-heart (as compared to external processes like gravity). However, cetanā is not always willful or even conscious intention. It takes a great deal of training and mental clarity to see it in its subtle forms. (See cetanā.)

wat

In Thailand a wat is a cross between a monastery and a community center. It is a place where monks often live. But many wats are also a place that lay Buddhists visit to learn or practice Buddhism.

wholesome/unwholesome

Wholesome qualities are ones that are beneficial. They have little tension in them or tend to reduce tension. Unwholesome qualities have tension or increase tension.

winking out

In the highest jhāna, the mind becomes so relaxed that it doesn't completely store memories or fully recognize phenomena. It's like looking through a pair of high power binoculars into a fogbank. In the text this is called "neither-perception-nor-non-perception." When the mind relaxes further, perception and memory go off line. This is called "nirodha" or "cessation of perception, feeling, and consciousness." When it relaxes even further, it's called "nibbāna." At first it may be hard for yogis to tell the difference between these three. Without perception or memory, subjectively they all feel like blacking out. However, unlike nodding off, when a yogi comes out of these, the mind is exceptionally clear and still. In conversations with yogis, I began collectively calling all three "winking out," because that's what they all subjectively feel like. There are subtle and important differences between them. But I use the term to distinguish between these refined meditation phenomena and ordinary grogginess. Recently, the term "winking out" has appeared in the urban dictionary to refer to a kind of spacing out. This is definitely not how I use the term.

wisdom

Seeing the causal relationships in Dependent Origination. In English, the word "wisdom" has a broad meaning. When the Buddha used the word, he was always referring to seeing the causal relationships. Seeing them is the core of the Dhamma. (See *paññā*.)

yana

A knowledge gained in meditation.

Yasodharā

The wife of Siddhārtha Gautama who became the Buddha. She was also his cousin and mother to their only child, Rāhula. She also became a Buddhist nun and became fully awakened.

yogi

A person who sincerely follows a spiritual path that includes a discipline like meditation. Narrowly, the term refers to someone proficient in yoga. I use the term more broadly to include any sincere meditator.

zafu

Meditation cushion.

zeal

Enthusiasm; energy. It is a common translation of *vīrya*. But it doesn't have the push or blind enthusiasm that may be implied by "zeal."

I. Resources

The invariable mark of wisdom is to see
the miraculous in the common.

– Ralph Waldo Emerson

Books

Johnson, David C., *The Path to Nibbāna: How Mindfulness of Loving-Kindness Progresses Through the Tranquil Aware Jhānas to Awakening.* Annapolis, Missouri: BTS Publishing, 2017.

Kraft, Doug. *Beginning the Journey: Initial Meditation Instructions Using the Buddha's Map.* Carmichael, California: Easing Awake Books, 2017.

———. *Buddha's Map: His Original Teachings on Awakening, Ease, and Insight in the Heart of Meditation.* Carmichael, California: Easing Awake Books, 2017.

———. *Circling Home: Spirituality Through a Unitarian Universalist Lens.* Carmichael, California: CreateSpace, 2010.

———. *God(s) and Consciousness: Mapping the Development of Consciousness Through Views of Ultimacy.* Carmichael, California: Doug Kraft Books, 2011.

———. *Kindness and Wisdom Practice: A Quick Guide to Mettā-Paññā Meditation.* Nevada City, California: Blue Dolphin Publishing, 2014.

Tejaniya, Sayadaw U. *Don't Look Down on Defilements.* Selangor Malaysia: Auspicious Affinity, 2006.

———. *Dhamma Everywhere.* Selangor Malaysia: Auspicious Affinity, 2011.

———. *Awareness Alone Is Not Enough.* Selangor Malaysia: Auspicious Affinity, 2008.

Vimalaraṁsi, Bhante. *Breath of Love.* Jakarta, Indonesia: Ehipassiko Foundation of Indonesia, 2012.

———. *Moving Dhamma, Volume 1.* Annapolis, Missouri: Dhamma Sukha Meditation Center, 2012.

Wilber, Ken. *Integral Spirituality*. Boston and London: Integral Books, 2007.

Websites

Dhamma Sukha Meditation Center:
http://www.dhammasukha.org

Doug Kraft:
http://www.dougkraft.com

Easing Awake Saṅgha:
http://www.easingawake.org

© Adam Eurich

J. List of Gathas

See simplicity in the complicated.
– Lao Tzu

"Gatha" is a Sanskrit term for a short phrase designed to illuminate the meditative process or spiritual understanding. Each chapter has at least one a gatha associated with it. Some chapter titles are also gathas. Below you'll find them all listed with the author and page where each appears. Ones without authors were created by me.

Gratitude

Be grateful to everyone.

— Atiśa

It takes a village to write a book. A veritable tribe of people prodded, pushed, edited, supported, critiqued, and encouraged this project and kept me going when I might have faltered.

First, I want to thank many teachers who have guided and trained me over the decades, especially my guiding teacher and mentor John Travis and my jhāna master and teacher Bhante Vimalaraṁsi. Their wisdom and kindness continue to inspire. Without them my meditation practice would be in shambles and this book would be a muddle.

I'm also grateful to Tony Bernhard and the members of his sutta study group that I've been a part of for years. His understanding of the text has been invaluable.

Second, I am grateful to my students who have had a larger impact on me than they may appreciate. Sometimes I didn't understand that I didn't understand something until finding I couldn't explain it to them clearly. The bright light of their open and sincere listening encouraged me to look deeper into how the Dhamma works. Without them I'd have been left muttering to myself.

Many people went the extra mile to read the manuscript and give concrete critique and suggestions. First amongst these is my wife, Erika Kraft, who read more drafts than anyone and still patiently and firmly pointed out difficulties. If you enjoy this book, you can thank her.

Others who have read various versions and given helpful feedback include Jens Tröger, Bill Storm, Liz McLaughlin, David Johnson, Ellen Lief, Dan Michele, Prashant Billore, Abhay Vardhen, Antra Priede, Scott Jordan, Gale Crow, Gus Koehler, Paul Johnson, Bob Adler, and Melisa McCambell.

Danielle Loesch and Cynthia Craft provided professional editing that cleaned up the text and my thinking. Jens Tröger's software, Bookalope, scanned the entire manuscript for subtle errors and magically created the e-book versions. Susan Gross patiently and skillfully led me through improvements to the cover design.

Photo Credits

David Dawson, Adam Eurich, Jess Gregg, Nathan Kraft, Mike Martin, John Travis, Jens Tröger, and Unsplash generously provided a treasure trove of beautiful photographs. The photographers, of course, retain all rights to the further use of their work. Some photos came from Unsplash, a website (www.unsplash.com) that offers free, high quality photos with very few restrictions. Photos or illustrations not shown below were created by me or were found in the public domain.

The following list describes each photo informally along with the artist and page where they appear. Unsplash photos have an asterisk(*) after the photographer.

Lila

And finally, I want to thank Lila, my cat, who meditates with me every morning and keeps vigil with me through many hours of writing at the computer.

Index

It is said that love comes through a window in the heart,
But if there are no walls, there's no need to have a window.

– Rumi

Made in the USA
San Bernardino, CA
26 November 2017